S0-AQL-313

The New Shell Guides
Devon, Cornwall and the Isles of Scilly

The New Shell Guides
Devon, Cornwall and the Isles of Scilly

Paul Pettit

Introduction by Winston Graham

Series Editor: John Julius Norwich

Photography by Martin Dohrn

Michael Joseph · London

First published in Great Britain by
Michael Joseph Limited, 27 Wrights Lane,
London W8 5TZ 1987

This book was designed and produced by
Swallow Editions Limited, Swallow House,
11–21 Northdown Street, London N1 9BN

© Shell UK Limited 1987

British Library Cataloguing in Publication Data:

Pettit, Paul
    The new Shell guide to Devon, Cornwall and
    the Isles of Scilly.
    1. Isles of Scilly — Description and
    travel — Guide-books
    I. Title
    914.23′504858   DA670.S2

Cased edition: ISBN 0 7181 2761 7
Paperback edition: ISBN 0 7181 2766 8

Editor: Raymond Kaye
Cartographer: M L Design
Production: Hugh Allan

Filmset by Wyvern Typesetting Limited, Central
Trading Estate, 277 Bath Road, Bristol BS4 3EH
Printed and bound by Kyodo Shing Loong Printing,
Singapore

The name Shell and the Shell emblem are registered
trademarks

Shell UK Ltd would point out that the contributors views
are not necessarily those of this company

The information contained in this book is believed correct
at the time of printing. While every care has been taken to
ensure that the information is accurate, the publishers and
Shall can accept no responsibility for any error or omission
or for changes in the details given.

A list of Shell publications
can be obtained by writing to:
Department UOMK/60
Shell UK Oil
PO Box No. 148
Shell-Mex House
Strand
London WC2R ODX

John Julius Norwich was born in 1929. He read French and Russian at New College, Oxford, and in 1952 joined the Foreign Office where he served until 1964. Since then he has published two books on the medieval Norman Kingdom in Sicily, *The Normans in the South* and *The Kingdom in the Sun*; two historical travel books, *Mount Athos* (with Reresby Sitwell) and *Sahara*; an anthology of poetry and prose, *Christmas Crackers*; and two volumes on the history of Venice, *Venice, The Rise to Empire* and *Venice, The Greatness and the Fall*, now published in one volume as *A History of Venice*. He was also general editor of *Great Architecture of the World* or more recently author of *The Architecture of Southern England*.

In addition, he writes and presents historical documentaires for BBC television and frequently broadcasts on BBC radio. He is chairman of the Venice in Peril Fund, a Trustee of the Civic Trust, a member of the Executive and Properties Committees of the National Trust.

Paul Pettit first became acquainted with the West Country as a visitor in the 1930s but since World War II, in which he served in the Middle East and Italy, it has been his chosen home. He has walked or motored with enthusiasm over every part of the region though admitting that the wilderness of Dartmoor and the rugged Land's End peninsula hold a special fascination for him.

He is the author of several books and some of his interests are indicated by membership of the Prehistoric Society, the Dartmoor Preservation Association and the Royal Society for the Protection of Birds.

Winston Graham was born in Lancashire but has lived the greater part of his life in Cornwall. A full-time novelist from the age of 23, he has written many novels, six of which have been screened, among them *Marnie*, and the Metro Goldwyn Mayer production of *The Walking Stick*. His novels of Cornwall include *The Grove of Eagles*, *The Forgotten Story*, recently a television series, and the *Poldark* novels, the first seven of which made up the immensely popular BBC television series of 29 instalments. This series has been shown in 37 countries and dubbed into 14 languages. Three more *Poldark* novels have been published since then, and his new modern novel, *The Green Flash*, came out in October 1986.

Winston Graham worked with Sir Alan Herbert on the campaign for Public Lending Right and for two years was Chairman of the Society of Authors. He is a Fellow of the Royal Society of Literature and was awarded the OBE in 1983.

Martin Dohrn was born in Christchurch, New Zealand in 1957. He moved to England with his family 10 years later. His interest in landscape and natural history stemmed from his schooldays where he took up photography as a humane alternative to collecting insects.

Front jacket photograph: Polperro, Cornwall (see p. 194)
Back jacket photograph: Fifteenth-century window, Probus Church, Cornwall (see p. 196)
Title-page: The Erme Estuary, Holbeton, Devon (see p. 96)

Contents

Introduction

WINSTON GRAHAM

To attempt an introduction to a Guide to Devon and Cornwall is rather like trying to describe an apple and an orange in the same breath. From an appropriate distance the two objects have a strong resemblance; the nearer you approach them the more different from each other they prove to be. No two adjoining counties in England are, I fancy, so dissimilar. It is even difficult for the casual tourist to move from one to the other without this fact being brought to his attention.

This is not due to any perverseness on the part of the inhabitants; it is because for ages they have been in effect a different people.

Inevitably there are a few areas where this is not so. From Launceston to Hartland, around Stratton and Holsworthy and Bude, it is not always easy to know whether to ask for Cornish or Devonshire cream. But as a generality the differences are marked. For the purposes of art, or at least of publishing, it might be convenient if a Guide to Devon and Cornwall could be a description of a homogeneous region and people. History has decreed otherwise.

For several centuries before the Romans came, and right up to our own time, Cornwall has been inhabited and cultivated by people of Celtic origin. These people were themselves invaders, arriving in Cornwall in the earliest centuries from Gaul, from Ireland, from the north. Refugees, driven west from Celtic Devon by later invaders from the Continent, swelled the numbers but did not dilute the blood. Cornwall became known as 'the land beyond the land', not immune from the waves of conquerors from the east but resistant to more than titular rule. Most of the waves of conquest became ripples and washed back across the Tamar.

The Romans founded the city of Exeter, built roads leading to it across the western counties and posted galleys to protect its sea approaches from Saxon and other raiders. They penetrated into Cornwall in search of metals, but once assured that it offered no threat to their security they tended to leave it to its own devices. After the power of the Roman Empire had been withdrawn, the Saxons drifted further and further west, first sharing Devon with the Celtic Britons, but gradually overrunning them and driving them across the Tamar; and in the succeeding centuries following them into the border areas beyond the river. Thus Poundstock and Whitstone in Cornwall have Saxon names, not Celtic. Devon has very many names that indicate towns and villages founded by the Saxons of Wessex, and later fortified against the Danes.

When the Norman Conquest came, it too lost much of its impetus by the time it had moved so far west. In Cornwall the new conquerors were content to be overlords: they built, or rebuilt, castles to establish their command, as at Restormel, Launceston, and Trematon, but except in church matters, where the monastic ways of early Celtic Christianity were superseded by a more hieratical system stemming from Rome, most of the population lived virtually unchanged lives.

Over the next centuries the English language, being the language of commerce, gradually overcame the old Cornish in the eastern parts of the county, and in the

St Nectan, Hartland (see p. 92)

ports and sea villages around the coast. The Tudors went further and anglicized the administration, so bringing the rocky peninsula more closely into the English influence. The later Tudors also created many new parliamentary boroughs in Cornwall, putting in Crown nominees in order to strengthen the royal party, and for nearly three centuries Cornwall returned 44 members to the Commons; as many as the thickly populated counties of Yorkshire, Durham and Northumberland put together.

Nevertheless, until the building of the railways and the invention of the car Cornwall remained obstinately a place on its own: 'the land beyond the land'. Devon was more important, Devon was larger, wealthier, more enterprising. When America was first discovered, and trade and conquest looked over the horizons of the sea towards new lands and new opportunities, it was from Devon that the seamen mainly came. Plymouth, the main port of the west after Bristol, is immortal in English history for the seamen it sent out to fight the Spanish, to defeat the Armada, to explore and to conquer and to trade. By the end of the 16th century Devon had become an important and influential part of England. When in November 1688 William of Orange with his 60 men-of-war and 700 transports, 'laden with the fate of empires', as Macaulay puts it, sailed from Hellevoetsluis in the Netherlands to claim the throne of England, it was to Torbay that he made his way, and in Exeter that four days later he shakily established his first headquarters.

Devon is characterized by its deep valleys. If you look at a relief map of the county you will see the way in which the rivers, rising in the extensive wet moorlands of mid-Devon, have made their way north to the Atlantic coast and south to the English Channel, creating the lush, deep valleys densely forested with beech trees, oak and ash, and the fertile farmlands which have given rise to the small market towns – of which it is said there were 38 even in Elizabethan times. By English standards it is a large county: 75 miles long by 73 in depth. Cornwall, by contrast, though some 80 miles long, is at its greatest depth barely 45 miles, from which it rapidly tapers away to a rocky, granite-hard, wind-swept, sun-and-shower peninsula. Wherever you go in it you can never get more than 20 miles from the sea.

Devon, apart from its great sea-going traditions and its many other activities, has always been a county of huntsmen. Until recent years anyone in Devon who was anyone hunted. It did not seem so much to matter whether it was stag, fox, badger, otter or hare, so long as it was something to gallop after. A writer in Victorian days said 'practically every parish in the county has its pack of harriers, and besides these not less than eight established packs of foxhounds and numerous other packs.' One enlightened gentleman called George Templar maintained two packs himself. With one of them he hunted wild foxes, with the other tame foxes which he had imported and kept in regular training. When one of these 'bag' foxes was turned loose a boy would run after it with a whip to get it going. Then the highly disciplined pack of hounds, which were known as the 'let 'im alone' pack, would follow in full cry. When eventually after a good chase they closed in on the fox, the first rider up would give his shout of 'let 'im alone!', whereupon the fox would fight his way out from the centre of the yapping, snarling pack unharmed – to be petted and fed and saved for the next time.

Many parsons of Devon and Cornwall were famous – and some of them infamous – for their hunting, their neglect of their duties, their many talents, their eccentricities,

New Street, the Barbican, Plymouth (see p. 119)

their enormous families. Two of the best known were both Devonshire men, though one is often described as a Cornish poet because he spent most of his life over the border. Robert Stephen Hawker, who was born in 1803, was a promising but indigent young man who married his godmother (21 years his senior) and she, a lady of modest means, was able to see him through his studies. In 1834 he was appointed to the living of Morwenstowe, then a wild, wind-swept and demoralized parish with a ruined vicarage and drunken, ignorant and debased parishioners. There had been no resident vicar for 100 years, but there Hawker lived in happiness with his wife for the next 40, lavishing charity on shipwrecked sailors and the poor and sick of his parish alike. He restored the church, built and maintained a school, and wrote books and poems about it all. His famous 'Song of the Western Men' ('And shall Trelawny die?') about the 17th-century bishop Sir John Trelawny, who was arraigned for high treason under James II, was for a time accepted as a contemporary ballad, and deceived such people as Walter Scott, Macaulay and Charles Dickens. When Hawker's first wife died he was 60, but the following year he married the daughter of a Polish aristocrat, by whom he had three daughters. To end it all, he caused a late scandal by becoming a Roman Catholic on his death bed.

The other, Sabine Baring-Gould, who was born in 1834 and lived to be ninety, came of an old Devonshire family and was vicar of Lew Trenchard, a parish halfway between Launceston and Okehampton and on the edge of Dartmoor. There he lived for 43 years, hunting, travelling and writing with unabated vigour. In all he wrote more than a hundred books, including *The Lives of the Saints* in 15 volumes, poems, hymns (including 'Onward Christian Soldiers'), and many romantic novels. He also wrote perhaps the best Cornish short story ever, *Polly Postes*.

Additionally he had five sons and nine daughters. There was an occasion when his wife decided to give a children's party, and there was much laughter and frolicking going on. Baring-Gould came down from his study, benignly tolerant of the noise, and saw a little blonde girl sitting on the last step of the stairs. He patted her on the head and smiled and said: 'And whose little girl are you?' She looked up at him and burst into tears. 'Y-y-yours, Papa,' she replied.

This was told me some years ago by a daughter of the 'little girl' whom I happened to meet in San Francisco.

Having accepted history as the dominant factor in the dissimilarity between the two counties, we see geography as the qualifying influence. Cornwall, geographically, is Devon writ small. Smaller rivers rising from narrower, lower central moorlands, cutting sharp, verdant, sparser, more wind-swept valleys on their way to the sea. If in earlier times the Devonshire man, surrounded by endless hills and dales, found communication difficult between village and village, town and town, in Cornwall it was more so. With roads scarcely existing – or when they existed scarcely connecting – the usual means of travel was by sea. Before the railways came Devon had a few good roads leading east and north towards the centres of power. Cornwall had none such. Devonshire men might like to think of Exeter as the centre or capital of Devon and Cornwall. Cornishmen would hardly know it. They went to London and Bristol by sea. They kept to their own communities, and interbred, and developed self-reliance, and did not need or much like strangers. Except for a few of the gentry, and except when outside events affected their religious observances, they cared little for what went on elsewhere. Rather like the early Greeks, they were tough, active, enterprising within their limitations, smallish and muscular, humorous and obstinate: though sometimes susceptible of the longueurs of the Celtic twilight. Their situation made them tremendously insular – or indeed peninsular – and this has persisted to the present day, and is not directed solely towards strangers. Some years ago I was talking with a man, himself elderly, about who was likely to be the then oldest inhabitant of Perranporth. I mentioned a man called Harry Mitchell. 'Gerraway,' said my friend with great contempt. 'That edn no good. Harry edn a Perranporth man. He come from B'lingey.' Bolingey is a mile from Perranporth.

Here and there in Devon, but more particularly in Cornwall, ruined chimneys still scar the landscape with memories of the days when mining was prosperous. Alas it is all gone, and alas some of the chimneys have fallen or been pulled down. Sufficient remain to remind us of the industrial revolution of the 19th century, when demand and opportunity released a spring of talent and genius in the Cornish character, and men like Richard Trevithick, Humphry Davy and Goldsworthy Gurney were in the forefront of mechanical and scientific invention and innovation. But later in the century the total collapse of tin and copper mining forced wholesale emigration upon the miners, so that the county was denuded of many of its most enterprising citizens.

When in 1859 Isambard Kingdom Brunel built his great bridge across the Tamar to carry the railway into Cornwall, he found the steep valleys of the Duchy constantly cutting across his progress. Travelling west by train today, you will find the line skirting one side of a valley until it can get no further without too steep a gradient, then a bridge has been built to carry it to the other side of the valley; and so round the corner to the next similar obstacle. The diesels of today, though proceeding with circumspection round the sharper bends, have so much greater acceleration than the

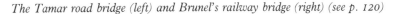

The Tamar road bridge (left) and Brunel's railway bridge (right) (see p. 120)

old steam trains that they easily knock half an hour off a 50-mile journey.

For the many thousands who never travel except by car, a train journey to the west is strongly recommended. Between Exeter and Newton Abbot there is the splendid run by the sea, in and out of tunnels and among the red rocks of Dawlish and Teignmouth; then out of Plymouth across Brunel's bridge with its splendid bird's eye view of the Sound; later, glimpses of the lovely lower reaches of the Tamar; mid-Cornwall, green and verdant; west Cornwall, treeless and ghost-ridden with old mine chimneys; then the slow unveiling of St Michael's Mount to crown it all.

Since the trains began to open up the west – and of course very much more so since the end of the Second World War, with the spread of the mass-produced car – many have come from other parts of England to settle in the more temperate seaside villages and towns of the West Country, either to retire, or to open or buy small businesses and make their living away from the rat race and the pressures of city life. The Cornish Riviera, so publicized by the old Great Western Railway, and the Devon Riviera with it, are to some extent advertising myths. The average rainfall in the West Country is much higher than in London, the winter winds can be as bitter as anywhere in England and rather more ferocious, and the snowfalls of Dartmoor are notorious. But the compensation is the underlying presence of the Gulf Stream, easing the frosts of the uplands, usually preventing them at sea level, the clarity of the high skies, the softness of the air, the washed blues and greys and purples of the hasty clouds. Semitropical plants, though buffeted by rough cold winds, flourish in a way they cannot do further east. Daffodils and most spring flowers are weeks earlier than in the rest of the country. In my garden on the *north* coast of Cornwall – where I created a large pocket of peaty ground – I used to feel aggrieved if I did not have

Detail of the west front of Exeter Cathedral (see p. 82)

camellias in flower by mid-December. I have an old horticultural map marking the limits of what was regarded as the most temperate part of England: this draws a line from Exmouth on the south coast, bisecting Exeter, and going up to Combe Martin on the north coast. And the further west you go from that line, and the nearer the sea, the better for most subtropical plants. For conventional gardening, however, covering the generality of flowers and vegetables and shrubs, the richer soils of Devon give much better results. I remember as a young man going to see my uncle, who lived in Newton Ferrers, and being astonished at the thickness and vigour of his rose trees compared to what I was able to grow in Cornwall.

So the South West – Devon, of course, but in a greater proportion Cornwall – has suffered, or enjoyed, a peaceful invasion of settlers, following in the footsteps of the Romans, the Saxons and the Normans trekking ever west; and whereas Cornwall threw back, often more by fortune than design, the other and earlier invaders, she has had no defences against these friendly people from up-country who have settled everywhere in the peninsula.

Nor could she have afforded to withstand them even if the wish had been there. The total collapse of the fishing industry, of copper mining, and then of tin mining, has left the county woefully dependent on tourism to sustain the barest standard of living.

There are, first, the tourists, who come yearly over barely a four-month period, flocking in their thousands like the pilchards that once flocked to her coasts, and then are as quickly gone: they provide a transfusion of life-giving money to the county, and much of Cornwall is now geared only to receive them. And, second, there are the people who come to settle, also in their thousands, buying bungalows and building small homes – 'they are smiling o'er the silvery brooks and round the hamlet fanes'; these also help to keep the county in a minimal degree of prosperity, and during the winter months too. My only fear is that there is a danger of turning the Celtic twilight into an Anglo-Saxon rest home.

Devon has been better able to assimilate and deal with these developments in West Country life because of her size and because she has had longer to do so. Also, as has been said, she is more closely integrated with the economics of the rest of the country. She has the great naval port of Plymouth, besides substantial market towns and some valuable light industries, additional to sheep and dairy farming. She is, over all, a richly verdant land, a place of ancient oaks and ancient inns, of long-woolled sheep, of heavy comfortable cattle, of clustered white cottages and moorland farms, and a substantial and not un-prosperous habitancy. The population of Exeter, the county town of Devon, is 96,000 as against the 16,000 of Truro, Cornwall's capital. Torquay has 108,000 inhabitants as against Newquay's 15,000. Plymouth has 225,000 compared with Falmouth's 18,000.

Yet each county, taken separately or with its neighbour, rewards the closest or the most casual exploration, as Paul Pettit's comprehensive gazetteer shows. There is nowhere like the West Country – though men will even differ as to what that phrase 'West Country' implies. To a Londoner it will include Salisbury and Bath. To a Cornishman the West Country ends at Exeter. It is a matter of perspective but not at all of appreciation. Devon and Cornwall have two of the finest cathedrals in the land, again greatly contrasting: Exeter is 12th to 14th century, its completion delayed by the epidemic of the Black Death – a gem, surrounded by a green close and cloistral

Pendennis Castle, Falmouth (see p. 172)

calm, with some of the best 13th-century woodcarving in the world. Truro
Cathedral, built between 1880 and 1910, is 19th-century Gothic and therefore
attracts criticism for its anachronistic style; but a superb building, designed like the
French cathedrals to exist in the very centre and bustle of traffic, fairly towering over
everything, physically and architecturally, particularly over some squalid modern
buildings which have done nothing to improve the charm of this attractive town.

In Devon and Cornwall you will find interesting churches galore, some of the most
individual and arresting villages, the best beaches in England, the clearest and most
brilliant sunlight, the cleanest rain, the wildest and most wayward winds, and escape
from pressure, economic, social, political, literary or romantic. Many men and
women have chosen to settle or to stay for a while in the West Country as a way of
escaping from their problems – or facing their problems in a new way – and
reassembling their lives. Those who were born here and have had to go away, long to
return. It used to be said in Truro of doctors that if they were appointed to spend a
year in the area, and outstayed the year, they would never leave again. Most of them
did not. Why should they?

Opposite: Daffodils, Sancreed

Dartmoor

The boundary of the National Park was wisely drawn to include large areas of 'border' country and many villages off the moor. Those villages and the settlements on the moor itself – Postbridge, Princetown and Widecombe – are described in the Gazetteer. This article deals with the high moor, 200 square miles of rolling hills and rugged valleys, the last wilderness of southern England.

It consists of the Forest of Dartmoor, the ancient royal hunting ground which has been Duchy of Cornwall property since 1337, surrounded by the extensive Commons of the border parishes. The great plateau slopes up from south to north, from 800 ft on the south-western edge to the northern heights of Yes Tor (2029 ft) and High Willhays (2038 ft) on Okehampton Common, and the great whaleback of Cosdon Beacon (1800 ft) so familiar to those travelling westward towards Okehampton on the A30.

The moor's characteristic features are its tors, the striking outcrops of granite often with daunting 'clitters' of boulders strewn down the slopes below them, and the large areas of blanket bog formed in late prehistoric times by the decomposition of vegetation in wet conditions. Intrusive are the china clay workings on Lee Moor, a number of high-level reservoirs and the grim conifer plantations of the Forestry Commission. In spite of partial destruction, and the constant threat of further exploitation, it remains a fascinating and challenging area for walking and riding.

The Dartmoor Tors

The 200-odd tors range from clusters of insignificant boulders to enormous rock piles weathered into fantastic shapes. Most visited is Hay Tor (1491 ft), two huge masses of granite easily accessible from the road up from Bovey Tracey. The all-round views from the summits across the moor and down the Teign valley to the English Channel are memorable. A few miles further along the road the huge bulk of Hound Tor is no less impressive and accessible. So are Combestone Tor (1156 ft) on the road up from Holne, dominating the beautiful valley of the Dart river around Dartmeet, and the great boss of Kestor (1433 ft) with its rock basin approached from Chagford. Vixen Tor near Merrivale is in a lowly position (987 ft) but stands nearly 100 ft above ground level on its south side, the highest rock on the moor. According to legend it was the home of a witch who enticed wanderers into the nearby mire. Magnificent piles to attract the walker are Great Mis Tor (1760 ft) towering above the Walkham valley and with a rock basin known as the Devil's Frying Pan; beautiful Hare Tor (1744 ft) rising over the gorge of the river Tavy; and above all Fur Tor (1877 ft), remote and formidable in the heart of the northern moor. In several places notable groups rear up along ridges – Belstone Tors and Higher Tor in the north; Littaford, Longaford and the White Tors north of Two Bridges; and near Widecombe the attractive Bonehill Rocks, Bell, Chinkwell and Honeybag Tors. Of modest appearance but of special interest is Crockern Tor, close to the Moretonhampstead road north-east of Two Bridges. The Stannary Parliaments which regulated the

River Walkham, below Merrivale

Vixen Tor

affairs of the tinners were traditionally held there for 400 years down to the 18th century.

Blanket bog and peat ties

The blanket bog or fen covers 20 square miles of the northern moor and is the source of the rivers Tavy, Taw, Teign and Dart. It should be approached with caution, particularly where the peat has become fissured, in places to a depth of 16 ft. Peat passes shown on 1/25,000 Ordnance Survey maps were cut in 1895–1905 to help huntsmen and stockmen to cross from one area of hard ground to another. Some are marked by granite posts with bronze plaques recording that they were made by Frank Phillpotts, a famous huntsman. He was a cousin of the anti-blood sports author Eden Phillpotts (1862–1960), many of whose novels have a Dartmoor setting. But Cut Lane across the north side of Cut Hill (1968 ft) is much older than the other peat passes, and almost certainly of medieval origin.

South of the east–west roads that bisect the moor a smaller area of fen is the source of the rivers Plym, Yealm, Erme and Avon. All over the moor mires should be avoided, particularly the notorious 'featherbeds', small patches of bright green moss which cover deep holes and shake when trodden. Another hazard for walker and rider are the old peat ties, regarded by William Crossing of *Guide to Dartmoor* fame as worse than the mires. Where peat has been cut for generations the ground becomes irretrievably broken, for example in the area south-west of Fur Tor.

Previous page: Saddle Tor

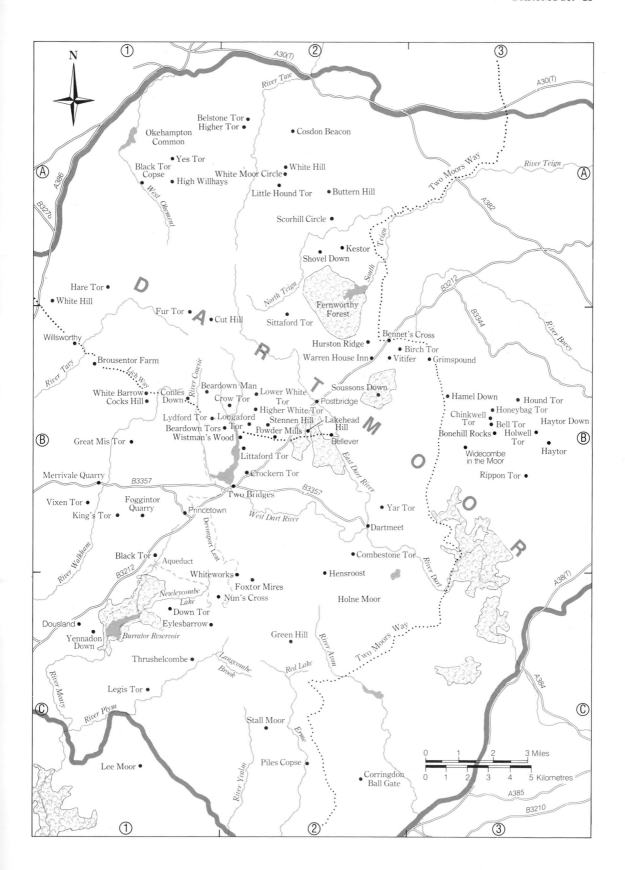

N

① ② ③

A30(T)

River Taw

A30(T)

Belstone Tor •
Higher Tor •

Okehampton
Common

• Cosdon Beacon

Two Moors Way

River Teign

• Yes Tor

Black Tor
Copse

• High Willhays

White Moor Circle

• White Hill

Little Hound Tor

• Buttern Hill

A382

Scorhill Circle •

West Okement

Hare Tor •
• White Hill

Fur Tor •

• Cut Hill

• Kestor
Shovel Down

North Teign

South Teign

Sittaford Tor •

B3212

Fernworthy
Forest

B3344

River Bovey

Willsworthy

River Tavy

Brousentor Farm

Lich Way

White Barrow
Cocks Hill

Conies
Down

River Cowsic

Beardown Man

Crow Tor

Hurston Ridge •

Warren House Inn •

Bennet's Cross
• Birch Tor
• Vitifer

• Grimspound

Lower White
Tor
• Higher White Tor
Stennen Hill
Powder Mills

Soussons Down

• Postbridge

• Hamel Down

Chinkwell
Tor
Bonehill Rocks

• Hound Tor
Honeybag
Tor
• Bell Tor

• Holwell
Tor

Haytor Down

Lydford Tor •
Beardown Tors •
Wistman's Wood

• Longaford
Tor

Lakehead
Hill

Great Mis Tor •

Littaford Tor •

Bellever

East Dart River

Widecombe
in the Moor

• Haytor

Merrivale Quarry

B3357

• Crockern Tor

Two Bridges

Rippon Tor •

Vixen Tor •

King's Tor •

Foggintor
Quarry

Princetown

B3357

West Dart River

• Yar Tor

• Dartmeet

River Dart

A38(T)

Black Tor •

Aqueduct

B3212

Devonport Leat

Newleycombe
Lake

Whiteworks •

Foxtor Mires
• Nun's Cross

• Combestone Tor

• Hensroost

Holne Moor

A384

Dousland •

• Down Tor
• Eylesbarrow

Burrator Reservoir

Yennadon
Down

Thrushelcombe •

Langcombe
Brook

• Green Hill

Red Lake

River Avon

Two Moors Way

River Meavy

Legis Tor •

River Plym

Stall Moor •

Erme

River Yealm

Piles Copse •

Lee Moor •

• Corringdon
Ball Gate

0   1   2   3 Miles

0 1 2 3 4 5 Kilometres

A385

B3210

① ② ③

D A R T M O O R

Dartmoor ponies

The moor's rough grazing supports Scottish blackface sheep, beef cattle and about 2500 ponies. The purebred pony is descended, like all native breeds, from the small horse brought to Britain by the Iron Age Celts and used for pulling war chariots rather than riding. The introduction of alien stallions from the First World War onwards has resulted in cross-breeding to such an extent that true Dartmoors are no longer to be found on the moor. Breeders of registered ponies tend to confine them strictly to their studs. The little herds of 'mongrels' that continue to roam wild are all owned by someone. In autumn the annual 'drifts' or round-ups take place and old mares, colts and some yearlings are auctioned in border towns.

Archaeological remains

The moor is of outstanding interest to the archaeologist, no other comparable area having such a wealth of prehistoric remains. The oldest are half a dozen Neolithic chambered tombs, much ruined, the best known close to Corringdon Ball Gate north-west of South Brent.

Attributed to Bronze Age times (c. 1800–800 BC) are many round burial cairns, a hundred of them containing kist tombs – stone boxes in which crouched bodies or ashes were placed. Good examples can be found close to the stream west of Legis Tor in the Plym valley and on Stennen Hill west of the upper Cherry Brook. An interesting group of 11 is strung out along the lonely valley of the Langcombe Brook, a left bank tributary of the Plym.

About 60 of the cairns have stone rows leading up to them, single, double and occasionally triple lines of unworked granite blocks which seem to mark a formal approach to the grave of an important person. A characteristic single row, about 160 stones irregularly spaced over 340 yd, goes to a cairn half a mile east of Down Tor above Burrator Reservoir. In the Erme valley a single row of small stones stretches for over 2 miles from Stall Moor to Green Hill, crossing the Erme and its tributary Red Lake. The double row on Hurston Ridge a mile north of Warren House Inn is typical: 50 pairs of stones, the largest next to the cairn, run up a gentle slope for about 150 yd. Triple rows on Holne Moor, Challacombe Down and at Yar Tor have been much robbed so that the restored rows at the foot of Cosdon Beacon, though cut by the peat track coming up from South Zeal, are probably the best example. They lead to the remains of a cairn which covered two kist burials.

Other monuments attributed to the Bronze Age are the crude stone circles of unworked granite blocks. A dozen are known scattered widely over the moor, the most impressive at Scorhill near Gidleigh with 23 erect stones. In a remote setting on the saddle between White Hill and Little Hound Tor, a mile south of Cosdon Beacon, the White Moor Circle is worth finding. A pair of circles, called the Grey Wethers from their resemblance at a distance to grazing sheep, lie between Sittaford Tor and Fernworthy Forest.

Groups of remains at four places indicate special importance in Bronze Age times: at Fernworthy among the plantations surrounding the reservoir; on Shovel Down near Kestor and at Merrivale on a small plateau above the Walkham river; and, most evocative of all, the rows and tombs at Thrushelcombe far up the Plym valley.

Apart from the monuments some 2000 foundations of Bronze Age buildings have survived, the majority in the southern valleys. Many are grouped in walled enclosures where traces of stock pens have also been found. Grimspound below the north end of Hamel Down is a well-known example. Associated with some settlements and also of Bronze Age date are the reaves or boundary banks, some of considerable length, perhaps marking grazing areas, and others forming field boundaries. Examples can be seen beside the road near Kestor and on the common south of Rippon Tor, the latter probably the largest system of prehistoric fields to survive in England.

Relics of medieval times include a ruined village 400 yd south-east of Hound Tor and many granite crosses that marked routes across the waste. One of the most interesting is Siward's or Nun's Cross close to a ruined farmstead 3 miles south-east of Princetown. It is over 7 ft high and was first mentioned in a document of 1240. Rough inscriptions read SIWARD on the east face and BOC LOND (Buckland) on the other. It stood on the route from the important Abbey at Buckfast on the Dart river to the equally important one at Buckland on the Tavy. The route is marked by other crosses, to the west above Newleycombe Lake and to the east in Fox Tor Mire and Newtake and on Ter Hill. Siward's Cross was also a boundary stone between the lands of Buckland Abbey and the Forest, still a royal domain in 1240. Near the Warren House Inn and close to B3212, Bennet's Cross is on the ancient route from Moretonhampstead to Tavistock which the modern road largely follows. The letters WB (Warren Bounds) were inscribed when it was used to mark the boundary of Headland Warren from which the inn takes its name. On the slopes to the south are Jan Reynolds' Cards, four enclosures said to represent the four aces which Jan dropped when carried off by the Devil for playing cards in Widecombe Church. They were carefully built to keep out the rabbits and used by the Warrener for growing winter feed for his charges.

Tin from Dartmoor

Also south of Bennet's Cross are the extensive remains of Birch Tor and Vitifer tin mines, a jumble of spoil heaps, 'gerts' (gullies) and shafts. Streaming for alluvial tin almost certainly began on the moor in prehistoric times and is recorded from the 12th century onwards. It was the medieval tinners who built the earliest clapper bridges of unmorticed granite blocks so that packhorses could carry their valuable loads in all weathers down to the Stannary Towns for weighing and stamping. The best known is at Postbridge; ruined bridges also survive at Bellever and Dartmeet lower down the East Dart river. By the 16th century shaft mining had replaced opencast working and production reached a peak. A revival in the 18th century continued until competition from abroad in the 1870s began the final decline, the last mine closing in 1930. The Birch Tor and Vitifer mines were 19th-century ventures on the site of earlier activity. Water for them, and for the Golden Dagger mine now hidden in the plantations on Soussons Down, was brought by gravity from the East Dart river along a 7-mile leat. Most of this abandoned waterway can be traced. Other mining areas of interest are at Eylesbarrow and Whiteworks south-east of Princetown, and at Hensroost and Hooton Wheals on Holne Moor. But all the moor valleys bear marks of the tinners' frantic search for ore through the centuries.

A feature of the old mining sites are the ruined blowing houses, used for smelting tin down to about 1740. Examples can be seen beside the river Walkham above Merrivale Bridge and at the delightful Black Tor Falls on the river Meavy, close to Black Tor with its logan stone and on the east side of the B3212 between Princetown and Yelverton.

Farming and quarrying

Side by side with the early tinners, farmers entered the Forest and began to enclose parts of the East and West Dart valleys. Through the centuries the drystone walls of surface granite were pushed out further and further from the original holdings to form 'newtakes', a distinctive feature of the landscape. Up to 1800 the farmhouses, too, were built of surface granite or 'moorstone' and quarrying did not begin until the 19th century. The quarry at Merrivale, opened in 1876, is the only one still in use. Disused quarries at Foggintor and King's Tor south-east of Merrivale are fascinating but sombre places to explore. The group of quarries at Hay and Holwell Tors on Haytor Down dispatched their stone along a remarkable tramway built in 1820. It was constructed of granite setts between 3 and 8 ft long with carefully cut flanges to guide the wagon wheels. The shorter setts were used on the curves. After the lines from the different quarry faces united, the single 'main' line ran down for 7 miles to the Teign valley. A dozen flat wagons, each capable of carrying 3 tons, formed a train. Horses assembled the train and went down behind the loaded wagons to haul them back after unloading. The section of track to Holwell quarry was the only place where teams of horses had to pull loaded wagons uphill. The layout on Haytor Down with its 'points' and branch lines is a protected monument. Along this unique tramroad passed granite for use on several buildings in London, including the British Museum and London Bridge. By 1860 the quarries were deserted.

The Dartmoor leats

Hundreds of leats once carried water to mines, mills and farms. Only a few remain in use. The longest and most elaborate is the Devonport Leat constructed in the 1790s to carry water from the West Dart, Cowsic and Blackbrook rivers high on the moor to the docks at Devonport. Originally 30 miles in length, a fine feat of engineering, it provided a separate supply from that of Plymouth which, since the days of Sir Francis Drake, had drawn water from the river Meavy. When Plymouth and Devonport were united (1914) the need for separate supplies ceased and the Devonport water is now piped from Plymouth's Reservoir at Burrator. Beyond the reservoir a stretch of the disused leat goes on over Yennadon Down to Dousland. Above the reservoir more-than 15 miles of leat are maintained and can be walked except for the section running through prison land at Princetown. From the weir on the West Dart the water runs along the hillside, flowing downhill but climbing steadily above the river. In many places the water gives the impression of flowing uphill due to the way the leat bank is built up on the lower side. It passes through Beardown plantations and comes out on the headland above the meeting of the Cowsic river and the West Dart. The original course curved up to the weir on the Cowsic, but it now crosses the river by a stone aqueduct and joins the Cowsic leat on the far side. The combined supply goes on under B3357 (Two Bridges–Tavistock) and soon enters the prison enclosures. It can be picked up again where it flows under B3212 (Two Bridges–Yelverton) half a mile north of Princetown and from there followed all the way to Burrator. A fine stretch of 4 miles leads to Fox Tor Mire and the watershed between the Dart and Meavy rivers at Nun's Cross Farm. This obstacle was overcome by tunnelling for 480 yd through the hill. The water emerges under a fine granite arch into a deep cutting. After a further 3 miles of smooth flowing round the valley of Newleycombe Lake the water suddenly cascades down 150 ft to cross the river Meavy on an aqueduct, one of the most unusual sights on Dartmoor.

From there it passes down through more plantations to the point where the flow is diverted at the reservoir.

The leat weir on the West Dart is best approached by the track from Two Bridges to Crockern Farm and on past Wistman's Wood, one of three ancient copses of English oaks on the moor. The others are Black Tor Copse in the deep gorge of the West Ockment river and Piles Copse beside the river Erme 2 miles above Harford. The woods are unique, their survival due to their position at the bottom of valleys where the clitter from tors has allowed seedlings to take root and to regenerate through the centuries. The trees have a stunted appearance, due to exposure and altitude, and moss and lichen cover their branches. They have been well described as the most curious woods in England.

Letterboxes

A recent addition to the moor's surprises are the so-called letterboxes. The first appeared about 1850 at Cranmere Pool, a depression in the peat of the northern fen. At first people left visiting cards in a bottle and then a metal box, but after 1905 a visitors' book was provided – the original is in Plymouth Library. Though Cranmere is an unremarkable spot, it was a challenge to moor walkers to find it. In 1921 the future Duke of Windsor was guided there and signed the book.

A second box was set up in 1938 at Ducks Pool near Plym Head in the southern fen. This remote hollow was also selected for the erection of a plaque in memory of William Crossing, author of many books about the moor in addition to his monumental *Guide* (1909). At both Cranmere and Duck's Pool it became customary to leave a postcard addressed to oneself which the next visitor would collect and post in his or her home village or town. Both places continue to be good objectives for a day's walk, but since 1960 the letterbox idea has run riot. The present count is said to be 450 or so! – ice cream cartons or small tins containing a rubber stamp and ink pad concealed all over the moor. 'Box hunting' has become a compulsive pastime for some.

The Lich Way

Of the many paths and tracks that cross the moor none is more rewarding to walk than the Lich Way (the Way of the Dead, from an Old English word for corpse, as in lich- or lychgate). It runs from the East Dart river westward to Lydford. This was the main route by which the early farmers in the Forest reached their distant parish church and along which the dead were carried for burial. The farmers also had to render 'suit and service' at the Forest Courts held in Lydford Castle. A dispensation from the Bishop of Exeter in 1260 allowed them to attend the much nearer Widecombe Church instead but the route to Lydford continued to be important for lay purposes. The starting point is Bellever Bridge across the East Dart river 1½ miles below Postbridge. The ruined clapper bridge beside it shows that this was an ancient crossing place, with the old farms at Babeny, Dury, Pizwell and Runnage only short distances from it. The route passes the Forestry Commission houses at Bellever, where there is also a Youth Hostel, and goes through Bellever Forest to Lakehead Hill. Among the trees are three kist burials and on the open space of the hill the enclosure wall of a prehistoric settlement and more Bronze Age graves. The path continues through woodland to the Postbridge–Two Bridges road (B3212). Half a mile beyond the road it crosses the Cherry Brook on a clapper bridge by the ruins of

Powder Mills, one of the moor's most interesting industrial sites. Gunpowder was made there for 50 years in the 19th century; the massive walls of the scattered buildings were designed to confine the blast in case of accident. The route from the Mills heads west-north-west towards the ridge between Littaford and Longaford Tors above the West Dart river. Longaford Tor (1595 ft) is a particularly impressive landmark, boldly placed in a commanding position. Once over the ridge the path descends to the northern end of Wistman's Wood and the West Dart river, which can be crossed at the Devonport Leat weir or higher up. A steep climb follows to Lydford Tor (1647 ft), leaving Beardown Tors to the south and little Crow Tor to the north. The path passes close to Lydford Tor and goes down to Traveller's Ford on the river Cowsic. Less than a mile up the valley and close to the insignificant rocks of Devil's Tor (1785 ft) stands Beardown Man, a prehistoric Standing Stone over 11 ft tall. The path continues over Conies Down where a ruined stone row runs up the slope. It is the highest row on the moor, the northern end 1600 ft above sea level and marked by a recumbent 9 ft pillar. A mile further on the path crosses the Princetown prison leat by a bridge and then the Walkham river at Sandy Ford. Ruins of a tin mine can be seen a short distance upstream. The path climbs the side of Cocks Hill to White Barrow (1610 ft), a ruined cairn marking the western boundary of the Forest. The view westward into Cornwall opens out and is breath-taking.

From the cairn the 2-mile descent to the river Tavy begins, across Wapsworthy Common to Bagga Tor Gate and the ancient farm of Brousentor. The track past the farm leads to a modern bridge over Bagga Tor Brook, but with permission from the farmer the ruined clapper a short distance below it, where the original route crossed, can be used. The right bank of the brook is followed down to the Tavy where a wood beside the river is called Coffin Wood, a reminder of the path's ancient use. Crossing the river at Cataloo Steps the path goes up Corpse Lane, another significant name, to Willsworthy high on the western side. This was the site of a Saxon farmstead recorded in Domesday Book.

The path turns left along a lane for a short distance and then right beside the Willsworthy Brook. After crossing the stream on a clapper the route runs uphill at the side of the Yellowmead enclosures to the slopes of White Hill and downhill for 1 mile to Beardon Gate on the Tavistock–Okehampton Road (A386). Then 300 yd northwards along the road a path on the west side runs down to cross the river Lyd above its gorge. Beyond the river the path goes under Lydford railway viaduct, another industrial relic, and climbs up to the historic village.

Wistman's Wood

The Celtic Saints

Christianity became the official religion of the Romans nearly a hundred years before they abandoned Britain to its own devices in about AD 400. But in Cornwall and most of Devon hardly any evidence has been found of the conversion of the native Celts before that time. They seem to have remained thorough pagans and it was only during the following centuries that missionaries from other Celtic tribes in Wales and Ireland came to convert them. Routes established back in prehistoric times across the seas and the peninsula itself helped the spread of these 'Celtic Saints' whose strange names survive in a hundred places to fascinate us today. 'More saints in Cornwall than in heaven' was the proud boast.

Landing on the north coast at such havens as the Taw, Camel and Hayle estuaries, the earliest missionaries were hermits who settled by springs or streams to convert and baptize their Celtic kin. Most of the holy wells in Cornwall, often pleasantly situated away from later churches or dwellings, mark their cells. They not only made converts but attracted followers and from these modest beginnings developed the earliest monastic communities in England.

The Saxons of Wessex had become Christians before their conquest of Devon and Cornwall in the 8th and 9th centuries and it is unlikely that they destroyed the existing religious houses. Nevertheless, the sites of pre-Saxon monasteries are not easy to trace. The cemetery and early buildings on the headland at Tintagel are believed to be the remains of one. A 10th-century charter relating to St Buryan near Land's End seems to confirm the ownership of land by an already well-established monastery. Other evidence points to communities at Braunton (St Brannoc) and Landkey (St Kea) in Devon, and in Cornwall at Gwithian (the oratory of St Gothian) and Padstow, formerly called Lanwethnoc after St Wethnoc and then Petrockstowe, St Petrock's holy place. From the holy wells, chapels and monasteries the names of many saints were transferred to the parish churches when they evolved in Saxon and Norman times.

By the 12th century the Celtic Church had been assimilated into the Roman, but the traditions of the saints remained firmly established in Cornwall. Their feast days continued to be celebrated. Not even the Reformation or the Puritans could pluck them from Cornish hearts and they played a considerable part in the persistence of Celtic custom and language beyond the Tamar. Devon was drawn earlier and more thoroughly into the English religious structure yet surviving dedications to the Celtic saints suggest that originally they had the same impact in west Devon as in Cornwall.

St Nectan

The story of St Nectan illustrates some of the difficulties that arise when trying to unravel the facts about individual saints. He is commemorated in Devon and Cornwall and both claim his burial place. He establishes his cell at Hartland, the chroniclers say, and during the 10th century his relics are found in the church there. Welcombe Church, not far away, is also dedicated to him. In Cornwall he appears as

One of two Saxon crosses in Sancreed churchyard (see p. 209)

the patron of a medieval chapel near Boconnoc, Lostwithiel, and his cell and burial place are claimed to be in St Nectan's Glen between Boscastle and Tintagel. This shows a typical accumulation of legends, often contradictory, in the centuries after a saint lived. Medieval chroniclers also identify Nectan as the eldest son of a King Brychan of Wales and record that he had 23 brothers and sisters, all of whom became hermits in Wales and the South West. The list of their names shows that some, such as Morwenna (Morwenstow), Juliana (St Juliot) and Cleder (St Clether) are still

Below: St Genny's Church, Crackington Haven (see p. 171)
Opposite: Stained glass at St Neot's church depicting scenes from the life of the saint (see p. 208)

commemorated but others are not heard of except in documents. Devout propaganda was characteristic of the Middle Ages and legends were created to fill out the sparse facts. One monk at least admitted that when material was lacking he had 'with the assistance of God' made up a suitable story. It may be that the names of some saints were also the product of medieval imagination.

St Petrock

The large number of surviving dedications to St Petrock suggest that he must have been one of the best known and influential of the missionaries. A 6th-century Welshman, he landed at or near Padstow and founded a monastery. This was moved to Bodmin in the 10th century because of the threat of Viking raids but continued to flourish until the Dissolution 600 years later. From the chronicles of later medieval monks he emerges as a Welsh prince's son who declines his inheritance in order to become a monk. He sails across to Cornwall on an altar stone and causes a never-failing spring to flow from a rock, like Moses in Horeb. For 30 years he leads a life of severe asceticism before travelling to Rome. A second visit to Rome is followed by a journey to Jerusalem, India and the 'Eastern Ocean', where he lives for seven years on a single fish. Returning to Cornwall he hands over his monastery and retires alone to 'the Valley of the Fountain'. After his death miracles take place at his tomb. His importance can perhaps also be judged by these efforts to connect him with Rome and to surround him with the mystique accorded to the early saints of the Roman Church.

St Piran

St Piran, too, is known from fact and legend. He came from Ireland to establish a cell on Penhale sands behind the beach that bears his name. About 1800 the remains of a small chapel, probably erected soon after his death, were discovered buried under the dunes. It had been abandoned in the 11th or 12th century and succeeded by a small church built less than half a mile inland, close to a Saxon cross. In time the wind-blown sands engulfed the second building though, since excavation, the ruins can be seen. In 1804 a third church was built at Perranzabuloe (St Piran-in-the-Sand) incorporating parts of the preceding building. The saint is also commemorated at Perranuthnoe on Mount's Bay and Perranarworthal near Penryn. A *Life of St Piran* appeared in the late Middle Ages but is now recognized as an adaptation of the life of another Irish saint, Ciaran, founder of the monastery of Saighir. According to this and later legends St Piran spends 15 years in Rome before returning to Ireland where his first disciples are animals—badger, boar, fox and wolf. The boar grubs out his cell for him. He sails to Cornwall on a millstone and lives for 200 years without losing his eyesight or his teeth. He performs many miracles and he becomes the patron saint of tin miners. The old Cornish expression 'drunk as a Perraner' is sometimes said to be based on the saint's fondness for strong drink, but is more likely to refer to the miners' exuberant celebration of his feast day in former times.

St Neot

Nothing is known historically of St Neot. The chroniclers make him a monk of Glastonbury Abbey, a dwarf 4 ft tall who prays or recites the Psalms standing up to his neck in water. He is fond of animals and when a hunted deer comes to his cell he stops the pursuing hounds with a glance and claims the hunter's horn as an offering to hang in his chapel. Each day two fish swim to his cell by the river and he takes one and lets the other go. One day in his absence a disciple cooks both fish but when the saint returns he puts one back in the river and it swims away. To enter his church he throws the key into the lock from the churchyard and the door opens unaided. This attractive little character is also commemorated outside Cornwall: St Neots in Cambridgeshire claims to be his burial place.

St Ia

A charming tale introduces St Ia, the patron saint of St Ives. She is an Irish virgin of noble birth who wishes to join St Gwinear on a missionary voyage to Cornwall, but he sails without her. She kneels to pray on the shore and notices a leaf in the water which she touches with her stick to see if it will sink. Instead it grows bigger and, assured that it has been sent by God, she embarks on it and crosses safely to the Hayle estuary. Another missionary, St Kea, is said to have made his journey in a·stone trough.

St Samson

St Samson is a more substantial character, his life recorded within 50 to 60 years of his death. He was a 6th-century Welsh bishop who founded the great Abbey of Dol in Brittany and another at Pental in Normandy. These are historical facts, but his visits to Ireland and Cornwall receive more imaginative treatment. In Cornwall he converts idol worshippers and raises a boy from the dead. He tackles a monstrous serpent which lives in a deep cave and terrifies the neighbourhood. The serpent in turn is terrified by Samson and tries to bite its own tail. He ties his girdle round its neck and hurls it from a high rock, bidding it die. Whatever the facts of his visit to Cornwall, he is commemorated at Southhill, north-west of Callington, where water from his well is still used for baptisms, and at Golant on the Fowey river. A cave half a mile from Golant church, down by the river, fits the description of the serpent's lair. His connection with the island of Samson in the Scillies was mentioned as early as 1193. Samson's importance was widespread, with many dedications in Brittany and his name honoured in Ireland, Italy and Bavaria. His travels in Cornwall, Wales, Ireland and Brittany show the constant intercommunication taking place between the Celtic countries on the fringe of Western Europe.

A multitude of saints

The catalogue of the saints is a long one. Signposts point to places like St Breock, St Keverne, St Teach, St Winnow and so on, or to villages whose names are derived from saints such as Crantock (St Carantoc), Lanivet (St Nevet), Egloskerry (St Keria) and in Devon Filleigh (St Fili). No other region in England preserves the traditions of so many saints.

In modern eyes the miracles attributed to them long after death tend to obscure rather than enhance their standing. But despite the labyrinth of myth and the scarcity of contemporary records, the achievement of the Celtic Saints is clear. In the centuries after the departure of the Romans they evangelized the South West. When St Augustine landed in south-east England in AD 597 to convert the heathen Saxons, the unconquered Celtic tribes of Devon and Cornwall had already accepted baptism. No wonder the saints endeared themselves to the Cornish and exerted a powerful and enduring influence.

The South West Coastal Path

The idea of long-distance paths originated in the United States in the 1920s and in 1935 a suggestion was made for the creation of a first path in England along the spine of the Pennines. But it was not until the passing of the National Parks and Access to the Countryside Act in 1949 that the Countryside Commission and local authorities were given the necessary legal muscle to develop them. A dozen or more paths have since come into existence. Of these the South West Coastal Path is far and away the most ambitious. It runs for 567 miles from Minehead in Somerset to Sandbanks (Poole Harbour) in Dorset and includes the 480-odd miles of magnificent coastline in Devon and Cornwall. It was opened in sections between 1973 and 1978 and has gradually been improved over the years, thanks to continuous prodding by the South West Way Association and the Ramblers Association, and with considerable assistance from the National Trust who fortunately own over a third of the route.

The path is described starting from the Somerset border on the north coast of Devon. The sections are arbitrary, each requiring from two to four days' walking depending on the mileage, the difficulties of the terrain and the fitness and determination of the individual. Only sponsored walkers or true adventurers are likely to attempt the whole path at one time, but long or short stretches can be selected for an afternoon's stroll or a day's outing, a weekend or several days of tramping. The path provides some of the most beautiful and challenging walking in England. Comparatively few easy stretches relieve the hard up and down slog and caution is needed in many places after rain or in bad weather. Cliff falls may cause diversions.

A 1/50,000 or 1/25,000 map and careful planning are essential for the serious walker. As with all long-distance paths, the Acorn symbol marks the way and also a limited number of signposts.

Devon border to Combe Martin (20 miles) All this section is in the Exmoor National Park. From Somerset the path enters Devon at Glenthorne Combe and can conveniently be joined by a path from the A39 between Wingate and County Gate. After $3\frac{1}{2}$ miles along the cliffs the path passes over The Foreland and plunges spectacularly down Countisbury Hill to Lynmouth, a fall of nearly 1000 ft in 2 miles. After climbing up from Lynmouth to Lynton (or taking the cliff railway) the Victorian North Walk provides an easy route to the famous Valley of the Rocks. Beyond this a minor road goes to Woody Bay and then a path through woodland and along the cliffs leads to the striking beauty of Heddon's Mouth Cleave. The path turns inland to cross the Cleave at Hunters Inn.

The experienced and agile can cross nearer the beach, but both the descent and ascent are extremely rough and steep. From Hunters Inn more cliff walking and a steep climb up the great bulk of Great Hangman (1044 ft), the greatest of the hog's-back cliffs, leads to the National Park boundary and the steep descent to Combe Martin.

Valley of the Rocks, Lynton

Combe Martin to Barnstaple (30 miles) Mainly road walking for the 5 miles to Ilfracombe, though the path out to Widmouth Head gives some relief with fine views eastward to Great and Little Hangman and the massive Exmoor coastline. Once through Ilfracombe easy stretches over open country go to Lee Bay, Morte Point with its sharp reefs and then the fine sands at Woolacombe. The path climbs gently out to Baggy Point and back to Croyde Beach. The next couple of miles to Saunton are also easy though rather less attractive. The final 10 miles are most interesting. After crossing the golf links the path runs inland of the famous Braunton Burrows to White House and Horsey Island, and along the edge of Braunton Marsh and historic Braunton Great Field to Velator. The disused railway line carries the path on past Chivenor airfield and along the north bank of the Taw into Barnstaple.

Barnstaple to Hartland Point (30 miles) A new section has been created on the south bank of the Taw using the disused railway line to Instow and Bideford on the river Torridge. In summer the ferry from Instow across the Torridge to Appledore can be used; at other times it is best to walk into Bideford and bus out to Appledore or Westward Ho! to resume the path. From Appledore the purists will want to pick their way round the peninsula at the mouth of the Taw–Torridge estuary and along the pebble ridge to Westward Ho! Alternatively a minor road conveniently cuts off the peninsula. A more exciting section now begins with much up and down walking, gradually increasing in severity, for the 19 miles to Hartland Point. Only the Hobby Drive near Clovelly provides a gentle 2-mile stretch. Hartland Point, the 'Hercules promontory' of the Romans, stands 350 ft above the turbulent tide race at the merging of the Bristol Channel with the Atlantic.

Hartland Point to Crackington Haven (25 miles) A dramatic section southward from the Point, nearly all the way on the exposed edge of the Atlantic cliffs and a great contrast to what has gone before. It is hard up and down work to cross the many streams that have carved openings through the cliff wall to reach the sea. The cliffs, contorted layers of rock lashed by the Atlantic, are rugged and magnificent. Hartland Quay, the fine waterfall at Speke's Mill Mouth and Welcombe Mouth lead to the Cornish border at Marsland Mouth and on to Morwenstow where the Reverend Robert Hawker's driftwood hut stands beside the path. After 16 miles Bude provides a break and the short stretch on to Widemouth Bay is unattractive. Beyond the Bay another fine cliff walk goes for 6 miles to the 450 ft drop into Crackington Haven.

Crackington Haven to Rock (30 miles) The good 7-mile stretch to Boscastle includes High Cliff (731 ft), the highest point on the whole Cornish coast, and the fine waterfall at Pentargon. Another good section goes on 5 miles to Tintagel, crossing Rocky Valley and passing above Tintagel Castle to the clifftop church beyond. From there to Port Gaverne is very wild with eight combes to negotiate, some very deep and steep-sided. The average walker should allow at least 4 hours to cover the 8 miles, with pauses to draw breath and to admire the wonderful views. The next section also includes some fine cliff walking round Kellan Head, Rumps Point (with its impressive Iron Age Promontory fort) and Pentire Point from which the views are exceptional even for the Coastal Path. The path turns back south-east from the Point to the sands of Polzeath and to very different, easy walking along the Camel estuary to Rock for the ferry across the river to Padstow.

Hawker's hut, Morwenstow (see p. 188)

Padstow to Perranporth (33 miles) An easy walk along the edge of the Camel estuary leads to Stepper Point and on by beach and comparatively low cliffs to the resorts of Trevone and Porthcothan with Trevose Head (240 ft) between them. The easy stretch continues for another 11 miles along the clifftop past Bedruthan Steps to Mawgan Porth and then above the impressive 2 miles of Watergate beach to Trevelgue Head and its interesting prehistoric remains. From there the path follows the streets of Newquay to the harbour. The route climbs from the harbour to Towan Head, passing the famous Huer's Hut, and turns south beside the golf links above Fistral Beach. At Pentire Point East it turns back eastward above the river Gannel and the yellow sands of Crantock Beach. In summer the Fern Pit ferry crosses direct to Crantock Beach; at other times the river may be waded with caution at low tide in good conditions. Another ferry upstream that crosses to Penpol Creek is also seasonal, though a tidal bridge near by over the main channel can be used at low tide. Otherwise the first road bridge over the Gannel on A3075 is over 2 miles from Fern Pit. From Crantock Beach it is easy going for the 10 miles to Holywell Beach, Penhale Point (skirting the military camp) and along Perran Beach to the small resort of Perranporth. The 'towans', the wind-blown sand dunes behind Perran Beach, are the highest in England.

Perranporth to St Ives (29 miles) A most interesting 3 miles to St Agnes through an area littered with the spoil heaps and ruined buildings of 19th-century mining. A scramble up and down is necessary at Trevellas Porth, otherwise it is easy walking along the cliffs that drop almost sheer to the sea. After climbing out of St Agnes another fine stretch goes to Porthtowan with birds, seals and wild flowers to observe and more mining relics, some spectacular, e.g. Wheal Coates. More cliff walking for 10 miles, with some stiff climbs to Navax and Godrevy Points, is marred for a couple of miles by having to walk beside the formidable fence of the Ministry of Defence establishment at Nancekuke. After Godrevy and the edge of Gwithian village the last few miles into Hayle are a rather dull slog along the beach of St Ives Bay beside another long stretch of piled-up 'towans'. Hayle also makes a dull interlude, relieved only by the varied bird life of the estuary and Carsnew Pool. Once round the latter and past Lelant Church, the path runs beside the railway into St Ives.

St Ives to Penzance (38 miles) This section covers the Land's End or Penwith peninsula and provides some of the most desolate walking anywhere in the South West. The path starts modestly from St Ives but soon becomes a hard slog along the cliffs over rough moorland with steep climbs and falls for a dozen miles to the headland known as Pendeen Watch. Turning south-west the path is easier but no less impressive through the Penwith mining area with its numerous relics. From Cape Cornwall another easy stretch, with the first sighting of the Longships lighthouse $1\frac{1}{2}$ miles off Land's End, leads to the magnificent sweep of Whitesand Bay and Sennen Cove with its lifeboat station at the southern end. Climbing out of the Cove an unspoiled mile of rugged cliffs carries the path to the curiously named Dr Syntax Head, the westernmost point of the mainland, and to Land's End itself where millions of visitors have eroded the clifftop. The fascination is obvious, with the jumbled stacks of black granite rock and the savage reefs running out towards the Longships lighthouse and the sea always turbulent and dangerous. On a clear day the Isles of Scilly can be seen 28 miles to the south-west. From Land's End the 5 miles round to Porthcurno is generally regarded as one of the finest stretches, if not the finest, of the whole path. It is superb cliff walking with only one small fishing village (Porthgwarra) on the way. Passing the open air Minack Theatre on the cliff at Porthcurno, the path goes down to the beach and up again for the short stroll to the rugged promontory of Treryn Dinas with its Logan Stone and Iron Age fort. A more exacting section, with a very steep climb at Porthguarnon, leads to beautiful Lamorna Cove, beloved of artists and a great contrast to the bare, exposed inlets of the north coast. From the Cove it is 2 miles to the road above Mousehole and the route at present then follows the coast road through Mousehole and round Penlee Point to Newlyn and Penzance.

Penzance to Mullion Cove (20 miles) A patchy section until Loe Bar has been crossed. East of Penzance the path goes along the beach to Marazion with fine views of St Michael's Mount and far ahead the Lizard Peninsula. Beyond Marazion it is nearly a mile along A394 before a path leads off across fields to regain the coast. After Perranuthnoe a more pleasant stretch passes attractive Prussia Cove where a pillar on the headland commemorates the wreck of the battleship *Warspite* in April 1947 when on its way to be broken up and the heroic rescue of the crew by the Penlee lifeboat. The path runs along the sheer cliff above Kenneggy Sands but at Praa the beach is again the best route to avoid using a road. The next stretch is cliff walking again past the ruined engine houses and stacks at Wheal Prosper and Wheal Trewavas and on to

Land's End

the small town of Porthleven, where the impressive harbour recalls its unfilled ambition to become a major port. More road work follows to Loe Bar, the shingle ridge between Mount's Bay and Loe Pool, and then a good 5-mile stretch along the cliffs and round the coves to the delightful Mullion Cove on the Lizard peninsula.

Mullion Cove to Helford (26 miles) The 6 miles to Lizard Point over exposed moorland is spectacular and passes Kynance Cove with its islands and colourful varieties of serpentine rock. The Point, the southernmost tip of the mainland, is as rugged and impressive as Land's End though far less visited. The route onwards is exacting in places, following the cliffs but with steep descents to the attractive fishing villages of Cadgwith and Coverack (9 miles) and on to Lowland Point. Offshore are the Manacles, the notorious reef where more ships have come to grief than at any other place along the south coast of Cornwall. An unattractive section, forced away from the coast by quarries, leads to Porthallow village where the path returns to the cliffs to reach Nare Point and the gradual descent to Gillan Creek. This can be waded at low tide to reach the pretty hamlet of St Anthony, otherwise it can be rounded at Carne. From St Anthony the path goes out to Dennis Head and on through private woodlands on the south bank of the Helford river to the pleasant village of Helford. The ferry across to Helford Passage is seasonal and at other times a very long detour through Gweek has to be made.

Helford Passage to Portholland (24 miles) The 9 miles to Falmouth is an easy section through the attractive hamlet of Durgan, below the National Trust gardens at Glendurgan, and out to Mawnan Shear and Rosemullion Head. Only short stretches of road at Maen Porth and Swanpool break the good cliff path, and on reaching Falmouth the walk out to Pendennis Head is worth while for the spectacular views. An all-year ferry from Falmouth crosses Carrick Roads to St Mawes, but then the river Percuil has also to be crossed to regain the path at Place Manor. It may be possible to arrange a boat direct to Place from Falmouth or on from St Mawes, otherwise a long diversion by road is necessary. From Place the path goes out to the lighthouse on St Anthony Head and the well-preserved remains of a coastal artillery battery constructed at the end of the 19th century as part of the defences of Carrick Roads. The path descends to the beaches at Porthbeor and Towan and runs along low cliffs to the fishing village of Portscatho (6 miles). A stiff climb round Gerrans Bay to Nare Head (330 ft) begins 9 miles of easy walking to the unspoiled cove at Portloe and the small beaches of Portholland on Veryan Bay.

Portholland to Fowey (24 miles) Good walking out to Dodman Point (370 ft), with its Iron Age fort and superb views up and down the coast, and on to Gorran Haven. A mile and a half beyond is 'Bodrugan's Leap' (National Trust) where Sir Henry Trenowth of nearby Bodrugan, a follower of Richard III pursued by Sir Richard Edgcumbe of Cotehele, rode over the cliff and escaped in a waiting boat to France. The path soon leaves the cliffs and follows the road for a mile through Portmellon to the old fishing port of Mevagissey (9 miles). The next 10 miles includes pleasant Hallane Beach and Black Head but from Pentewan onwards the dominance of the china clay industry is apparent, the sands whitened by waste formerly washed down the St Austell river and the sea bed affected over a wide area. From Porthpean the walk to Charlestown and on through the developments at Carlyon Bay and the port of

Par can only be described as a chore. From Polmear east of Par the path picks up again and runs through open country for 5 miles round Gribbin Head to Fowey. An all-year ferry crosses the estuary to Polruan.

Polruan to Stonehouse/Plymouth (30 miles) Climbing out of Polruan the 7 miles to Polperro is hard going but very rewarding – a beautiful and unspoiled coastline, and the path mainly on National Trust land and well maintained. An easier stretch goes on to Looe passing the two pairs of landmarks above Talland Bay and near Looe Island, a measured nautical mile apart, for use in speed trials at sea. A seasonal ferry crosses Looe harbour, otherwise a stroll through the streets of West and East Looe makes a pleasant interlude. The next dozen miles to Rame village are unsatisfactory, with a lot of road walking, a military range at Fort Tregantle and much holiday development. If the tide is right and no red flags flying, the sands and boulders of Whitesand Bay offer some relief for the last 3 miles. Climbing up from the beach or moving on from Rame, a good path goes round magnificent Rame Head (300 ft) with its ruined 14th-century chapel and, in good weather, a sight of the Eddystone Lighthouse 10 miles out to sea. The walk on to Penlee Point and round to the twin villages of Cawsand and Kingsand gives breath-taking views of Plymouth Sound and its great breakwater. Along the edge of the Sound the path comes to the wooded Mount Edgcumbe Country Park and to the hamlet of Cremyll with its historic ferry across the Hamoaze to Stonehouse.

Stonehouse/Plymouth to Bigbury-on-Sea (25 miles) The first 7 miles are from Admiral's Head at Stonehouse through Plymouth and its suburbs east of the river Plym and back westwards to the start of the proper path at Turnchapel near Mount Batten Point. The walk along Plymouth Hoe to the Barbican area and Sutton harbour with the many monuments and historic buildings should not be missed. From Turnchapel a good path along the eastern cliffs of the Sound is rewarding for its views but at Wembury Point naval gunfire may cause a diversion. The easy stretch goes on through Wembury, where the church stands alone on the cliff edge, to Warren Point and the beautiful, wooded estuary of the river Yealm (7 miles). A summer ferry crosses to Noss Mayo, otherwise a long diversion is necessary to cross the Yealm. A nicely graded track runs out from Noss Mayo towards Gara Point and the path continues up and down along the cliffs to the river Erme, the fine coastal views culminating in the unspoiled river mouth. It can be forded in normal conditions for an hour before and after low tide by an old crossing to a point ½ mile north of Wonwell Beach. The path climbs slowly east of the river and the going becomes strenuous with some very steep slopes for most of the 4 miles from the Erme to Bigbury and the mouth of the river Avon.

Bigbury-on-Sea to Torcross (24 miles) A summer ferry crosses the river Avon to Bantham, otherwise a long diversion must be made up to the bridge at Aveton Gifford. An easy 4-mile stretch goes on to Thurlestone and to the popular Hope Cove. The next 7 miles to Salcombe are exacting and magnificent – high, rugged cliffs from Bolt Tail to Bolt Head, with a steep fall and climb at Soar Mill Cove, and then the beautiful entrance to the Kingsbridge estuary. The path descends to Salcombe for the all-year ferry across to East Portlemouth. Good and strenuous walking continues for 8 miles to Prawle Point and Start Point. Beyond Start Point the

Sea campion near Helston

path goes through the villages of Hallsands and Beesands to Torcross.

Torcross to Brixham (20 miles) After a slog along Slapton Sands to Strete Gate the route at present takes to the main road (A379) until beyond Stoke Fleming village, unpleasant walking for 3½ miles. A minor road then leads to the National Trust Car Park at Little Dartmouth farm and paths go on to the coast. A fine stretch follows for 1½ miles to Dartmouth Castle. The lower ferry for cars at Dartmouth is the shortest route across the river to Kingswear, but a passenger ferry runs from the Quay for those who wish to see more of this historic town. A mile of quiet roadway leads out of Kingswear to Mill Bay Cove where a strenuous section begins across the steep valley and through Warren Woods to Inner Forward Point and along the coast to Man Sands. This stretch was only opened in 1984, most of it on land formerly owned by Lt Colonel H. Jones, the Falkland VC, and dedicated to his memory. Good cliff walking continues to Berry Head at the south end of Torbay and so down into Brixham.

Brixham to Exmouth (24 miles) A difficult and unexciting section, mainly road walking for 10 miles round Torbay to Marine Drive, Torquay, where a path runs out to Hope's Nose, the northern limit of the Bay. The path struggles on by Anstey's Cove, Oddicombe beach and through woodlands to Watcombe Head. Open country is at last reached beyond Maidencombe with some very steep climbs in the 3 miles to the red promontory called the Ness at the mouth of the river Teign and the resort of Shaldon. An all-year ferry crosses to Teignmouth. A stroll along the front leads to a stretch of the sea wall between Brunel's railway line and the beach. After a mile or so the railway enters a tunnel and Smugglers Lane carries the path up to the A379 for another section of unpleasant walking into Dawlish with only one diversion at

Dartmouth Castle (see p. 79)

present to the cliffs. From Dawlish the best route is along the beach at low tide all the way to Dawlish Warren, the great spit at the mouth of the river Exe. More roadwork has to be faced to Starcross for the summer ferry to Exmouth, otherwise it is the road again to Powderham Church, and then the pleasant estuary bank to Turf Lock and the canal towpath to reach the ferry across to Topsham.

Exmouth to Dorset border (26 miles) The whole of the East Devon coast has been declared 'an area of outstanding natural beauty'. After the long promenade or sandy beach at Exmouth, the path climbs to the red cliffs of the High Land of Orcombe (250 ft) and is good walking all the way to Budleigh Salterton, marred only by the enormous caravan park at Sandy Bay and the rifle range that denies access to Straight Point. At present no bridge crosses the narrow mouth of the Otter at the end of Budleigh Salterton beach but a good path runs about ½ mile inland to White Bridge and back to the cliffs. The 3-mile stretch onwards is very enjoyable walking until another huge caravan park disfigures the approach to attractive Ladram Bay. The going then becomes harder with a 500 ft climb to pass through the plantation below the summit of Peak Hill and down, up and down again into the pleasant resort of Sidmouth. The next 9 miles to Seaton are even more exacting with two formidable combes before reaching Branscombe Mouth. Another steep climb leads to Hooken Cliff and its famous chalk landslip – 10 acres of land that fell into the sea one night in 1790 – and to the striking 400 ft-high chalk cliffs of Beer Head. Beyond Beer village and Seaton a bridge crosses the river Axe and the path climbs to Seaton golf course before going down into the Dowlands Landslip, a National Nature Reserve where walkers must keep strictly to the path.

China Clay

The region's manufacturing industries are small-scale and employ only a fifth of the work force, well below the national average. The exception is the extensive quarrying and refining of kaolin or china clay.

Few visitors to Cornwall can escape at least a glimpse of the impressive ugliness of the landscape round St Austell. It is a vast, grey labyrinth of yawning quarries and towering heaps of waste that have replaced the granite moorland of Hensbarrow. It has often and rightly been called a lunar landscape. Other workings can be seen elsewhere in Cornwall, particularly on Bodmin Moor, and on Lee Moor in Devon, but so far it is only round St Austell that 30 square miles of countryside have been totally obliterated. The reason is that the Hensbarrow area has been worked since the industry began and produces the best quality clay. Historically, the industry is merely the latest of innumerable ventures to wring wealth from the Cornish rocks and at the present time a remarkably successful one.

China clay was formed about 300 million years ago when the granite backbone of Devon and Cornwall was cooling and acidic vapours partly decomposed the felspar element in it. The Chinese first discovered that it could be used for making fine porcelain. While the Saxons conquered England they were already quarrying it in the Kaoling Hills after which it is named. But the method of making porcelain was a closely guarded secret until early in the 18th century when it became known in Western Europe and the search for local deposits began.

Cookworthy and the start of porcelain manufacture

William Cookworthy (1705–80), born in Kingsbridge, Devon, was a Quaker who established himself as a wholesale chemist in Plymouth. He studied an account by a Jesuit priest of the manufacture of porcelain in China, obtained specimens of the clay from America and set out on a systematic hunt for it in Cornwall. The identification of a small deposit on Tregonning Hill near Helston was soon afterwards followed by the discovery of more extensive deposits at St Stephen-in-Brannel in the area west of St Austell which is still being worked. Cookworthy took some years to master the technique of manufacture but at last found the right mixture of clays and, in primitive kilns, raised the necessary firing temperature of 1300–1400°C to produce the first true porcelain made in England. He patented the process in 1768 and opened a factory in Plymouth, a short-lived venture which moved to Bristol two years later. The long-term results of his discovery would certainly have surprised him.

The Staffordshire potteries, Wedgwood, Spode, Minton, soon took over the process and supplies of clay were shipped north through the harbour constructed at Charlestown close to St Austell in the 1790s. Although the cost of transportation was high, it was cheaper than bringing in sufficient quantities of coal to establish potteries in Cornwall. The demand for porcelain increased in spite of the wars with France (1793–1815) and it was not long before the use of the clay in papermaking started. It was both an effective filler and coating, producing a whiter, heavier paper better able

'The Cornish Alps', near St Austell

to take printing ink. Its value as an 'extender' was also exploited in less desirable ways. In 1814 a man was prosecuted at Truro for diluting flour with china clay. About this time fewer than 10 pits were operating in the St Stephen area with an output of barely 2000 tons a year.

Growth despite reverses

From these modest beginnings the industry grew slowly during the 19th century. New harbours were built at Pentewan and Par in the 1820s to handle the traffic, and new pits were opened on Bodmin Moor and elsewhere in Cornwall and on Lee Moor in Devon by 1860. Fowey harbour was then brought into use. The industry survived many setbacks – strikes, falling prices from 1870 onwards, the First World War – and by 1939 annual production had risen to 700,000 tons.

The Second World War proved another serious setback due to the industry's dependence on overseas markets and production dropped by nearly two-thirds. Since then, however, it has risen to 3 million tonnes a year, almost 20 per cent of world production. In the ceramic industry it is used not only for tableware and sanitary products but in tiles, glazes, enamels and furnace linings where its heat-resisting quality is of value. Paint, rubber and plastic manufacturing processes require it, also many pharmaceutical products, but a staggering 80 per cent of production goes to the papermaking industry.

Extracting the clay

Originally a process similar to tin streaming was adopted to extract and refine the clay, with the important difference that tin was heavier than its impurities, whereas in clay the unwanted elements of quartz sand and mica are heavier than the clay. The overburden, the varying depth of soil above the clay, was removed by pick and shovel. Streams of water from launders were directed on to the exposed clay to break it from the pit face, helped by the tools and boots of the quarrymen. This made a 'slurry' of which more than 80 per cent was waste. The slurry was carried down to pits where the sand dropped to the bottom, to be removed by horse and cart to the tips. It was then driven on manually or by water-powered pumps through launders and drags at different speeds where the gluey micaceous waste and any remaining sand were separated and, until 1974, discharged into rivers to pollute them and, in time, the sea. The clay, still in suspension, went to settling pits where the water could be drawn off. It was then allowed to dry naturally, packed in casks and carted away in horse-drawn wagons. This laborious process could take up to eight months to complete. The introduction of steam pumping engines and of coal-fired kilns were important improvements during the 19th century. The men who worked in the industry grew into close-knit communities as proud of their special skills and product as the tin miners whose age-old industry was collapsing while the extraction of china clay continued to expand.

With machines and the application of high technology the process has become vastly more elaborate and efficient. Drilling reveals the extent and depth of a deposit and the quality of the clay before a start is made. Mechanical excavators uncover the clay bed and dump trucks remove the overburden to tips. Water cannon, automatically controlled, wash the clay from the quarry face to the bottom of the pit from where it is pumped to a sand separation plant. From this the sand is taken to tips by conveyor belts. The slurry passes on to centrifugal separators where the finer micaceous waste is drawn off. A series of special dewatering tanks thicken the clay and any remaining particles of sand, mica and undecomposed felspar are removed during further refining. Filter presses and turbo or rotary driers complete the drying. Daily analysis of the slurry is carried out at most stages, chemicals are added to whiten the clay and make it more buoyant, and computers select the necessary blend to give the clay the required consistency. The whole process from pit face to delivery at the quayside can take a mere eight hours.

Disposing of waste and healing the scars

A huge problem for the industry and for the environment is the disposal of the overburden and of the sand and mica waste which form such an overwhelming proportion of the excavated material. Over 10 million tonnes of sand, for example, are produced a year. Of this barely a tenth is used for road material and precast and ready-mix concrete. Distribution costs are high so that it can only be used locally. Otherwise none of the waste has any commercial value. The industry has shown a determination to explore every means by which the battered landscape can be improved and reclamation plans have been in operation for a decade. The lunar aspect of Hensbarrow is slowly beginning to change. Though the waste sand is porous and acidic and contains no nutrients, the old conical tips can be colonized naturally by gorse and other assertive plants, but this takes 30 years and hardly improves the scenery. As a result of the Aberfan disaster in South Wales in 1966, tips of all kinds must now by law be flat-topped. Using up-to-date botanical skills and machinery they can be landscaped and seeded with grass and clover while still in use.

The micaceous waste, instead of being discharged into the rivers, is now carried away through miles of piping either to worked-out pits or to specially constructed storage lagoons. The white, powdery silt retains sufficient moisture to support grass and, in the long term, can become permanent pasture or even grow wheat or vegetables, and trees are planted round the lagoons to soften their unnatural appearance. Regeneration takes time, but the effort is being maintained and over the years will help to restore some parts of the devastated areas to usefulness. Research and the carrying out of reclamation work has cost the industry £12 million and a yearly outlay of £750,000 continues to be allocated for the purpose. All this reflects modern concern for the environment which in the past was totally disregarded. Perhaps the greatest achievement so far has been the change in the rivers (Par, Fowey, St Austell), from industrial 'drains' to proper habitats once more for birds, fish and human beings.

A valuable industry

While reclamation continues, and new pits are opened and old ones become larger and deeper, the industry's importance to the region and to the national economy remains evident. It gives employment to thousands of people and 80 per cent of production is exported. The clay goes mainly to Continental Europe through the ports of Fowey and Par in Cornwall and Plymouth in Devon. The ports have been specially adapted to handle china clay and in Cornwall private roads connect the Hensbarrow quarries to them or the clay is piped to the quay as a slurry for customers who require it in this form. From Lee Moor all the output is piped to a plant at Marsh Mills on the outskirts of Plymouth and distributed by road or rail, or taken to Millbay Dock for shipment.

Tourism

The region's holiday industry began some 200 years ago. Up to the middle of the 18th century only intrepid 'foreigners' like Celia Fiennes and Daniel Defoe braved the long and difficult journey. Roads, where they existed at all, were the responsibility of parish councils who thought no good purpose would be served by maintaining them for the benefit of people passing through. Few wheeled vehicles were in use and people rarely travelled for pleasure. When they had to travel it was often quicker and easier by water than by land. This began to change when the Turnpike Companies were created in the 18th century with power to charge tolls for the making and upkeep of better roads. The first turnpike in the region brought the London road to Exeter in the 1750s, and during the next 30 years others were made to the principal towns in Devon. Cornwall also built – piecemeal – a network of turnpikes, notably the road from Launceston across Bodmin Moor in 1769, the precursor of the A30. But the roads in Cornwall attracted few visitors at first. They catered for Government and Admiralty dispatches and mail, landed gentry and travellers on official business. Cornwall maintained its isolation into the 19th century.

It was otherwise in Devon. The merchants of Exeter had begun to use Exmouth for 'bathing and diversion' early in the 18th century. An Assize Judge spread its reputation further afield and by the end of the century it was an established resort, the earliest of the region's watering places. Teignmouth was not far behind, and Dawlish and Sidmouth were developing by the 1790s. Medical opinion recommended the benefits of sea bathing and the climate and scenery of the South West were attractive to the moneyed classes. The long wars with France (1793–1815), which it was estimated prevented 40,000 people from travelling on the Continent, boosted all the English resorts. Because Plymouth still lacked a breakwater to give protection from the south-westerly gales, the Fleet anchored regularly in the shelter of Tor Bay and at the northern end the little harbour of Tor Quay developed rapidly into an all-year resort.

The more rugged north coast of Devon did not attract visitors in any number until a little later. The first hotel at Lynton opened in 1807 and by the 1820s the small port and market town of Ilfracombe had been discovered and had grown equal to Exmouth and Sidmouth in population. The railway at last opened up Cornwall to visitors. Once Isambard Kingdom Brunel's great bridge at Saltash spanned the Tamar (1859), the trains carried people in increasing numbers to Newquay, Falmouth, St Ives and Penzance. The little fishing village of Newquay with a hundred inhabitants grew steadily into a town of 15,000 residents living on the holiday trade. The through line to Penzance opened in 1859 and about the same time the first steamer service across the turbulent waters to the Isles of Scilly began. Visitors to the islands were comparatively few until after the Second World War when better and larger boats, and helicopter services, made access easier both for day trips and holidays.

Detail of fan vaulting, Exeter Cathedral (see p. 84)
Overleaf: Sidmouth and Salcombe Hill cliff (see p. 128)

Replica of the Golden Hind, Brixham (see p. 68)

The region's comprehensive rail network was completed in 1898 by the opening of the line to Bude. Bank Holidays, legalized by Act of Parliament in 1871, enabled all classes to swarm to the seaside if only for the day. When holidays for all started soon afterwards, the use of the railways increased dramatically and all the region's resorts became busier and less selective.

The car and the motor coach introduced the modern expansion of the industry. Holiday travellers by road in the 1920s may have been few, but by the 1930s cars had begun to challenge the railways and new and improved roads became necessary. The bypass built to divert traffic round Exeter, the gateway to more than half of Devon and to the whole of Cornwall, was notorious for its traffic jams even before 1939.

The explosion of the industry in the last 30 years has been due to the immense increase in car ownership, and more recently to the opening of the M5 motorway from Bristol. This penetrates across the river Exe into the heart of Devon and brings millions of people within a few hours' driving time of the resorts. The railways, once the pride and mainstay of the region, can now claim less than 10 per cent of holiday traffic. Another aspect of easy road access is the spread of tourism to the remotest parts and through all months of the year. The April–September season still dominates with 70 per cent of all visitors, but the rest come in the winter months, lured by the prospect of milder weather than elsewhere in Britain and uncrowded beaches and countryside.

So tourism has become an essential part of the region's economy. Visitors spend an estimated £800 million a year, nearly a tenth contributed by people from overseas; and 45,000 jobs depend on it. People flock to an environment that provides nearly every form of outdoor recreation including the best surfing in England and the unusual excitement of shark fishing. Every effort is made to provide other holiday attractions against the background of the superb coasts, rivers and countryside. The lists on pages 215–217, by no means exhaustive, show how the region caters for a tremendous variety of leisure interests. The attractions are open all the year round except as stated. In addition, most towns have their own museums, many first class and no longer the dry-as-dust places they used to be. Water Authority, Forestry Commission and National Trust properties offer picnic sites and nature trails. Lifeboat stations usually welcome visitors. Some of the lighthouses are open at certain times. The local authorities maintain Tourist Information offices in all the important centres.

The Tavistock canal (see pp. 137–40)

DEVON

Watersmeet, near Lynmouth (see p. 105)

Watersmeet, near Lynmouth (see p. 105)

Editorial Note

If a name within the text of an entry is printed in capital letters, this indicates that it has a Gazetteer entry of its own.

Entry headings are followed by a map reference in parentheses, thus: Holberton (2/5A). The figure 2 is the map number; 5A is the grid reference, with 5 indicating the across, and A the down reference.

Previous page: Torquay Harbour

Devon Gazetteer

Appledore *see* Bideford

Arlington Court (2/3A) The home of one branch of the Chichester family beside the A39 6 miles north-east of BARNSTAPLE. The house, contents and nearly 3500 acres of grounds passed to the National Trust on the death of Miss Rosalie Chichester in 1949. The family came to Arlington in the 14th century but the present house was built in 1820–3 to the design of a Barnstaple architect, Thomas Lee. It is a plain-looking building decorated only by Tuscan pilasters at the corners and a semicircular porch with Doric columns on the east side. It was extended in 1865 and the attractive stable block built at the same time. This contains a fine collection of horse-drawn vehicles, some of which are used to take visitors round the grounds. The nearby church

The grounds, Arlington Court

was rebuilt in the 19th century, although some earlier Chichester memorials survive and the National Trust has added a monument to Miss Chichester designed by John Piper. The collections in the house – *objets d'art*, model ships, shells, costume, furniture – reflect her Victorian background and tastes. A watercolour by the visionary poet and painter William Blake, displayed in the ante room, is unexpected. This rare piece was found lying on top of a store cupboard after the National Trust took possession.

The grounds, surrounded by an iron fence 8 miles long, were already a nature reserve in Miss Chichester's lifetime. The lake is a wildfowl sanctuary, and roaming the park are the descendants of her Shetland ponies and Jacob sheep. Her famous nephew, Sir Francis Chichester, was born two miles away in the small village of Shirwell where his father was rector. After many epic solo flights and voyages he became the first

person to sail round the world single-handed.

The house is open from April to October, the grounds all year round.

Ashburton (2/3C) A small, quiet town on the old EXETER–PLYMOUTH coaching road and roughly halfway between the two cities. The name derives from the river Ashburn which rises on Dartmoor and flows through the town to join the Dart below BUCKFAST. Although a market town from Saxon times, its real prosperity was bound up with Devon's historic industries, tin and wool. Tin mining developed on Dartmoor late in the 12th century and Ashburton became one of the four collecting places round the Moor for weighing and stamping the metal before sale, i.e. a Stannary town. The other three were CHAGFORD, PLYMPTON and TAVISTOCK. About the same time the river provided power for several fulling mills where cloth was cleaned and thickened. Attractive slate-hung houses in the town date from the 16th and early 17th centuries when the cloth trade was at its height. During the 17th century, although the tin trade had become much diminished, the town was busy with increasing traffic between Exeter and Plymouth. This ceased when the railway line to Plymouth, which did not pass through the town, opened in 1846. About the same time the decline of the cloth trade finally ended the town's importance. It is now a place for retirement and a good base for exploring south-east Dartmoor. The interior of St Andrew's Church suffered a necessary but intrusive restoration in the 1880s, but the 15th-century tower remains. Its three stages are gracefully tapered and beautifully proportioned: one of the best in Devon. A headstone in the churchyard commemorates François Guidon, a young French officer of the Napoleonic period, who died while on parole from the war prison on Dartmoor.

Ashprington see Cornworthy

Ashton (2/4C) One of several attractive villages in the Teign valley, situated off the B3193 4 miles north of Chudleigh. Alternatively it can be approached by negotiating the network of lanes and by-roads that cross the Haldon Hills west of EXETER. The buildings, many of traditional cob and thatch, are scattered down the valley of a tributary stream. The church on a rocky mound at the higher end lies a mile distant from the Manor Inn down by the Teign river. In spite of restoration the church has retained the atmo-

sphere and fittings of a medieval building: carved bench ends, ancient glass, a wall painting and 15th-century screens. The canopy of the rood screen was added in the early years of this century, but some of the paintings on the panels and on the parclose screen that stands between chancel and Lady chapel are remarkable examples of medieval work.

Ashwater (2/2B) An agricultural village in the Carey valley 2 miles east of the Holsworthy–Launceston road (A388). Poor clay soil predominates here, but the valley fields are moderately fertile. Although the buildings are of no special note they are attractively grouped around the triangular village green. Ashmill bridge over the river was medieval, but was replaced early in the 19th century. The 14th- to 15th-century church of St Peter incorporates parts of earlier buildings to which the handsome Norman font and 13th-century lancet windows bear witness. The font is one of the most interesting in Devon. A moulded, square-topped bowl is rounded beneath and cushioned by four semi-circular panels with angel faces between them at the corners of the square moulding. The panels have plain rims terminating in dragon heads and are uniquely decorated. One shows a lion and another a salamander; the latter symbolizes the upright man who overcomes luxury and lust, for the salamander traditionally put out fires. The general design of the font resembles several in North Cornwall, which is not surprising with the Tamar river less than 4 miles away. The other interesting feature of the church is the six-bayed arcade between nave and aisle.

Atherington see High Bickington

Axminster (2/5B) A small and busy market town on the Dorchester to EXETER road (A35) less than 3 miles from the Dorset border. It is one of only two places in Devon – the other is Exminster near Exeter – where the suffix 'minster' has survived. The name derives from a Saxon monastery founded in the Axe valley about AD 700 and the town probably dates back to the second half of the 7th century. The main road curves through Axminster making an unusual and attractive High Street that will look even better when through traffic can use a proposed bypass. The interesting George Hotel is an 18th-century

Opposite. (Above) Grey heron, the Axe Estuary (see p. 60); (below) Axminster

coaching inn, and many 18th- and early 19th-century buildings can be found along the main road and in the narrow streets surrounding the church and market. The church is a Norman and 13th-century building with a central tower, not a common feature in Devon. Axminster carpets are well known. The manufacture was started in 1755 by a local man, Thomas Whitty. It was the custom to ring the church bells when a carpet was completed. George III and his Queen visited the factory in 1789 and the carpets found their way into many stately homes, including Saltram House (*see* Plympton). The business was carried on by the family until a grandson of Thomas Whitty went bankrupt in 1835 and the looms were sold to the Wilton factory.

Axmouth (2/5B) A very attractive village on the Axe estuary, a mile inland from the sea. The pebble bar across the river mouth and the narrow, tortuous outlet formed in medieval times make it difficult to realize that Axmouth's historical importance was as a harbour. Here or hereabouts the Romans had a safe anchorage to land men and stores. This part of East Devon has so far been more productive of evidence of Roman occupation than anywhere else outside EXETER. Four hundred feet above the village on Hawksdown Hill an Iron Age fort reveals even earlier activity in the area and it is not surprising that, after the Romans sailed away, the Saxons established a military base and trading centre. These continued into Norman times but the blocking of the river mouth, notwithstanding many attempts through the centuries to re-open it, ended Axmouth's prosperity. The result is today's small and delightful village with its unpretentious but pleasing main street and side lanes, the buildings ranging in date from Tudor times to the 19th century. Two inns, one a very old and thatched 'local' with a large garden for its summer visitors, perhaps reflect the time when the population was much larger than today.

The country to the east is worth exploring. If not following the designated Coastal Path from Seaton or Lyme Regis, the best approach to the famous Dowlands landslip is along lanes and footpaths running south-east from the village. All the cliffs along this part of the coast are susceptible to landslip and at Christmas 1839 something like an earthquake occurred. A huge section of cliff slipped seawards to create a deep chasm three-quarters of a mile long and several hundred feet wide between the new, sheer cliff and a detached 'island' consisting of an estimated eight

million tons of earth. This gorge is a unique place, a natural jungle, now part of the National Nature Reserve which stretches for several miles towards Lyme Regis. The Coastal Path runs through the Reserve and walkers must keep to it unless they obtain a permit from the Nature Conservancy Council. The Reserve is of special interest to geologists (strata, fossils); botanists (completely natural vegetation); and to bird-watchers (many resident and migrant birds).

Barnstaple (2/2A) The most important town in North Devon at the head of the estuary of the river Taw. A Saxon settlement became a walled Norman town with an important castle. Of these, however, only the 60 ft high mound of the castle remains. Gone, too, are the medieval wool trade, the ocean-going ships that once crowded the Quay, and the right to elect two members of Parliament. A once flourishing pottery industry is much diminished. But Barnstaple is still a robust, active place, the market town and agricultural centre for a large area, as it has been for centuries. Its three churches are not of outstanding interest except for the splendid broached spire of St Peter's, comparable with the best elsewhere. Shop fronts in the busy, narrow streets often obscure good 17th- and 18th-century buildings. Penrose Almshouses (1626) in Litchdon Street is the most agreeable of such foundations in the town: 20 dwellings round a courtyard aproached through a granite-columned colonnade. Close to the Royal Fortescue Hotel, the Woolwich Building Society premises have a fine plaster ceiling dated 1620, an example of the local plasterers' skill at its best.

Queen Anne's Walk on the Quay is an open portico where bargains were made at the height of the town's commercial prosperity. The glass-roofed Pannier Market, 445 ft long, was built in 1854 to replace an earlier building. Farmers' wives and smallholders still come to sell their produce on Tuesdays and Fridays, and the farmers on Fridays attend the cattle market beneath the castle mound. The 16-arched bridge over the Taw was built in the 15th century and has been much altered and widened since. The original width of less than 10 ft can be detected in the masonry under the arches. John Gay was born in Barnstaple in 1685 and educated at the grammar school (now St Anne's Chapel Museum) before he went to London to achieve popular success with *The Beggar's Opera*.

Barnstaple Pannier Market

Beer (2/5B) A fishing village in a small bay 1 mile west of Seaton that has become an agreeable small resort. Three roads converge steeply down the combe (as small valleys are termed in the West Country) to the shingle beach, and in the side lanes local materials have given many cottages a distinctive appearance. Some have rough flint walls and stone quoins, others alternate courses of flint and stone, very different from normal construction in other areas of Devon. Building stone has given Beer an importance out of all proportion to its size. Neolithic man knapped fine black flints on Beer Head, the chalk cliff rising 400 ft above the village, the last outcrop of the chalk ridges that run across southern England. The whitish Beer stone was first exploited by the Romans and quarrying continued at times down to the 19th century. The old quarries lie three-quarters of a mile west of the village, a cold labyrinth of caverns open for guided tours in the summer months. The stone was used not only in Roman villas in East Devon, in EXETER's Cathedral and Guildhall, and in many churches all over Devon, but also in London and elsewhere. Bovey House, now a hotel, was built mainly of the local stone in Tudor times.

Bere Ferrers (2/2C) A pleasant village on the Tavy 7 miles south of Tavistock and 'capital' of the broad peninsula that runs down to the meeting of the Tavy and Tamar rivers. The church of St Andrew is of particular interest. It retains more 14th-century work than is usual in a Devon church: for example, some of the windows and the unbuttressed tower. The outstanding feature is the glass in the east window depicting Christ and the kneeling figures of Sir William de Ferrers and his wife who built the church in the 14th century. It is reputed the oldest stained glass in Devon except for some in EXETER Cathedral. Other features are the late Norman font in limestone from Hurdwick quarry north of Tavistock, the 16th-century benches and the medieval tombs of the Ferrers.

Berrynarbor (2/2A) A small village in a deep valley 1 mile inland from COMBE MARTIN Bay on the North Devon coast. Along the coast road holiday chalets, camping sites and Watermouth Castle, a castellated 'Gothick' mansion built about 1825 and now a tourist attraction, are in marked contrast to the largely unspoiled village

Opposite. (Above) Beer; (below) The Tavy at Bere Ferrers

where ground has had to be levelled on the hillside to provide a small car park. The remains of a 15th-century manor house stand near the mainly 15th-century church. The 96 ft high church tower with its diagonal buttresses is one of the best in North Devon. The nave arcade is of Beer stone, which must have been brought mainly by sea from the famous quarry far away in the south-east of the county. Old cottages surround Ye Olde Globe Inn, a slate-roofed inn with slate and limewash floors in the bar, the latter often used in the past in country kitchens. The discerning visitor may 'discover' the village during the summer months but in its sheltered valley its character is well preserved.

Berry Pomeroy (2/3C) A village 2 miles east of TOTNES and approached by lanes from the NEWTON ABBOT (A381) or PAIGNTON (A385) roads, one of many places in Devon that has preserved much of its old-time tranquillity in spite of lying near main thoroughfares. The church of St Mary with its tall tower continues to preside over the cluster of houses. It was rebuilt late in the 15th century by Sir Richard Pomeroy, whose family had owned the manor since the Norman Conquest. He lies in an ornate tomb in the chancel. A monument in the north aisle to Sir Edward Seymour (son of the Lord Protector of Edward VI), and to his son Edward and his wife and their 11 children, commemorates the only other family to own the estate down to the present time. The church also has the distinction of having two vicars who between them spanned a hundred years: John Prince, author of a locally famous book, *The Worthies of Devon*, from 1681 to 1713; and Joseph Fox who served until 1781.

The ruins of Berry Pomeroy Castle are a mile away along a delightful wooded drive. Though the Pomeroys possessed it earlier, the oldest parts date from the 14th century: a powerful gatehouse with grooves for a double portcullis, two angular towers, a massive south curtain wall with a semi-circular tower projecting at the eastern end, and part of the western curtain. After nearly five centuries the Pomeroys sold to the Seymours who built a Tudor mansion and the customary service block inside the medieval walls. The three-storeyed mansion, though roofless, survives with a plain but powerful façade. Late in the 17th century the Seymours made their home in Wiltshire and the castle fell into decay. Isolated on the wooded heights above the Gatcombe brook it is one of the most romantic places in Devon and open to the public all year.

Bickleigh (2/4B) A pleasant village on the EXETER–TIVERTON road (A396) which is popular with people who work in either of those places. The Exe valley, here bounded by partly wooded hills that rise to over 600 ft above sea level, with vivid patches of ploughed red soil on the lower slopes in season, makes a glorious setting. The old mill near the bridge over the Exe is a craft centre open to the public. The bridge, rebuilt in 1809 after flood damage, together with the 17th-century thatched Trout Inn and cottages close by, is a well-known beauty spot. Across the bridge Bickleigh Castle (open from April to early October) was a fortified manor house rather than a castle. Part of the moat, the strong gatehouse and traces of a great hall are the fragmentary remains. Outside the castle on the west bank of the Exe stands a simple, thatched, 12th-century chapel. Although much restored in the 15th century and later, it gives a good idea of how a small Norman church must have looked.

Bideford (2/2A) A bustling North Devon town on the west side of the Torridge estuary. It rose to prominence as a seaport in Elizabethan times and prospered from overseas trade, particularly in tobacco, for 250 years. Some original merchants' houses survive in Bridgeland Street, which was laid out towards the end of the 17th century parallel to and north of the High Street. Across

Bideford bridge

the river part of the Royal Hotel in East-of-Water was also a 17th-century house. The rest of the town is mainly Victorian but delightfully sited on the steep hill beside the river. The church of St Mary, rebuilt in 1865 except for the tower, retains its large, Norman font complete with moulded base and unusual decoration. An informative plaque in the church commemorates Sir Richard Grenville, of *Revenge* fame, who did much to enhance the town's importance in Elizabethan times.

The bridge across the Torridge is 667 ft long with 24 arches of varying span. The latter feature arose because the 15th-century stone structure was built round an earlier wooden bridge constructed of oak timbers of different lengths. The finest medieval bridge in Devon, it has necessarily been repaired and widened over the last 400 years but is justly famous. The Quay at the west end was built out from an older quay to form a pleasant promenade by the river with a statue of Charles Kingsley in his professorial gown, pen in hand. His story of the Elizabethan seadogs, *Westward Ho!*, begins with an affectionate description of the town. He stayed at Northdown House, now a convent, while writing its 250,000 words in a scarcely credible period of less than seven months. A charming bow-fronted building facing the Quay was once the Ship Inn where, in the novel, the lovers of the ill-fated Rose Salterne formed their 'Brotherhood of the Rose'.

North of Bideford the resort of **Westward Ho!**

developed after the tremendous success of Kingsley's book and is named after it. Only the well-known golf links on Northam Burrows, and the long pebble ridge that does not always protect them successfully from the Atlantic rollers of Barnstaple Bay, are noteworthy. These and the gorse-covered hill west of the resort called Kipling Tors (National Trust) were the background for the exploits described in *Stalky & Co*, based on Kipling's own schooldays at the United Services College, now a terrace of houses.

Also north of Bideford, on the peninsula between the sea and the estuary, **Northam** has a ruthlessly restored church but the tall tower was a landmark for centuries for ships entering the estuary at Bideford bar. A mile north of Northam, at the tip of land overlooking the meeting of Taw and Torridge, **Appledore** is a delightful and unspoiled fishing village, with old houses in narrow streets and shipbuilding continuing on a modest scale. The North Devon Maritime Museum contributes to its attraction.

Bovey Tracey (2/3C) A small, straggling town astride the river Bovey 5 miles north of NEWTON ABBOT on the A382. From the 13th century it was a market town and later traded in cloth, lignite and pottery. It is now simply a 'gateway to Dartmoor', particularly to such well-known places as Haytor and the Becka Falls near MANATON. The Bovey basin continues to be important for its ball clay and potteries, but these industries are centred outside the town.

The church of St Thomas of Canterbury is a handsome building with a tall, unbuttressed 14th-century tower. The spacious interior is mainly 15th century; an outer north aisle was added in the 19th century. The capitals of the Beer stone arcade and the lavish carving of the 15th-century stone pulpit are noteworthy. A rood screen of 11 bays (1427, well restored in the 19th century) is a fine one and earlier in date than most of those surviving in Devon.

The bridge over the river dates from 1643, widened in the 19th century. The substantial building beside it with a wooden waterwheel, erected 1854, was not a mill but stables and servants' quarters for Riverside House near by. The wheel raised water for domestic use to a cistern in the stumpy tower of the building.

On the outskirts of the town, on the B3344, a late Georgian house and 200 acres called Parke were given to the National Trust in 1976. The Dartmoor National Park has its offices and an information centre there. A mile further along the road is the Yarner Wood National Nature Reserve where pied flycatchers, once scarce in Devon, have been encouraged to nest with notable success. Two Nature Trails are open to the public, but a permit is required to leave the marked paths. Four miles of the Bovey valley above the town, including the beautiful Lustleigh Cleave, are another National Nature Reserve with public rights of way through it.

Bradworthy (2/1B) A remote village in the valley of the river Waldon, a tributary of the Torridge, 8 miles north of Holsworthy. Minor roads converge on it from all directions through unspoiled countryside, mostly pasture fields and moorland. In layout it is a good example of an early Saxon village built compactly round a square. The buildings are modest but pleasant, the older ones dating from the 18th century. The aisleless church of St John the Baptist, with transepts of unequal length, was originally built late in the 12th century, no doubt on Saxon foundations. It was rebuilt again a hundred years later after being struck by lightning. The embattled tower is dated about 1500. In the church some typical medieval Barnstaple tiles are decorated with floral patterns. Three miles south-west the reservoirs known as the Tamar Lakes have facilities for fishing and sailing, a hide for birdwatching, a picnic area and walks. The upper lake dates back to 1825 when it was formed to supply water to the Bude canal (*see* Cornwall).

Braunton (2/2A) The largest village in Devon, 5 miles north-west of BARNSTAPLE on the A361 to ILFRACOMBE. Unfortunately its growth since the Second World War has been a suburban-like spread as a dormitory for Barnstaple, but much of interest remains. Some pleasant old houses survive in the original streets of the village and the large parish church indicates that Braunton was of considerable importance in medieval times. It is dedicated to St Brannoc, one of those Celtic saints more commonly found in Cornish contexts. He came over from South Wales in the 6th century and his bones are said to lie under the high altar. The aisleless building is mainly 13th century, but the south tower is Norman with a broached spire, now a little crooked, added later. The nave has a fine wagon roof of *c.* 1500 ornamented with gilded bosses. It is possible that the rebuilding at that time did away with an earlier aisle, resulting in the present unusually wide nave. The carved oak and chestnut pews were made throughout the 16th century and are

one of the best collections in Devon. Adjoining the churchyard is the usual Church House with wooden mullioned windows and a double stair at one end which gave direct access to the upper floor from the churchyard and the street. The ground floor is occupied by a small local museum.

South and west of the village the open country bounded by the sea and the Taw estuary is of exceptional interest. Close to the built-up area is Braunton Great Field, a fertile open field of several hundred acres. Though reduced in size since late medieval times and now farmed by only a few people, it represents a rare survival of the ancient open-field system. Its southern boundary is a medieval hedge dividing it from Braunton Marsh, once the common grazing land of the village. Enclosure and extensive drainage works completed early in the 19th century have altered its character. West of the Marsh and the Great Field, beyond a high embankment, are Braunton Burrows. This huge area of sand dunes, which rise to ridges nearly 100 ft above sea level, is famous for insects, mosses and wild flowers and as a stopping place for migrant birds. The southern portion of the Burrows is a National Nature Reserve of great importance where trails have been laid out through the dunes. West of the Burrows the 3-mile stretch of Saunton Sands is one of the finest beaches in south-west England.

Also close to the village is the RAF airfield at Chivenor, well known as a base for the helicopters that carry out many rescue missions along the north coast.

Brentor (2/2C) A famous landmark on the western border of Dartmoor approached along by-roads from TAVISTOCK, LYDFORD or MARY TAVY. It is a steep, isolated hill of volcanic stone rising over 1100 ft above sea level. The small church on the summit is dedicated to St Michael – like many others built on rocks all over Christendom. It is a plain building of nave and chancel, partly 12th but mainly 13th century, with an early 14th-century tower, built of stone quarried from the hillside itself. Tristram Risdon in his *Chorographical Description or Survey of Devon* of 1630 summed it up in often-quoted words: 'a church full bleak and weather beaten, all alone, as it were forsaken, whose churchyard doth hardly afford depth of earth to bury the dead . . .' But it is still in use, not forsaken, and many visitors scramble up the hill today to marvel at it and at the magnificent views.

St Michael's church, Brentor

Bridford (2/3B) An upland village in the hills west of the Teign river, and 9 miles south-west of EXETER. Abandoned mines and quarries (granite, barytes, lead) are set amid wonderful scenery, but it is the 14th- to 15th-century church that is rewarding after the 700 ft climb from the river along narrow lanes. The small building with its medieval glass, bench ends and wagon roofs contains probably the finest rood screen in Devon. Other good screens have survived (e.g. CULLOMPTON, CHULMLEIGH, KENTISBEARE and KENTON) but this is so unexpected in a remote and hilly village. The gentle colouring contrasts with the exuberant carving. The Tudor roses, and the pomegranates of poor Catherine of Aragon, suggest a date about 1530. Nowhere is the genius of the Devon woodcarvers better expressed. A mile north-west rears a huge granite outcrop known as Heltor Rock, giving all-round views of crowded hills and valleys leading up to Dartmoor and its tors.

Brixham (2/4C) A historic fishing port at the southern end of Tor Bay, once famous for its deep-sea trawlers. The fleet numbered 300 vessels at the beginning of the present century. Fishing declined dramatically between the wars and recently the holiday trade has become more important, as in so many coastal towns. The mainly early Victorian buildings are pleasant without being notable. The harbour retains its fascination, a haven for yachts and small boats of all kinds as well as for the small fleet of fishing boats. William of Orange landed here in 1688 and his statue on the Quay records his promise: 'The liberties of England and the Protestant religion I will maintain.' Berry Head, the promontory that protects the harbour to the east, is both a Local Nature Reserve and a Country Park. The dual designation is intended to protect the wild flowers and the important sea bird colonies (which include kittiwakes, fulmars, guillemots and razorbills) while allowing the public to enjoy the scenery which has long drawn people to the Head. The remains of two forts built on the promontory in Napoleonic times are listed buildings. Berry Head Hotel, erected as a military hospital in 1809, was subsequently lived in by the Reverend H. F. Lyte, author of 'Abide with me', inspired by the sun setting over Torbay.

Broadclyst (2/4B) A large village north-east of EXETER on the road to Taunton (B3181). The Saxon settlement, according to the Anglo-Saxon Chronicle, was burned by the Danes in 1001.

Most of the village is owned by the National Trust, forming part of the Killerton estate given by Sir Richard Acland in 1942–3. It has many cob-and-thatch cottages, a pleasant green, and almshouses built and endowed by Henry Burroughs in 1605. The Red Lion Inn, a striking building close to the churchyard, may have been the Church House. A double lychgate leads into the churchyard where a medieval cross survives and the village stocks have found sanctuary. The 15th-century church tower is one of the noblest in Devon, nearly 100 ft high and similar in design to many in Somerset: tall windows and pinnacles, tapering corner buttresses, decorated parapets, finely carved gargoyles. The interior of the church, mainly 14th century, has suffered from Victorian 'improvements' but contains a fine nave arcade and some notable monuments. The tomb of Sir John Acland (1620) is the most lavish Jacobean monument in Devon. The Aclands, one of Devon's best-known families, lived at Landkey near BARNSTAPLE in the 12th century. During Elizabethan times they came south to Columbjohn, 2 miles north-west of the village, and erected a mansion of which only an Elizabethan arched gateway and a rebuilt chapel remain. The rest was demolished when the family built Killerton House (now National Trust) in the 1770s. The house, which is open from April to October, stands in beautiful landscaped grounds with 15 acres of garden, open all year. On the great hill behind the house, where rhododendrons and conifers particularly flourish in acid soil, trees from all over the world are Killerton's chief attraction. Good walks circle the hill and go on to Columbjohn. Two miles to the south-west the 600 acres of Ashclyst Forest, another part of the estate, provide parking places and forest walks.

Broadhembury (2/5B) One of the prettiest villages in Devon lying snugly under a spur of the Blackdown hills 1 mile north-east of the A373 HONITON–CULLOMPTON road. The single street of thatched cottages slopes up towards some larger houses, the 14th- to 15th-century church and the Drewe Arms Inn. The church has tombs of the Drewe family who built the large house outside the village called Grange early in the 17th century. The inn was originally the Tudor Church House, a building used for meetings, parish feasts and other entertainments, rather like a later parish hall. It has interesting windows and ceiling beams and a low arched entrance passage which goes straight through to the back yard.

A mile to the south-west at the end of the Blackdown spur is **Hembury Fort** from which the village takes its name. It is the most impressive of Devon's Iron Age hill forts and one of its most fascinating prehistoric sites. There is a comparatively easy access on the east side but a scramble over the three banks and ditches at the north-west corner, or a climb from Hembury Fort cottage on the main road up the original hollow way to the west entrance, gives a better idea of the immense strength of the defences. The ramparts enclose a roughly triangular space of 7 acres. The fort was excavated in the 1930s and more work has been done recently. The first excavations revealed that the southern part of the fort overlaid an earlier Neolithic settlement. This was protected by a ditch and bank interrupted at intervals by entrances, a type of 'causewayed camp' long known from Windmill Hill in Wiltshire. This exciting discovery pushed the occupation of the spur back to the beginning of the 3rd millennium BC. A fine view from the tip of the spur, stretching down to the sea and westwards to the Haldon Hills beyond EXETER, rewards the visitor.

Buckfast (2/3C) The abbey stands beside the river Dart half a mile north of the A38(T) road. Founded in Saxon times it prospered under Cistercian rule from cattle and vast flocks of sheep. Apart from the abbey barn and a tower of the abbot's lodgings, everything was swept away after the Dissolution (1539). The Benedictine Order bought the site in 1882 and embarked on a rebuilding, carried out by the monks themselves, which followed the ground plan of the medieval abbey. Construction of the church began in 1907 and it was consecrated 25 years later. The combination of Norman and Early English styles is not unpleasing and represents a considerable achievement by a handful of devoted monks. From Buckfast in medieval times a track called the Abbot's Way went up to the edge of Dartmoor at Cross Furzes and then across the wilderness to the abbeys at Buckland and TAVISTOCK, a good route today for explorers of the southern Moor.

Buckfastleigh, a mile southward, was a clearing of woodland by the abbey in the 13th century. It became a small market town, and in the heyday of the wool trade a mill town, but it was always overshadowed by ASHBURTON a few miles away. The railway came up from TOTNES in 1872 on its way to Ashburton. It was closed in the 1960s but has been reopened by the Dart Valley Railway

Co. Steam locomotives once more puff up and down beside the beautiful stretch of the Dart between Buckfastleigh and Totnes.

Buckland in the Moor (2/3C) Four miles northwest of ASHBURTON a row of picturesque stone and thatched cottages lie in the lovely combe where Ruddycleave Water, a typical Dartmoor stream, runs under the road and plunges down 400 ft through woods to the river Dart in its deep gorge. The main part of the unspoiled village is a quarter of a mile away up a steep hill. St Peter's Church, like most of the cottages, is built of 'moorstone', the West Country name for surface granite. Strewn all over Dartmoor, it has been used undressed since the Bronze Age, and cut and dressed since Saxon times. The first church was late 12th century (the Norman font survives), rebuilt in the 13th and 15th centuries. It is probable that the handsome rood screen was the final embellishment. A wooden staircase to the rood loft, instead of the more usual stone steps, is elaborately carved. The clock on the church tower has no numerals for the hours but gilt letters which, starting from nine o'clock, read 'My dear Mother', a tribute from a former lord of the manor. High above the village the rocks of Buckland Beacon (1282 ft), one of the best-known landmarks on southern Dartmoor, give

The clock, St Peter's Church, Buckland in the Moor

breathtaking views over the Moor and the Dart gorge and south-east to the English Channel. Two slabs of moorstone on the Beacon were incised with the Ten Commandments in the winter of 1928–9. On the summit another inscription records the lighting of a fire, one of a chain, to celebrate the Silver Jubilee of George V's reign in 1935 – 'and all the people shouted and said God Save the King'.

Buckland Monachorum (2/2C) Of the 30 or so monasteries in Devon at the time of the Dissolution (1539), Buckland Abbey is a rare survivor. It was sold to the Grenville family at the Dissolution and they abolished many of the buildings, but daringly converted the abbey church into a Tudor mansion. The great nave was divided into several storeys, and the central tower retained with good effect. In 1581 Sir Richard Grenville (of the *Revenge*) sold the estate to Sir Francis Drake who used it as his principal residence when not at sea. It remained in the Drake family for

Buckland Abbey

three and a half centuries. Since 1948 Buckland Abbey has been National Trust property run as a Drake, Naval and West Country Folk Museum by Plymouth Corporation. Drake's Drum, which fortunately survived a fire at the house in 1938, is a precious exhibit. The fine medieval tithe barn near by, 154 ft long, was also preserved by the Grenvilles and houses a collection of historic vehicles. Recently the National Trust has acquired more land adjoining Buckland Abbey including farm buildings, some of 15th-century date, which complement the tithe barn.

The village, a mixture of old stone cottages and modern buildings, lies 1 mile to the north, west of the A386 TAVISTOCK–PLYMOUTH road. St Andrew's Church is almost entirely 15th century, with many crocketed pinnacles decorating the tower and transepts, the south porch and the west end of the aisles. Inside it is tall and spacious, the south chancel aisle distinguished by a large monument erected here in 1795 to Lieutenant-General George Augustus Eliott, Lord Heathfield, who married a Drake heiress from the abbey and is remembered for his resolute defence

of Gibraltar against the French and Spaniards (1779–83).

A walk north-west from the village along lanes and paths leads to Double Waters, the confluence of the river Walkham with the Tavy in deep woodland, one of the most beautiful sights of the Dartmoor border country.

Cadbury (2/4B) A hamlet among the steep hills west of the river Exe, approached by a lane off the Bickleigh Bridge–CREDITON road (A3072). The lovely scenery can be appreciated from the hill to the north where the ramparts of a small Iron Age fort occupy a typically commanding position. Some excavations in the 1840s by George Fursdon, the landowner, uncovered a well shaft, 58 ft deep and lined at the bottom with puddled clay. From this were recovered bronze bracelets and rings, beads and pottery all of Roman date and most unusual finds for Devon. They were mainly women's possessions and, together with a few Roman coins found in a lane near by, proved some activity at the fort as late as the 4th century AD. The finds were similar to votive offerings at sacred hill-top sites elsewhere in England and indicate that the well was associated with a pagan shrine used by the Celtic inhabitants of the district. In the hamlet St Michael's Church is a small and simple 15th-century building on an earlier site. It contains a Norman font, a medieval stained-glass panel of Christ showing His wounds, and a carved Elizabethan lectern. East of the church the small estate of Fursdon has been owned by that family in unbroken succession since the 13th century. The house is late Georgian with slightly projecting wings and a small colonnade at the centre of the main façade. Inside, visitors can see traces of an earlier building and many old family possessions.

Chagford (2/3B) An ancient market and Stannary town on the edge of Dartmoor, reached from the MORETONHAMPSTEAD to Whiddon Down road (A392). The historic activities have ceased but it remains a town of character and a good centre from which to explore northern Dartmoor and the upper valley of the river Teign. The setting above the river, backed by granite hills, is beautiful. The bridge over the river to the west is 16th century, replacing an earlier structure. Rushford bridge to the north-east cannot be much later in date, nearby Rushford being an Elizabethan farmhouse. Many other centuries-old farmhouses in the area are worth more than a passing glance. Impressive granite buildings can also be found in most of the town streets which all lead to the Square and its restored Market Cross. The tall west tower of St Michael's Church is all dressed granite, a good example of the medieval masons' mastery of this difficult material. A fine monument in the chancel is to Sir John Wyddon, a Justice of the Queen's Bench who died in 1575. At one time he owned the house facing the south side of the churchyard which is now the Three Crowns Hotel, a particularly striking granite building with its porch and mullioned windows. The former Church House adjoining it is another. A mile south-west of the town stands one of the many ancient, weather-beaten granite crosses of Dartmoor and its borderland. This one is spectacularly placed on the summit of Week Down (1050 ft) and marked an old trackway over the hills to Moretonhampstead.

Chittlehampton (2/3A) A large village 5 miles west of SOUTH MOLTON off the B3227. It is centred around a wide, attractive square of thatched and slated cottages with porches. Formerly these stood on all four sides but the northern row was demolished more than a hundred years ago and the site incorporated in the churchyard. The church therefore occupies the fourth side, a spectacular rebuilding of the 15th century. The west tower is immensely strong and tall (115 ft), yet as harmonious as any of the famous towers of Somerset. Tapering, pinnacled buttresses and tall windows, gargoyles and a frieze below decorated battlements, and lofty pinnacles forming a sort of crown make it the finest tower in Devon and an outstanding piece of architecture. The church is the only one dedicated to St Hieritha or Urith, an early martyr said to have been born at East Stowford a mile to the north and to have been cut to pieces with scythes by the pagan villagers of Chittlehampton. The first church was erected over her supposed burial place and it became a place of pilgrimage throughout medieval times. Winson Cross half a mile south-east of the village, though mounted on a rather ridiculous 18th-century octagonal pedestal, may have once marked a route for pilgrims.

A fine cross beside the lane running south-west to Brightly Barton may have marked a trackway ascending from the river Taw. In the church a statue of St Hieritha on the 15th-century stone pulpit shows her holding the palm of martyrdom and a small block of stone, perhaps a book or the foundation stone of the church. The modern statue placed in an old niche on the tower shows her as a comely young woman holding a scythe over her right shoulder and a replica of her head in her other hand.

At Cobbaton, north-west of Chittlehampton, there is a collection of Second World War fighting vehicles.

Chulmleigh (2/3B) A small and ancient market town east of the river Taw, roughly halfway between CREDITON and BARNSTAPLE on the old road over the hills. The market pens used to be put up against the churchyard walls where cars now park and the large church of St Mary Magdalene shows what an important place it must have been. It is mainly a 15th-century rebuilding, magnificently sited on a hill 450 ft above sea level, the tower of massive granite blocks visible from great distances. Wagon roofs throughout the building have carved bosses and some notable angels with outspread wings supporting the ribs. The fine rood screen, restored in 1914, stretches across nave and aisles. The old road from Crediton and EXETER climbed steeply from the valley of the Little Dart river and the toll house at the south end of the town is now a cottage. The old coaching inn, the Kings Arms, was also converted to dwellings some 30 years ago but its impressive façade still faces the town square with its well-preserved town pump. Behind the inn horses were stabled and revived in extensive outbuildings after the long pull from either direction. At the northern end of the town the Barnstaple Inn is a thatched, granite building bearing the date 1663, but it may well have older origins. In spite of disastrous fires in the 19th century many old buildings and cobbled alleyways in the town have survived. It lost its importance when a new road was built along the Taw valley (1830) and the railway followed (1854), attracting markets to its stations. These in their turn have gone but the old town lives on, a friendly and rewarding place.

Clovelly (2/1A) Ten miles west of BIDEFORD, a favourite village with visitors to the north coast since the latter part of the 19th century. It can be reached from the west along the B3237 or from the south-east along a toll road called Hobby Drive, which starts at Hobby Lodge on the A39(T). In either case cars must be left at the park above the village. Clovelly occupies a cleft in the spectacular wooded cliffs of Bideford Bay. The long cobbled street, so steep it is stepped in places, was the bed of a rivulet plunging down to the sea. The cottages and shops seem to stand one on top of the other and at the bottom are a small beach and harbour. The latter was constructed in the 16th century, the only safe anchorage on the Devon coast west of APPLEDORE. From the harbour pier the village can be seen in its wooded setting, a picturesque place indeed. The church stands inland, a 15th-century building much restored but interesting. A yew avenue leads to the door and monuments to the Cary family include one to the Will Cary whom Kingsley made such an attractive character in *Westward Ho!* Clovelly Dykes, at the junction of the B3237 with the main road, are Iron Age earthworks forming concentric enclosures that cover 23 acres. They seem too large and not well-sited for defence and are thought to have been a centre for cattle rearing, perhaps an early marketplace, accessible from three directions along ancient ridgeways.

Clyst St Mary (2/4B) A village close to EXETER on the A3052 to SIDMOUTH, notable for the ancient bridge across the river Clyst and its water meadows. Stretching for 200 yd on low arches, it dates from the 13th century and is the oldest in Devon. Although not so impressive as the famous bridges at BIDEFORD and BARNSTAPLE, it is more evocative of the leisurely traffic of medieval times. It seems scarcely possible that this bridge carried the main road until a few years after the Second World War, when the present dual carriageway was made to bypass it and the village.

Cockington *see* Torquay

Colyton (2/5B) A delightful small town in East Devon on the river Coly, a mile north of Colyford on the Lyme Regis–EXETER road (A3052). This favourable site above the Coly (a Celtic name), surrounded by fertile countryside, was occupied early in Saxon times. A Saxon cross is preserved in St Andrew's Church. After a fire in 1933 it was discovered, in pieces, built into the fabric of the church tower. It was painstakingly extracted and put together. The town clusters round the church and contains many good buildings, particularly the Vicarage (1529) and the Great House on the Colyford road built for an Elizabethan merchant. The fine Old Church House has the date 1612 on the front, but this recorded the enlargement of a much earlier building by the addition of the top storey. It was then used as a grammar school until 1928 when the school moved out of town. The church is one of the most interesting in Devon. A 15th-century lantern surmounts the Norman tower, a rare feature in England. The great west window, the largest in any parish church, fortunately lost only a few pieces of its magnificent glass in the 1933 fire. Some intriguing tombs and two fine screens, one Tudor the other Jacobean, continue the history. In the 18th century the nave was heightened and the south aisle extended to give the church its spacious look. The two fine candelabra in the nave, each to hold 36 candles, were installed in 1796. The north aisle was enlarged in the next century.

The church is a wonderful example of 'history in stone' and, with its attractive churchyard, is immaculately kept.

Combe Martin (2/2A) A large village on the north coast, east of ILFRACOMBE on A399. The setting is everything, a beautiful and fertile valley down which the houses straggle between sloping market gardens and small fields. The earliest settlement was a mile inland where the church stands and through the centuries it expanded down to the sandy beach, ready to receive 20th-century holidaymakers. Once it was a mining village; silver-lead mines brought prosperity in late medieval and Tudor times, and some mining continued spasmodically down to 1875. A ruined chimney on Knap Down to the east commemorates this activity. The only building of interest apart from the church is the Pack of Cards Inn, an eccentric house built on a cruciform plan with 52 windows and many tall chimney stacks, said to look like a card house. The red sandstone church of St Peter ad Vincula has 13th-century lancet windows in the chancel, but is mainly 15th century with impressive façades to north and south. The tower is compared with other famous towers on the north coast in the saying:

> Hartland for length,
> Berrynarbor for strength,
> Combe Martin for beauty

Combpyne (2/5B) A hamlet of stone houses in a deep valley less than a mile north of the A3052 road into Devon from Lyme Regis. Manor Farm, next to the church, may have been a medieval religious house of some kind. The church of St Mary the Virgin is unusual for Devon with a saddleback tower; and, though mainly 13th century in date, it has many resemblances to a Saxon building. Through the centuries much restoration has been necessary but many features confirm an early foundation. The south porch gives access to the base of the tower, not to the nave

where there is little room for an entrance. The 15th-century windows of the nave do nothing to change its small size, typical of a Saxon building. The east window has three good 13th-century lancets and the font of Beer stone is of similar date. The most interesting feature, the sketch of a ship on the south wall of the nave, is believed to be of the 14th century. Although the hamlet appears landlocked the drawing recalls that the sea is less than 2 miles away.

Towards the sea stands Rousdon, an imposing mansion built about 1880 in imitation Tudor style, now occupied by All Hallows School.

Compton Castle (2/4C) A fortified manor house rather than a castle in the hills west of TORQUAY, approached from either A381 (NEWTON ABBOT–TOTNES) or A3022 (Torquay ring road). The spectacular defensive walls, towers and gatehouse were built about 1520 and mask the earlier house within them. Some parts are 14th century, but most of the present building dates from the middle of the 15th century. It was the home of the Gilbert family down to 1800. The most famous of them was Sir Humphrey Gilbert, a half-brother of Sir Walter Raleigh, who founded the first colony in Newfoundland in 1583. Returning to England he went down with his ship *Squirrel* in a storm off the Azores. His son Raleigh founded a colony in Maine in 1607 and it was a descendant of his, Commander Walter Raleigh Gilbert, who bought the castle in 1930 when it was very decayed with only a few rooms in use as a farmhouse. For 20 years he and his wife carried out major restorations. In 1951 he gave the property to the National Trust, which has continued to maintain it as one of Devon's most interesting historic houses. It is open three days a week from April to October.

Copplestone (2/3B) At the junction of A377 and A3072 4 miles west of CREDITON, the village takes its name from a Saxon cross, the *Copelan stān*, referred to in a 10th-century document. The shaft survives standing by the roadside, indicating the meeting place of three parishes and a landmark for travellers for centuries. In medieval times and perhaps earlier the route from EXETER divided here, one branch going west to Cornwall, avoiding the border hills of Dartmoor, the other north-west to the Torridge estuary. The shaft is mainly decorated with a characteristic interlacing

Overleaf left: Clovelly; (overleaf right) Compton Castle

pattern, but on one side are carved crosses and a niche high up for an image. Still standing 10 ft tall, it must have been even more imposing when complete with its crosshead.

Cornwood (2/3C) A village 10 miles north-east of PLYMOUTH on the river Yealm, a centre for many ancient farms which occupy the sheltered land close to the south-west border of Dartmoor. It makes a good base for exploring the Moor between the rivers Plym and Erme with its multitude of Bronze Age remains: open and enclosed settlements, stone rows, and cairns. A good example of an enclosed settlement can be found 3 miles north of the village on the left bank of the Yealm not far from the attractive little waterfall known as Yealm Steps. Reminders of Dartmoor's industrial past are near by: two ruined blowing houses, one above the falls on the right bank, the other lower down on the left bank. This type of building was used for smelting tin on the Moor over a period of 400 years up to the middle of the 18th century and these must therefore be over 200 years old at least. Blowing houses were always sited in river valleys, a small water-driven wheel being used to work the furnace bellows. Traces of the leats that brought the water to the blowing houses can be seen at Yealm Steps.

Cornworthy (2/3C) One of three villages – the others are Ashprington and Dittisham – among the unspoiled hills on the west bank of the river Dart between TOTNES and DARTMOUTH. As you approach Cornworthy along the lane from Bow Bridge, the ruins of a 14th-century gatehouse stand on the hill above the village, all that remains of an Augustinian priory. In the steep valley below the houses climb attractively up the slopes, on the east side rising to the battlemented, double-buttressed tower of St Peter's Church. The south porch of the church is entered from the west side, the first of several unusual features, and has stone benches along three walls for the meetings that were once held in it. The church, built of local slaty rock, is mainly 14th century with a circular Norman font of red sandstone surviving from an earlier building. The granite pillars of the nave arcade lean markedly outwards, the arches of mixed granite and Beer stone. The attraction of the rough-looking rood screen is that it has never been restored and seems of two distinct styles: 15th-century tracery across the nave and earlier Decorated tracery across the aisles which may be late 14th-century work. Box

pews, a Georgian pulpit, the wooden tracery and clear glass in the windows are all 18th-century fittings which subsequently escaped molestation by the Victorians. The result is a light and spacious building altogether different from most parish churches in Devon.

Ashprington is another attractive village among the hills. The church, one of few outside Wales dedicated to St David, is noted for its tall, unbuttressed tower with a stair turret that for some reason stops short of the top stage. The interior was drastically restored in the 19th century but the fine Norman font of red sandstone survived, similar to Cornworthy's but larger.

Dittisham lies close to the river with its moored yachts, 2 miles north of Dartmouth. The church of St Peter has one roof spanning nave and aisles. The rood screen was carefully restored in the 1950s and is impressive, but the most remarkable fitting is the 15th-century stone pulpit. It is shaped like a wineglass and carved with vine leaves and crude figures in arched niches, all coloured, unique in Devon.

Between Ashprington and Cornworthy lies Bow Creek, wooded and tidal, through which the river Harbourne flows into the Dart. Bow Bridge over the river is a well-known beauty spot. On the south side of the creek the hamlet of Tuckenhay was once a small port, its quays, warehouse and papermills now either derelict or converted to other purposes.

Crediton (2/4B) A very ancient market town 7 miles north-west of EXETER on the BARNSTAPLE road (A377). Only 40 years ago cattle were sold in the widest part of the long High Street and sheep pens stood at the bottom of Market Street. 'Kirton [Crediton] was a borough town', the inhabitants boasted, 'when Exon [Exeter] was a vuzzy [furzy] down.' This was not true but the town does not forget that it was the seat of the bishopric for 140 years before it was transferred to Exeter in 1050. The town is too near Exeter ever to have attained any eminence since then – a dormitory now for some, but still 'the town' for many in the area of fertile farms and estates on the tongue of red soil that protrudes west of the river Exe.

A series of fires in the 18th century destroyed most of the old buildings and the High Street is mainly respectable 19th century. Fortunately the church of the Holy Cross, one of the finest parish churches in any town, survived. It is a large 12th-century cruciform building, a collegiate church, rebuilt early in the 15th century. It became the parish church in 1547 and the Lady chapel at the east end was then used as a grammar school until 1859, when the school moved to its present location at the west end of the High Street. The church exterior, with its fine central tower, two south porches and bold clerestory, is russet-coloured and very pleasing. The oldest part of the interior is the crossing, supporting the great weight of the tower: pointed arches with simple mouldings and piers with simple capitals. The monuments include one to Sir John Sully (d. 1387), a follower of the Black Prince in his many campaigns. Another commemorates a later hero, General Sir Redvers Buller VC, known for his relief of Ladysmith in the Boer War. He was born at Downes, the Georgian mansion on the road to Exeter. But the town's most famous son was undoubtedly St Boniface (Winfrid, or Wynfrith, was his original name), missionary to the heathen tribes of Germany in the 8th century. After his martyrdom in 755 he was buried at the great monastery he had founded at Fulda in Hesse and has been venerated there ever since. His native town seems to have given him scant recognition until the 12th centenary of his death, when the statue in the public garden west of the church was unveiled.

Cruwys Morchard (2/4B) A manor house, church and a few farms in the hills 5 miles west of TIVERTON. The old rhyme

> Crocker, Cruwys and Coplestone
> When the Conqueror came were all at home

may not be accurate so far as the Cruwys family is concerned, but the manor was recorded in Domesday Book and the family was here at least by the 12th century. With the estate passing only

Detail of the rood base, Cullompton

once through a daughter, her husband assuming the name of Cruwys by royal licence, the family is still in possession. The tenacity of the Devon squire, surviving civil war, economic disasters and disputed successions, was never better demonstrated. The present house is Georgian but it stands on a medieval site and many features date back to Tudor times.

The small church of the Holy Cross close by is a 14th-century building with a south aisle added in the 16th century. Damaged by fire in 1689, it was preserved by sensible refitting early in the next century. Good box pews include special ones for children. The chancel and parclose screens, the best of this date in the county, are in classical style with Corinthian pillars, architrave and pediment, demonstrating the continuance of the great tradition of woodcarving in Devon.

Cullompton (2/4B) If you enter Devon by the old road from Taunton (B3391) or by the M5, one of the first landmarks to catch the eye is the splendid tower of the church of St Andrew. Rising 100 ft over the rooftops, the local red sandstone is set off by decorated battlements of lighter Ham Hill stone from Somerset, Beer stone shafts on the buttresses and, on the west side, a 17th-century clock. This superb tower was built in 1545–9 to complete the early 15th-century building, with an extra aisle added in the 1520s by John Lane, a wealthy clothier of the town. The whole reflects prosperity from the wool trade, the exterior lavishly decorated, the interior all light and colour helped by a clerestory, an uncommon feature in parish churches. The grey Beer stone of the nave arcade contrasts with the vivid colouring of the wagon roof and of the magnificent rood screen which stretches across the whole width of the church. Parts of the base of the rood itself are preserved: two great oak baulks carved to resemble rocks littered with skulls and bones, with a socket for the foot of the cross, and showing how large the rood must have been. The Lane aisle has a west window of six lights and beautiful fan vaulting to match that of the rood screen. The west gallery, supported on Ionic columns, is a very good example of Jacobean woodwork.

The town is mainly one street which broadens towards the north end into the old marketplace. Walronds and the Manor House on the west side of the street are Elizabethan buildings, the latter subsequently enlarged, but most of the older houses were destroyed by fire in 1839. No longer

a market town, no longer enriched by the wool trade, it is a good shopping centre set in a fertile agricultural district.

Dalwood (2/5B) A village in a pleasant valley north of the AXMINSTER–HONITON road (A35). The parish contains one building of exceptional interest: the Baptist Meeting House, one of the earliest to survive, at Loughwood Farm. Its origin can be traced back to the 1650s when the site was hidden in thick woodland. The fittings of the thatched chapel date from the early 18th century and the building and the stable close by now stand on open farmland. Though only a few hundred yards downhill from the main road, the chapel remains peaceful and admirably simple. The whitewashed walls, pine pews and dominating pulpit serve as a tranquil reminder of the years when the Baptists were a persecuted sect and could only gather for worship in remote places. The National Trust acquired the property in 1969 and carried out much-needed restoration with its usual scrupulous care.

Dartmouth (2/6A) It is fitting that the town at the mouth of Devon's most beautiful river should be such a dramatic and fascinating place. It stands on the west bank beside the deep-water harbour that made it important from the 12th to the 18th centuries. An assembly place for many military expeditions, from the Crusades down to June 1944, its prosperity was based on the import of wine, the export of cloth and a share of the lucrative cod fishing off Newfoundland.

The best approach is by ferry from KINGSWEAR on the east bank, to see during the passage the buildings rising steeply from the waterfront and to the north the vast bulk of the Britannia Royal Naval College (1899–1905), which perhaps aptly dominates it. The Quay is a good starting place for an exploration of the narrow streets with their wealth of 16th- and 17th-century merchants' houses and the famous Butterwalk, battered by bombing during the Second World War but happily restored. To the south the old quay at Bayard's Cove has a terrace of 17th-century houses and the Old Customs House (rebuilt in 1739). Near by are the ruins of a fort built in the early 16th century to augment the defences provided by the 15th-century Dartmouth Castle (open all year), which stands 1 mile to the south at the mouth of the river. This was another fort rather than a castle, a two-tiered platform from

Britannia Royal Naval College, Dartmouth

which musketry and artillery could cover the entrance to the anchorage. The large, square gunports were the first of their kind. Through a timber-framed opening a chain could be stretched across to Kingswear Castle on the opposite shore. The upper storey of the fort provided accommodation for a small garrison.

Behind and above the fort stands St Petrox Church, remarkable for its exciting setting. It is a 17th-century rebuilding in Gothic style of a former chapel. It contains a Norman font, good brasses to town merchants, and the central east window is a memorial (1927) to George Parker Bidder, the famous 'calculating boy' and engineer who was born in MORETONHAMPSTEAD and died at Dartmouth in 1878.

St Saviour's Church near the Quay once stood at the water's edge. Ships moored to its church-yard wall until more land was reclaimed late in the 16th century. It has a magnificent 15th-century rood screen and 17th-century west gallery. Of outstanding interest are the brasses in the chancel showing John Hawley (d. 1408) and his two wives. He is in full plate armour and the women in sideless surcoats and pleated skirts

Drewsteignton

reaching to the ground. He was the most famous of the town's medieval merchants, thought to have been the model for Chaucer's Shipman in the *Canterbury Tales*.

Another famous native of the town was Thomas Newcomen, inventor of the earliest industrial steam engine. He is commemorated by the ramped road called Newcomen Street and one of his engines is on display near the Butterwalk. Another engine dated 1725 can be seen at the National Trust property at Little Dartmouth, 1 mile south of the town on the coast.

Dawlish (2/4C) A small seaside resort 10 miles south of EXETER on A379. It takes its originally Celtic name from the 'black stream' that flows through it. The historic village stood two-thirds of a mile inland, but after visitors started to arrive at the end of the 18th century the ground towards the sea was landscaped, the stream stepped to make little waterfalls and building on either side extended the town down to the beach. The Strand on the north side has many very pleasing Georgian buildings. Jane Austen visited in 1802 and refers to the town in *Sense and Sensibility*. In 1846 Isambard Kingdom Brunel pushed through the extension of the railway

Castle Drogo built by Sir Edwin Lutyens between 1911 and 1930

from EXETER to NEWTON ABBOT along the coast, and a low granite viaduct carried the line over the mouth of the 'black stream' so that access to the beach was not impeded.

Devonport *see* Plymouth

Dittisham *see* Cornworthy

Dolton *see* Iddesleigh

Dowland *see* Iddesleigh

Drewsteignton (2/3B) An attractive village and walking centre 1 mile north of the great gorge of the Teign river. Many cottages are of granite, as are the simple moorland church at one end of the square and the Church House near by. The Drewe Arms, an unspoiled inn, occupies a central position. It managed without main water and electric light well into the 1930s. The district abounds with good walks, particularly down to Fingle Bridge on the Teign, a famous beauty spot, and along the river banks in both directions. The handsome granite bridge with pointed piers

downstream as well as upstream is at least 400 years old.

On the hills rising from the river are good examples of Iron Age forts, Prestonbury to the east and Cranbrook to the south.

The gorge of the Teign is spectacular and best appreciated by walking the Hunters' Path high up along the south-facing escarpment from Fingle to Castle Drogo. The 'castle' is a large country house built of local granite by Sir Edwin Lutyens between 1911 and 1930 for Julius Drewe, the founder of the Home & Colonial Stores. It is now owned by the National Trust and is open from April to October. Lutyens was a very great architect but here he worked with difficult material and his original plan was continually whittled down during the long period of building. The result, though a unique building structurally and the last great country house likely to be built in England, appears cold and unattractive to many. Even so the site on the promontory above the gorge is splendid, with wide views over the Teign valley to CHAGFORD and Dartmoor. The gardens are not extensive compared with other great houses, but full of variety, their creation and maintenance on the windswept promontory a notable achievement. A mile to the west is Spinster's Rock, the remains of a Neolithic cham-

Wild daffodils, Dunsford

bered tomb consisting of three uprights and a capstone re-erected in 1862.

Dunchideock (2/4B) A scattered hamlet 3 miles outside EXETER at the foot of the Haldon Hills. The red sandstone church, a medieval building and a farm stand alone in a beautiful setting. The medieval building, now in multiple occupation, may have been the Church House or the old rectory. St Michael's Church is a small, one-aisled 14th-century building restored in the 19th century but rich in fittings. The rood screen is complete with doors and cornice and ingeniously encases three sides of the octagonal aisle pillar without disturbing the overall harmony. Roof bosses, a font of the early 15th century, some bench ends of the 16th century and then, another surprise in this out of the way place, a dignified mural monument to Major-General Stringer Lawrence (1697–1775), 'the father of the Indian Army'. It was erected by his friend Sir Robert Palk, of nearby Haldon House, to whom he had left a fortune. Sir Robert also commemorated Lawrence by building the tower on the hill above

Haldon Belvedere. Triangular in plan with 'Gothick' windows and turrets at the corners, it is a famous landmark visible from Dartmoor to the west and from most of East Devon.

Dunsford (2/3B) An attractive village 8 miles west of EXETER off the B3212 and just inside the Dartmoor National Park boundary. Many thatched buildings of cob and of granite are overlooked by the battlemented tower of St Mary's Church. Although much restored, the church contains the tombs of the Fulford family, of Great Fulford outside the village, who can claim unbroken male succession since the 12th century. The monument to Sir Thomas Fulford (d. 1610) and his wife, their seven children depicted kneeling on the wall behind their recumbent effigies, is particularly notable. A mile south of the village Steps Bridge over the Teign marks the lower end of the great gorge of the river. The National Trust owns Bridford Wood south of the river and there are picnic places and beautiful woodland walks. The walk along the north bank upstream to Clifford Bridge is delightful at all seasons, but especially so in the spring when the woods are carpeted with wild daffodils.

East Budleigh (2/4C) One of the most delightful villages in East Devon, 2 miles inland from the mouth of the river Otter. It has many old buildings of cob and thatch, a stream from the heights of Woodbury Common running down the main street, and a red sandstone church well-known for its association with the Raleighs. Hayes Barton, the thatched E-shaped farmhouse where Sir Walter Raleigh was born, probably in 1552, lies in the peaceful valley to the west of the village. His father was a churchwarden of All Saints Church and the family pew, where young Walter worshipped every Sunday, is dated 1537 and has a defaced shield which bore the family coat of arms. Sixty-two other bench ends, mostly 16th century, depict material rather than divine subjects. A splendid early 16th-century ship, a pair of fishes, the head of a Red Indian, tools of the wool trade, a cook with a trussed fowl and a spit turned by a dog combine to give a vigorous picture of Tudor occupations. The church itself was built between 1420 and 1455. Restoration in the 19th century and extension of the chancel have not disturbed the Beer stone arcade, the roof beams with their fine bosses regilded in medieval

Opposite: The Nave and west window, Exeter Cathedral

*Stone boss representing the martyrdom of St Thomas
A' Beckett*

colours, the large south porch with its stone seats,
and the curious squint in the south aisle which
passes through the rood stairs.

Two links with America after Raleigh's time
are recorded in the church. The arms of the
Conant family appear on a modern pew end:
Roger Conant of East Budleigh was one of the
founders of Massachusetts in 1623; and a small
window in the chancel commemorates Vice-
Admiral Preedy who, as Captain of HMS
Agamemnon, was responsible for laying the first
submarine cable across the Atlantic in 1858.

Exeter (2/4B) One of the great historic cities of
England. On the spur above the river Exe, protected by deep valleys to north and south, the
Romans first built a legionary fort (AD 55–60) and
later a city. The line of the Roman walls continued to mark the limit of building until the 18th
century.

Although the city was badly damaged by
bombing in 1942 the principal medieval monuments, Cathedral, Castle and Guildhall, escaped
destruction. The rebuilding of the devastated
areas has lasted 40 years. Deserving of praise are

the wider part of the High Street, a quite pleasing
composition for the 1950s; and in Queen Street
the preservation in the layout of the new shopping centre of two Georgian porticoes and of the
tiny medieval church of St Pancras.

Viewed from the surrounding hills, in spite of
some competition from recent building, the two
Norman towers of Exeter Cathedral still seem to
dominate. They rise over the transepts like castle
keeps rather than ecclesiastical towers, their
solidity in contrast to the buttresses and varied
window tracery of nave and choir and to the
profusion of images on the west front. But the
interior is the chief glory, nearly all in Decorated
style and completed in 90 years (*c.* 1275 to 1365).
The vaulting extends without a break over nave
and choir, a rare feature which enhances the
impression of harmony and spaciousness. The
stone bosses of the vault, the Minstrels' Gallery
and many corbels in the nave and choir are lively
masterpieces of medieval stonecarving. The
13th-century misericords of the choir stalls are
the oldest set in England and include a celebrated
representation of an elephant. The organ,
occupying a central position over the screen
between nave and choir, is by John Loosemore
(1665). Medieval stained glass in the fine east
window and elsewhere was fortunately removed

to safety during the Second World War. A bomb that fell in the south choir aisle, blasting the south-east corner of the Cathedral, would otherwise have damaged it. All the bomb damage was painstakingly repaired, many thousands of fragments of the original structure being picked from the debris during the months following the raid.

Within a short distance of the Cathedral half a dozen small, medieval parish churches, in addition to St Pancras, have survived. St Martin's edges into the Cathedral Close itself and has a fine west window. Its chancel is set at an angle to the nave, no doubt due to its cramped site. St Mary Arches gave its name to the street in which it stands and has Norman arcades, well restored after bomb damage, and monuments to many prominent citizens. St Mary Steps adjoins Stepcote Hill, a stepped and cobbled medieval street climbing up to the centre from the site of Westgate. The round Norman font is one of the best in Devon with four bands of interesting decoration. The intriguing clock on the tower is known as 'Matthew the Miller and his two sons' from the three figures in the canopied alcove above the clockface. They are more likely to represent Henry VIII and two guards, the king nodding his

Castle walls, Exeter

head at the hours and the guards striking the quarters. But for the parishioners the clock commemorates a tradesman noted for his punctuality, so much so that they had taken the time from his comings and goings. An old rhyme perpetuated the legend:

> Adam and Eve would never believe
> That Matthew the Miller was dead
> For every hour in Westgate tower
> Old Matthew nods his head

Rougemont Castle is an early Norman stone castle erected soon after William conquered the city in 1068. It was formed by building a wall with a strong gatehouse across the northern corner of the existing city walls to form a subrectangular enclosure. The impressive gatehouse with its lofty barbican appears to have served also as a keep and was preserved when a new entrance to the courtyard was made beside it in 1770. The main building inside, now used as Law Courts, was built in 1774, the wings added in this century. A deep, steep-sided moat protected the walls and part of this can be seen in the delightful Rougemont Gardens adjoining the castle.

The third great medieval building is the Guildhall, the oldest municipal building in England and still used by the City Council. The hall was built in the 14th century, the lofty timbered roof

Mol's Coffee House, Exeter

erected 1468–9 and the heavy portico over the High Street pavement added in the days of Elizabeth I. The portico pillars are granite, the superstructure is of Beer stone. The Mayor's parlour above the portico is a charming room with views up and down the High Street. In the hall are two good portraits by Sir Peter Lely, one of Devon-born General George Monck, the other of Charles I's daughter Henrietta who was born in Exeter.

Beneath the bustle of its everyday life the city is full of other treasures. The medieval city walls on Roman foundations are remarkably well preserved and a walk tracing their course is rewarding. In Fore Street, behind the nondescript façade of Tuckers Hall, is a beautiful timber-roofed and panelled room where the Guild of Weavers, Fullers and Shearmen have assembled for 500 years. Further up the hill St Nicholas' Priory was founded in the 11th century and preserves its Norman crypt. The eastern end of the medieval bridge over the river Exe is now exposed, although the church on it has unfortunately been allowed to decay beyond repair. The underground passages, some of which can be explored, were water conduits probably originating in Roman times and documented from the 14th century onwards. They may also have been used for communication between different parts of the city in times of trouble. Apart from the Guildhall portico several buildings in High Street are of Tudor date and also, among many attractive buildings in the Cathedral Close, the shop called Mol's Coffee House with its many-paned upper windows. A century later the handsome brick Custom House was built down on the Quay.

In Georgian times the city at last expanded significantly outside its Roman/medieval girdle and splendid terraces such as Barnfield and Colleton Crescents and the old Devon & Exeter Hospital in Southernhay East resulted. Within the walls the Assembly Rooms in the Cathedral Close built about 1768 became the Royal Clarence Hotel 30 years later, reputedly the first 'hotel' in England. In South Street, close to the South Gate (since demolished), the Unitarian George's Chapel was built in 1760. The charming Rougemont House near the Castle entrance, now part of the City Museum, dates from 1820 and the towering warehouses on the Quay from 1835. A ferry from the Quay crosses to the canal basin where the Exeter Maritime Museum exhibits boats from all over the world: a reed boat from Lake Titicaca, coracles from Wales, and afloat in the Basin an Arab dhow and other vessels. The Exeter Canal is the oldest in England to have pound locks. It was cut to Countess Weir in 1564–6 to bypass the weirs in the river which prevented shipping reaching the city. Later it was extended to TOPSHAM and then to Turf, 1 mile below Topsham, a distance of 5 miles.

Exeter has grown vigorously during the last 30 years, not least by including Pinhoe and TOP-SHAM within its boundary. North-west of the city Exeter University, which has expanded fourfold since constituted in 1955, occupies a magnificent campus. The large, purpose-built blocks are set in superbly planned and maintained grounds.

Exmoor (2/3A) Only the western part of Exmoor National Park lies in Devon, barely a third of the whole. It differs from Dartmoor and the rest of the county in many ways. The long, bare ridges are moulded by Devonian shale, slates and sandstone, not granite, and though some peat has formed there are no blanket bogs or dangerous mires. Cultivated land restricting the moor to the highest levels, deep-cut valleys and a majestic coastline combine to give great variety to the scenery.

The rivers flowing north – Heddon, West Lyn, the East Lyn and its tributary streams – are all of modest length. They rush down from the moor through spectacular wooded valleys to force narrow outlets to the Bristol Channel, very different from bigger rivers like Taw or Exe with their wide estuaries. The coastline of hog's-back cliffs rising to over 1000 ft bears no resemblance to the southern coast, nor to the flat-topped cliffs further west that resist the full force of the Atlantic.

The high western moor is grassland and heather where hardy Exmoor ponies run wild, many cross-bred but some still retaining the characteristic pale muzzle of the native breed. The moor also shelters numerous herds of red deer, although these shy animals are not often glimpsed by visitors. Across the high land many

Doone Valley, Exmoor, (see p. 88)

ancient ridgeways provide good pony trekking and walking. A track climbs from the West Lyn valley and goes south for 5 miles past Saddle Gate to Mole's Chamber and then continues as a by-road to the southern edge of the moor. Many Bronze Age hut circles and burials can be found close to it. Setta Barrow, one of a group 1 mile south from Mole's Chamber, has a good retaining kerb of stones. At Kinsford Gate, Five Barrows, a group of nine, include a well-preserved bell barrow with berm and ditch. At 1600 ft the site is the highest point of the Devon moor, and the all-round views are breath-taking. Another track leads west from Saddle Gate over Challacombe Common where Chapman Barrows are a well-known linear cemetery strung out along the ridge. A quarter of a mile south-east the 9 ft high Long Stone is the tallest standing stone on the moor. Near Mole's Chamber yet another ridgeway goes south-west towards the Bray valley, running over Shoulsbarrow Common where the earthworks called Shoulsbury Castle are something of a mystery. A bank and ditch enclose an area of four acres, with another bank and ditch on three sides. Often described as an Iron Age hill fort, the nearly rectangular plan and the low ramparts closely resemble the remains of two Roman fortlets not far away near the coast.

Badgworthy Water on the county boundary is 'Lorna Doone country'. A memorial to R. D. Blackmore stands on the left bank a mile upstream from its junction with the East Lyn river. Further up the site of a medieval village in Hoccombe Combe is thought to have been the lair of the lawless Doones whose exploits inspired the novel.

Exmouth (2/4C) A large seaside resort with a fine sandy beach 2 miles long. It was once a port of some importance, vessels anchoring in the estuary until the small dock was opened in 1865.

It is Devon's oldest resort, attracting the citizens of EXETER early in the 18th century and then by 1800 many substantial visitors from elsewhere. Since then the population has grown from 2000 to nearly 30,000 and the holiday trade overrides any other industry. The great sea wall was begun in 1841 and finally extended to Orcombe Point in 1915 to make one of the best promenades in the region. The Lifeboat Station stands proudly on the front surrounded by tourist attractions.

In spite of severe damage by bombing in the Second World War some attractive late 18th- and early 19th-century buildings survive. Most notable is the terrace called the Beacon, an interesting example of Georgian architecture apparently built piecemeal from 1792. No. 19 was occupied for several years by poor Lady Byron who arrived shortly before the poet's death in Greece. At No. 6, when not using her London house, the rejected Lady Nelson lived from 1816. In 1830 she had her son by her first marriage, Josiah Nesbit, and his four young children, interred in the churchyard at Littleham, an ancient parish now part of the town. Ten months later she was buried in the same grave.

The tower of Holy Trinity Church is a prominent landmark from the sea and the estuary. The building dates from the 1820s when growth as a resort necessitated something larger than the chapel that had previously sufficed. It was poorly rebuilt early in this century and then badly damaged by bombing. A replacement stained-glass window dedicated in 1957 portrays Sir Winston Churchill in his Garter robes.

North of the town in Summer Lane, Courtlands Cross, are two curious buildings. A La Ronde is said to have been inspired by the 6th-century octagonal church of San Vitale in Ravenna. It is a 16-sided house with a central octagonal hall and odd-shaped rooms radiating off it. The hall is 60 ft high and the staircase and the gallery above are lined with shell designs, only one of many eccentric fittings. The house was built by the Misses Jane and Mary Parminter in 1798. Later they built Point in View near by, a small, low chapel with a four-sided spire surrounded by a group of one-storey almshouses. These are occupied under the terms of the original trust by elderly women of good character, and services are still held in the chapel.

Farway (2/5B) A rambling village among a tangle of lanes in the Coly valley south of HONITON. By the ford over the river stands an attractive tiled mill house but the village is mainly thatched. Netherton Hall, now a school, is an early 17th-century mansion built by a celebrated lawyer, Sir Edward Prideaux. He is buried in St Michael's Church situated nearly a mile away uphill towards the greensand ridge of Farway Common. His effigy in barrister's robes lies in the north aisle, which was rebuilt about the time of his death (1628). The church has a good 15th-century tower with a polygonal stair turret, gargoyles and pierced stone windows in the upper storeys. Three stout, squat pillars in the nave survive from the Norman church, their scalloped capitals partly cut away when the arcade was rebuilt in the

13th century. The altar is unusual, a small and
elegant Jacobean table. Another memorial in the
north aisle commemorates Humphry Hutchins,
the man who paid for its rebuilding, traditionally
with gold coins discovered during ploughing in a
field on Farway Common. The field is still known
as 'Money Acre'. On the same ridge a remarkable
Bronze Age cemetery extends 2½ miles southwards to Broad Down. Over 50 round barrows of
simple bowl type have been identified. Those that
have been excavated contained rich grave goods
datable to 1700–1400 BC and cremated bones.
The largest group of barrows is at Roncombe
Gate, a road junction 1 mile south-west of the
village.

Gidleigh (2/3B) A scattered hamlet of cottages
and ancient farms on the edge of Dartmoor, 3
miles south of Whiddon Down on A30. The
c. /1300 castle is very ruined, only a square tower
containing one room over a cellar and a stair
turret remaining. Holy Trinity near by is a simple
moorland church of granite with a low west tower
and inside a restored 16th-century rood screen
and some medieval glass in the south aisle. A
good walk from the hamlet leads to the steep,
wooded valley of the North Teign plunging down
from the moor and crossed by the footbridge at
Glassy Steps. Other walks lead up to the moor
itself where many prehistoric remains include the
impressive stone circle on Scorhill Down, and
relics of later activity such as tinners' workings
and the long pot-water leat to Scorhill and
Creaber farms. The hamlet was a resting place on
the old track known as the Mariners' Way which
crossed the county from BIDEFORD to DART-
MOUTH, reputedly used by sailors to get from one
port to the other. It is difficult to trace now but its
20th-century successor is the ambitious long-
distance path created during the last decade, the
Two Moors Way, which crosses and links Dartmoor and EXMOOR. This runs less than a mile
south of the hamlet.

Great Torrington (2/2A) An ancient market
town on the OKEHAMPTON–BIDEFORD road (A386)
remarkable for its setting on top of a steep hill
above the river Torridge. Castle Hill and its car
park give spectacular views over the river valley
and the unspoiled countryside stretching south to
HATHERLEIGH and beyond. Nothing remains of
what must have been an important castle.
Perhaps the town's most memorable event
occurred at the end of the Civil War after its
capture by Fairfax for the Parliament in 1646.

A Georgian building in Great Torrington

The Royalist gunpowder stored in St Michael's
Church accidentally blew up killing 200 people
and sending the roof skywards. The church was
rebuilt soon afterwards but suffered a drastic
restoration in 1864. Nearby Palmer House was
built in 1752 by John Palmer who had married
Mary Reynolds, a sister of the great Devon painter. The Black Horse Inn in the Market Square is
17th century, much restored, and the Torridge
Inn probably as old. The impressive Town Hall
was Georgian but rebuilt in 1861. Other Georgian
buildings have survived but most of the town is
unexciting Victorian. The glass factory, which can
be visited, is a tourist attraction and has brought
a much-needed light industry to the town.

Three bridges cross the Torridge. Rothern
Bridge on the Bideford road is 15th century,
much widened. Taddiport Bridge, probably 17th
century and later widened, carried the old road to
the south. New Bridge was erected in 1843 to
carry the present road to the south. All three
feature in *Tarka the Otter* by Henry Williamson.
At Town Mills Bridge, over a small tributary of
the Torridge close to New Bridge, the otter
hounds met to hunt Tarka to his death far down
the river.

Overleaf: View from Castle Hill, Great Torrington

Halberton (2/4B) A large village 3 miles east of TIVERTON on A373. It is divided into Higher and Lower Town, and between the two is a large pond fed from a warm spring so that the water never freezes. The village contains some interesting buildings including the red sandstone, Georgian-styled Rock House close to the road bridge over the Grand Western Canal. The Church of St Andrew is also of red sandstone, older and better preserved than many in Devon. Much is early 14th century, the Norman font surviving from a previous building. Embellishments of the early 15th century include the octagonal, finely carved pulpit and the fine rood screen, the latter with plain but excellent tracery and complete with doors to chancel and both aisles. The Grand Western Canal makes a great loop round the village. It was a branch to Tiverton opened in 1814, part of a grand scheme to link Taunton with TOPSHAM which was never completed. The canal fell into disuse in 1924 but, after much prodding by the local Preservation Trust, it has been restored by the County Council and designated a Country Park. The towpath provides good walking through mainly unspoiled countryside for the 12 miles from Tiverton to the Somerset border.

Harberton (2/3C) A village 2 miles south-west of TOTNES in the fertile valley of the Harbourne river. Many of the farms date from Saxon times and people were busy hereabouts much earlier. At Hazard Hill, a mile north-west, flints and pottery turned up by ploughing led to the discovery in 1950–1 of an important Neolithic settlement of the first half of the 3rd millenium BC.

The narrow streets climb up to St Andrew's Church, a lovely 14th- and 15th-century building. The superb painted and gilded screen is marred only by replacement panels inserted in 1871. They are not wood but metal sheets painted with figures of saints straight out of a Victorian book for children. Thirteen of the original panels, preserved under glass in the north aisle, show how unsympathetic were the restorers. The red sandstone font is a particularly beautiful example of Norman work. The 15th-century stone pulpit is richly carved, but the statuettes in the niches are probably later replacements for those destroyed by reforming zeal. The south porch is large with a stair turret to give access to an upper room and the bold 14th-century vaulting has carved bosses that include two heads believed to be Edward I and Queen Eleanor. Externally the fine tower and the battlements and buttresses throughout give the building a rugged, satisfying appearance.

Beside the churchyard stands the 15th-century Church House Inn which retains many original features. A round-headed oak door leads to the former brewhouse with a wide chimney breast at the west end of the building. Most of the windows are replacements but the lintels, and the lintels of two blocked-up doorways, remain. Inside some fine panelling and many dark oak beams make it one of the most impressive examples of a Church House used as an inn.

Harford (2/3C) A quiet moorland hamlet beside the river Erme, $1\frac{1}{2}$ miles north of Ivybridge. The small moorstone church with low unbuttressed tower is typical of the Dartmoor borders. Inside a brass in the chancel commemorates a Speaker of the House of Commons, Thomas Williams (d. 1566), who was born at nearby Stowford House. East of the church a lane runs up to the moor gate which gives access to the southernmost tip of Dartmoor between the rivers Erme and Avon. Paths lead northwards over Harford and Ugborough moors with their wealth of prehistoric and industrial relics, east to SOUTH BRENT and south to the great bastions of Ugborough and Western Beacons that dominate the EXETER–PLYMOUTH road between South Brent and Ivybridge. They both rise to over 1000 ft and give views across most of the area between the rivers Dart and Plym known as the South Hams.

Hartland (2/1A) A small town in the thick wedge of land, the Hartland peninsula, that forms the north-west corner of Devon. Reached by minor roads off the A39 from BIDEFORD to the Cornish boundary, it is a pleasant place with some good early 19th-century houses and shops. St John's Church was built for the benefit of the townsfolk in 1839 because the parish church of St Nectan lies $1\frac{1}{2}$ miles away in the hamlet of Stoke. The tower of St Nectan is the tallest in North Devon, 130 ft high in four stages with buttresses, gargoyles, battlements and tall pinnacles. It is a landmark all over the peninsula and far out to sea. The church interior is large and lofty, mainly 14th to 15th century, with a highly decorated Norman font, well-kept wagon roofs and a magnificent rood screen. The peninsula has a tiny population scattered about in farms and hamlets, none more than 4 miles from the sea. The western cliffs, the finest in the West Country, meet the northern at Hartland Point, a headland of rugged grandeur rising 325 ft above the sea. The tide race is dangerous even on a calm day and a lighthouse, built on a shelf two-thirds of the way down the cliff in 1874, warns ships to keep their distance. The view of the island of LUNDY, 11 miles out in the Bristol Channel, forecasts the weather:

> Lundy high, sign of dry.
> Lundy plain, sign of rain.
> Lundy low, sign of snow.

Two miles south of the Point is Hartland Quay, formerly a little harbour for coastal vessels. A hundred years ago the harbour walls were intact but they have since been swept away by the furious seas that lash this 'iron' coast. Startling cliffs with tilted and contorted layers of sandstones, slates and shales surround the Quay. Nothing but ocean lies between them and America. All along the coast the waves and grinding pebbles have worn away soft strata to form caves, and short streams plunge over the cliffs in attractive waterfalls. A series of waterfalls at Speke's Mill Mouth, a mile south of the Quay, is the most impressive. On the north coast the National Trust owns 120 acres at East Titchberry Farm with access down 260-odd steps to Shipload Bay and its shingly beach.

Hatherleigh (2/2B) A market town 7 miles north of OKEHAMPTON on A386. The main street climbs from the river Lew to the marketplace and the 15th-century red sandstone church of St John the Baptist with a shingle spire. Although the town suffered from fires in the 1840s, the church and other older buildings survived. Two by the churchyard entrance are rebuilt or restored parts of a medieval College of Friars, and the attractive George Hotel is c. 1500. The side road from the town to Monkokehampton passes along the northern edge of Hatherleigh Moor with fine views southward over unspoiled farmland to Dartmoor. Hatherleigh Moor is typical of much common land in West Devon. Its gift to the parish was erroneously attributed in an old rhyme:

> I, John of Gaunt
> Do give and do grant
> Hatherleigh Moor
> To Hatherleigh poor
> For evermore.

Whoever the real donor, over 400 acres survive from medieval times as the common land of the parish and the commoners are still known by their traditional name of 'Hatherleigh potboilers'. The rough, wet grazing was requisitioned and fenced during the Second World War by the Agricultural Executive Committee and eventually handed back to the commoners much improved.

Hawkchurch (2/6B) A pleasant village, 3 miles north-east of AXMINSTER, among the hills close to the Dorset border. It was not included in Devon until the boundary was altered in the 19th century. In medieval times it was owned by the great abbey of Cerne in Dorset and the connection is recorded on the 15th-century tower of St John the Baptist Church. Below the fine west window a row of shields and quatrefoils is similar to one on the surviving gatehouse at Cerne and the central shield bears the abbey arms. The body of the church was, of necessity, restored in 1859–60, but as much older work as possible was retained. The plain font may have stood in the original Saxon church. The north arcade pillars with scalloped capitals are Norman, the south arcade 13th century, the capitals decorated with foliage interspersed with heads and figures: a ram playing a fiddle, a goat playing a horn, a boy with a dog. Both sets of pillars are short so that the capitals, unusually, are at eye level and can be examined comfortably. The arcades are markedly at odds with the rest of the building for both the floor and roof of the nave were raised, the clerestory inserted and the chancel enlarged during the 19th-century restorations. It was fortunate that the preservation of the older work was considered more important than a loss of proportion.

Hembury Fort *see* Broadhembury

High Bickington (2/3A) In hilly, unspoiled country west of the EXETER–BARNSTAPLE road (A377) where it runs beside the river Taw, the village is nearly 600 ft above sea level. In the by-streets many thatched cottages are jostled higgledy-piggledy by some less attractive buildings. The 16th-century George Inn and the adjoining cottages, once a brewhouse, form a particularly pleasing group. An arched passageway through the Victorian school building leads to the churchyard and makes an unusual lychgate. The church tower dominates the village and the surrounding farmland and can be seen from great distances. A Saxon foundation, the first stone church was a

Overleaf: A view from Hartland Quay

Norman building of which many traces remain: the south door arch with dog-tooth moulding, a small blocked-up doorway in the north aisle, the fine font, the south wall of the chancel and the lower storey of the former tower now used as a vestry. Many alterations and enlargements took place in the 14th century and again late in the 15th century when the west tower was built. The church is full of interesting things, of which the 70-odd pew ends are outstanding. Some are 15th century, some probably older, some 16th century and some Victorian restorations or additions. The Victorians repositioned the pews and mixed up the different styles of carving in this remarkable collection. On the front of the choir stalls the 1904 carvings maintain the tradition well. They depict birds and animals, illustrating the lines from the Benedicte: 'All ye Fowls of the air, bless ye the Lord . . . All ye Beasts and Cattle, bless ye the Lord . . .' A small memorial plaque on the south wall of the nave records that Colonel Bernard Channer of the Rajput Light Infantry was the first officer to be awarded the Distinguished Service Order after its creation in 1886. Other plaques commemorate his three sons, all of whom served in the Indian Army.

Two miles north along B3217 the village of **Atherington** shared High Bickington's church and priest in Saxon times. In the 13th century it built its own church but since 1979 the two places have once more shared a rector. Atherington is another hill-top village, the church tower another landmark. The church has a 15th-century octagonal font and a fine window of medieval stained glass in the north aisle. Interesting tombs include that of Sir John Bassett of Umberleigh (d. 1529) with brasses of the knight in armour, his two wives and his twelve children in two groups below their respective mothers. The unique feature of the church is the medieval rood loft across the aisle, the only one of many hundreds to survive in Devon. The oak screen and the loft were brought to Atherington from Umberleigh in the Taw valley when the chapel there was destroyed in 1800. The carving is magnificent, a supreme example of the skill of Devon's 16th-century woodworkers.

Holbeton (2/5A) A village in the area south of Dartmoor known as the South Hams. Narrow roads lead from the A379 KINGSBRIDGE to PLYMOUTH road to the village and continue west of the river Erme down to the sea. The mouth of the Erme, unlike most other debouchments in Devon, is totally undeveloped and unspoiled. All

Cottages in Holbeton

Saints Church stands impressively above the village. The tower and spire erected c. 1300 reach a height of 113 ft. The interior is spacious with tall arcades and two aisles. The south and west doors, the rood screen above the wainscoting, the reredos, choir stalls and pews are all modern and all of excellent design and execution. A remarkable 17th-century monument to three generations of the Hele family has 22 kneeling figures in tiers and a semi-recumbent effigy of a knight in armour. From the church the village runs down steeply towards the Erme and it is an easy ten minutes' walk to the beautiful, wooded riverside.

Holne (2/3C) A pleasant village on the south-east edge of Dartmoor, 4 miles west of ASHBURTON. At the Vicarage (rebuilt 1832) Charles Kingsley was born in 1819. Though he only lived there for six weeks, he kept returning to Devon throughout his lifetime. He considered himself a true native and Devon was to inspire his best novel, *Westward Ho!* The village stands high above a beautiful stretch of the river Dart where it comes down from the high moor. To the north-west it flows through Holne Woods (National Trust) and north-eastwards it twists and turns in a deep, wooded gorge round the peninsula of Holne Chase crowned by an Iron Age fort. The road from Ashburton cuts the neck of the penin-sula, Holne Bridge at one end and New Bridge at the other, both medieval. The car park at the latter is a good place from which to walk the river banks. A mile south of Holne Bridge is the River Dart Country Park. Holne Church, where Kingsley's father acted as curate, is unpreten-tious. It is a cruciform building of about 1300 with aisles of unequal length added 200 years later. The west tower is early, unbuttressed but its base inclined outwards for greater strength like a castle bastion. There is no stair turret – the stairs go up in the thickness of the wall. The early 16th-century carved pulpit is of unusual design but the screen of the same date has not lasted as well as others in Devon. The Church House survives as an inn, an attractive granite building, mid-16th century, with an unusually large and striking porch.

Honeychurch *see* Sampford Courtenay

Honiton (2/5B) A busy market town in East Devon on the A30. The long High Street has mainly Georgian houses and shops, with many bay windows, making a very pleasant whole.

Fires in the 18th century destroyed most of the earlier town but an exception is the fine Jacobean building called Marwood House at the north-east end of the town. It was built in 1619 for the physician John Marwood, the second son of Elizabeth I's physician Thomas Marwood who died in the town in 1617 at the age of 105 and was buried in the parish church. Near the centre of the town another building of interest is the former All Hallows School, now a museum of local history with an emphasis on lace. The making of fine Honiton lace by hand was a cottage industry for centuries in East Devon, and became famous when Queen Victoria ordered her wed-ding dress to be made of it. Traditional lace and the local hand-painted pottery are still produced on a small scale and can be bought in the town. The All Hallows Museum also contains the bones of prehistoric animals (elephant, giant ox, hip-popotamus) discovered in 1965 when work began on a much-needed bypass.

On the hill south of the town stands the former parish church of St Michael. By the early 19th century it was too small and too inconvenient to serve the flourishing community. A new parish church (St Paul's) was therefore built in the High Street in 1837–8 on the site of the former chapel of All Hallows. Rather unhappily a 'Norman' style was adopted without any consideration for

New Bridge, Holne Woods

the thoroughly Georgian setting.

Copper Castle, where the road to AXMINSTER leaves the town, is an early 19th-century castellated toll house with the original iron gates still in position. Also on the outskirts, on the EXETER road, stands St Margaret's Hospital, a medieval foundation for the lepers who were not allowed to enter the town. It was rebuilt and re-endowed as almshouses in the 16th century and looks very attractive with its thatched roof and much later 'Gothick' windows. North of the town the river Otter wanders quietly along its lovely valley beneath the last spurs of the Blackdown Hills, Hembury, St Cyres and Dumpdon with its clump of trees, all familiar sights to travellers on the A30.

Iddesleigh (2/2B) A village on the narrow B3217 which winds through the hilly farmlands between the Taw and Torridge rivers. The buildings are a delight, nearly all cob and thatch, some of the best in Devon. The 15th-century church stands above the village, with views south-eastwards to the distant heights of northern Dartmoor. The west tower has diagonal buttresses, battlements and modest pinnacles. Jack Russell, the famous hunting parson, succeeded his father as rector in 1826 and stayed seven years before moving on to SWIMBRIDGE where his exploits became legendary.

The rector now also looks after the tiny hamlet of **Dowland**, a mile or so to the north, and the

Holy Trinity, Ilfracombe

village of Dolton a mile further on, along the B3217. At Dowland the church of St Peter is undisturbed Norman to 15th century and the aisle arcade of oak pillars and arches, not stone, is one of only two such in Devon. The long, thatched building adjoining the churchyard was the Church House. Substantial stone chimney stacks rise at either end and the small windows facing the churchyard with round-headed oak frames are notable features of a picturesque building.

Dolton has a particularly interesting font in its otherwise Victorianized church. Two square slabs of stone placed one on top of the other are completely covered in carving, mainly of interlaced snakes and plaited rope. A ferocious face on the upper block is upside down, showing that the block was turned over so as to taper downwards and the bowl hacked out of the broader end. Altogether a curious piece that may well be two parts of a Saxon cross, probably of the 10th century.

Ilfracombe (2/2A) The largest resort on the north coast, approached from the east by A399 and from the south by A361. It was a market town and a small port before the first visitors began to arrive by boat from Bristol and Swansea in the early years of the 19th century. For a long time access by road was difficult and it was not until the last third of the century that better roads and the arrival of the railway (1874) doubled the population. Apart from earlier buildings like Montpel-

lier and Hillsborough Terraces and the Tunnel Baths, the town is therefore mainly late Victorian but distinguished by its hilly setting, the attractive harbour and wonderful cliff scenery.

Lantern Hill on the north side of the harbour made it a safe anchorage on a dangerous coast. On the hill stands St Nicholas's Chapel, a medieval building with a lantern at its west end that has served as a lighthouse for centuries. The rubble masonry of the walls could be 14th century and it was already a place of pilgrimage early in the next century. Though long disused as a chapel and much altered, it is a most picturesque and interesting building.

East of the harbour is Hillsborough Hill and its pleasure grounds, and to the north-west the rocky promontory of Capstone Point with good paths to the summit and views of LUNDY and the coast of Wales on clear days. The old town lay on the slopes west of the harbour, the parish church of Holy Trinity half a mile from the quayside. It is a 14th- to 15th-century building but the low, unbuttressed tower over the north transept may be earlier. The beams of the wagon roof of the nave rest on figures of angels with gargoyles beneath them, an uncommon feature in Devon. Also noteworthy are the decorated panels in the roof above the vanished rood screen, the Norman font, the Elizabethan pulpit and the 15th-century south door with its knocker.

Ilsington (2/3C) A small village in the Dartmoor National Park 2½ miles south-west of BOVEY TRACEY. It lies on the eastern edge of the high moors and the parish includes three of the best-known tors – Rippon, Saddle and Haytor Rocks – which rise 900 ft above the village. The houses cluster round the church of St Michael, the friendly inn on the south side of the churchyard and the long, attractive medieval Church House, converted into cottages, on the west. The modern lychgate has a room over it and replaced former structures with this unusual feature. The church is of granite, limestone and shale mostly covered by roughcast to try and keep out the damp. The early 14th- to 15th-century building has a good south porch, a richly carved oak screen, a mutilated effigy of a woman in the north transept of c. 1350, and the only medieval bench ends in Devon with the leaf and flower ornament known as 'poppy-head'. The wagon roofs have some fine carved bosses. The most remarkable feature is the crossing where there are no walls above the nave arcades so that the great semicircular beams connecting the wagon roofs of nave and transepts

Tapeley Park House, Instow

spring across like arched bridges. John Ford, the early 17th-century dramatist, was born at nearby Bagtor House and baptized in the church in 1586.

Instow (2/2A) A small resort on the east of the Torridge estuary, looking across at the stepped houses of Appledore. The extensive sands and dunes spread northwards to the river Taw and its junction with the Torridge. Everything else is small-scale, a tiny quay, barely half a mile of promenade and a population that has altered little in number in the last 100 years. The front is separated from the main A39 by the line of the BARNSTAPLE–BIDEFORD railway, now a public footpath and part of the Coastal Path. The old town is on a hillside half a mile inland. The pleasant church of St John the Baptist was a Norman building altered and enlarged in the 14th and 16th centuries. Among some interesting memorials a tablet commemorates Humphrey Sibthorp, the famous 18th-century botanist, who died at nearby Fullingcourt, now a farmhouse. A stained-glass window in the north aisle is in memory of Augustus Cleveland of Tapeley Park, who fought at Waterloo, and also of his son who rode with the Light Brigade at Balaclava and died of wounds received at Inkerman. Tapeley Park, a mile to the south, was a Georgian House built by the Clevelands but altered in the 19th century and in this. It was the home of the late John Christie, the founder of the Glyndebourne Opera. His daughter welcomes visitors to see the fine furniture in the house and the delightful gardens.

Kentisbeare (2/5B) In fertile farmland 3 miles north-east of CULLOMPTON (Junction 28, M5), the village is a mixture of old and new. Cob and thatch, cob and stone, slate and stone and small modern developments intermingle. Apart from St Mary's Church the most interesting building is the medieval Church House at the corner of the churchyard with its mullioned windows and many other original oak features. Externally the church is unusual for Devon, the stair turret and buttresses of the tower having a handsome chequered pattern formed by blocks of whitish Beer stone and of local red sandstone. The gargoyles projecting from the corners below the battlements are said to represent the Four Horsemen of the Apocalypse. The building is mainly 15th century and among many notable features the lovely rood screen is outstanding. Its ten bays, all of a different width, stretch across both nave and aisle. It bears the arms of John Whiting, a Merchant Venturer of London, who died in 1529 and is buried with his wife in the south aisle. The screen has been dated to the reign of Henry VII (1485–1509) and has fan vaulting and varied tracery in the panels. It is one of the best to survive, intact except for the doors and a crest along the top of the carved cornice; altogether a fine example of the skill of Devon woodcarvers of that time. In the chancel, by contrast, is a typically elaborate 19th-century marble memorial. It commemorates the Reverend George William Scott, Rector of Kentisbeare, who died at the age of 26 of scarlet fever. Carved on a scroll is a poem by the rector's cousin, Sir Walter Scott, written not long before his own death:

> To youth, to age alike, this tablet pale
> Tells the brief moral of its tragic tale . . .

Kenton (2/4C) A large village west of the Exe estuary on the EXETER–DAWLISH road (A379). It stands in the shadow of **Powderham Castle**, the home of the Courtenay Earls of Devon for the last 600 years. The original building must have been a fortified manor house rather than a castle, although in a strong position, the river Kenn on the south side and on the east the Exe reaching nearly to the walls over what is now parkland. The medieval building is lost beneath the additions and alterations of the 18th century, when the beautiful park was enclosed, and further rebuilding in the 19th century. It is open to the public (but not all week) from Easter Sunday to 23 September. A herd of fallow deer graze the park and the long-established heronry is one of the largest in Devon. At the northern corner of the park, close to the Exe, Powderham church is a small 15th-century building of red sandstone, its romantic setting disturbed by the railway passing close by on an embankment. Across the railway a good walk along the seawall, a favourite with birdwatchers, goes north to the beginning of the Exeter Canal at Turf. In the fields north of the park a circular, brick dwelling was a former dovecot. The tower on the ridge north-west of the castle is a triangular Belvedere erected in 1773.

Kenton village is surrounded by rich, red farmland and All Saints Church, one of the finest of the county's red sandstone parish churches, reflects a prosperous community. It is a very handsome and harmonious building, all of it dating from the second half of the 14th century and lovingly preserved. The pulpit is a scrupulous reconstruction of the medieval original. The rood loft is modern but the screen is a gem with much old colouring. Not surprisingly, the painted figures of saints and apostles on the panels are interesting but inferior to the wonderful woodcarving. The 120 ft tower and the superb two-storeyed, battlemented south porch are in keeping with the rich and spacious interior.

Kingsbridge (2/5A) An important town in South Devon, the 'capital' of the South Hams, at the head of the broad estuary which stretches for 5 miles inland from SALCOMBE harbour. The town owes its prosperity both to the fertile farmland of the district and to its position where the estuary can be rounded. The waterfront is now a promenade for watching ducks, swans and small craft, but in the past coastal and ocean-going vessels moored at the quays and a shipyard flourished on the east bank of the creek. The attractive main street climbs from the waterside along a narrow ridge and has good shops and inns and several interesting buildings. The King's Arms Hotel, opened in 1775, was the town's coaching house. The Old Grammar School (1670) houses the Cookworthy Museum of Rural Life in South Devon, mainly devoted to the work of William Cookworthy, a Quaker, born in the town in 1705.

He discovered china clay in Cornwall and was the first maker of porcelain in England. The Shambles, a striking market house built in 1796, has an arcade incorporating granite pillars from an Elizabethan building.

At the higher end of the street, half a mile from the quays, the Georgian Knowle House was the home of the ornithologist Colonel George Montagu who identified the species of harrier that now bears his name. This is a rare bird of passage in Devon, but the estuary and its tidal creeks attract many divers, grebes and waders, seen at their best in the winter months when visitors and boats cause least disturbance. Geographically, the estuary is a good example of a submerged river valley or 'ria' into which no stream of any significance flows. The parish church of St Edmund is a 13th-century cruciform building with aisles added in the 15th century. The fine central tower and spire look down on the busy main street. The town's other church, dedicated to St Thomas of Canterbury, served Dodbrooke in the valley to the east, another one-street town united with Kingsbridge in 1893. The tower is 14th century, the remainder 15th century except for the north aisle rebuilt in 1887. It contains a Norman font and a 16th-century screen survives across the nave and south aisle.

King's Nympton (2/3A) A village well worth the 2-mile diversion from the EXETER–BARNSTAPLE road (A377) at its junction with the B3226 to SOUTH MOLTON. After a stiff climb the whitewashed cottages and thatched inn, the attractive church and Church House (now a dwelling) form a delightful picture. 'Nympton' or 'Nymet' appears in several village names in Devon; of Celtic origin, it means a place, often a grove, consecrated to a pagan deity. The early Christians took over such sites and the sill of the south door into St James's Church is the recumbent shaft of a Saxon cross. The 14th-century, or even older, church tower supports a fine copper spire, a modern replacement incorporating windows from a former wooden one. The interior of the church is full of interest. The north wall of the nave, thought to be the oldest part of the structure, has no windows. The roof bosses of nave and south porch and the good rood screen are medieval, two doorways typical Tudor, the altar rails Jacobean. Equally of note are 18th-century features: box pews, an extraordinary wooden reredos in classical style, a painted chancel ceiling and an unusual white marble font with a small, fluted basin on a bulbous stem.

Kingswear (2/6A) A small town on the east bank of the Dart estuary opposite DARTMOUTH. The situation is superb, the houses climbing a precipitous hill and looking out south-west over the river. The only level ground is the car park down by the railway station. From earliest times a ferry crossed to Dartmouth. The arrival of the railway in 1864, and later of the car, greatly augmented the ferry traffic. The railway was axed in the 1960s and is now privately run by the Dart Valley Railway Company. In summer and at Easter authentic Great Western trains steam along the edge of the estuary, a nostalgic sight. Close to the station a large marina provides an up-to-date amenity.

Kingswear Castle stands at the river mouth, built c. 1500 to complement the one at Dartmouth in defence of the anchorage. The square tower occupied an exposed position not far above sea level, so iron cannon became corroded and had to be replaced by brass ones. It ceased to be of military use in the 17th century when the increased range of cannon enabled those at Dartmouth Castle to cover the river mouth unaided. Two hundred years later it was converted and enlarged into a residence by Charles Seale-Hayne, whose fortune also endowed the well-known agricultural college near NEWTON ABBOT named after him.

Landcross (2/2A) At the junction of A386 and A388 2 miles south of BIDEFORD lies the smallest parish in Devon. It occupies a narrow-necked, rounded peninsula formed by a great loop of the river Torridge and a tributary, one of many streams in Devon called Yeo. The small 15th-century church of Holy Trinity has a good set of bench ends and a font of early Norman type: a short pillar moulded at top and base, a cushion capital forming the bowl. Baptized in this font in 1608 was George Monck, born at Great Potheridge several miles up the Torridge valley, who became one of Cromwell's finest generals and the decisive figure at the Restoration of 1660.

Lapford (2/3B) A village on a hill above the EXETER–BARNSTAPLE road (A377) north-west of CREDITON. Its position has helped to preserve something of its character, but when industry developed beside the main road and railway in the Yeo valley it was inevitable that new estates would be built. The church of St Thomas of Canterbury is a 15th-century building notable for its woodwork. The exquisitely carved rood screen, the varied bench ends and the beautiful

Dart Valley Railway Company train, near Kingswear (see p. 101)

carving of the roof timbers, particularly the canopy or ceilure above the rood, are all worth close examination. William Radford, rector at the beginning of the 19th century, was a man of great physical strength and a formidable boxer. His son, known as 'Parson Jack', also earned a reputation as a fighting man who revelled in boxing and wrestling.

Both men, and others of the same family, were also rectors of **Nymet Rowland**, a hamlet on a promontory 1 mile to the west between the Taw and Yeo rivers. There the little 15th-century church of St Bartholomew has a wooden arcade to the north aisle, one of only two examples of this in Devon. The curious post supporting the western arch of the arcade was put in 200 years later. The Norman font is also unusual in having incised decorations above and below the double moulding of lozenges round its middle, rather crude additions to a simple and early tub font.

Lundy (2/1A) An island 11 miles off Hartland Point marking the beginning of the Bristol Channel. It is administered by the Landmark Trust for the National Trust who acquired it in 1969. It can be reached by boat from BIDEFORD or by

helicopter from a landing ground near Hartland Point. The island is three miles long and averages half a mile in width, a flat plateau mostly of granite where cattle graze 400 ft above the sea. The cliffs are spectacular and a landing can only be made at one place.

The name, of Old Norse origin, means 'Puffin Island' and these comical birds have bred on the cliffs for centuries.

Evidence of prehistoric and Saxon occupation has been found and marauders and pirates used the island intermittently as a base down to the 17th century. The square keep called Marisco Castle was built in the 13th century and takes its name from the Marisco family, of whom the notorious William de Marisco was hanged in 1242 for his depredations along the coasts of Wales and Devon. The highest point of the island is Beacon Hill (471 ft) and there the Old Lighthouse was built in 1819, its light so far above the sea that it proved to be of little use to ships in cloudy weather. In 1897 two new lighthouses were erected nearer sea level at the north and south ends of the island.

An ancient chapel once existed near the Old Light but the present church of St Helena is late Victorian. The walls are faced with granite, but the interior is lined with bricks from North Devon and the roof is of Cotswold slate. Granite was quarried on the island from 1863 to 1911; the other materials had to be shipped from the mainland.

The pleasure of Lundy is to find an accessible but unspoiled island with 7 miles of wild cliffs and no 'entertainment' apart from a small hotel and the Marisco Tavern. Above all it is a place for watching the birds that breed on the cliffs or pause on migration unmolested by human interference. Breeding guillemots and razorbills outnumber puffins at the moment, but the latter have increased after years of decline. Wonderful views can be obtained of all these and of the kittiwake and fulmar colonies, of shags and ravens. Spring and autumn migrations bring exotic species, woodchat shrike, golden oriole, rose-coloured starling, hoopoe, and rare buntings and warblers.

Luppitt (2/5B) A hamlet 4 miles north of HONITON lying in a deep valley between two spurs of the Blackdown Hills. Approached by narrow, winding lanes it seems a remote place and in hard winters can be cut off for days. Several farms in the valley are recorded in Domesday Book, showing that the valley was cleared and settled in Saxon times.

St Mary's Church, a cruciform building on a shelf of the steep hill above the hamlet, continues the story. The oldest furnishings are a rare Norman pillar piscina and a remarkable font of which the bowl and a few inches of the shaft survive. The bowl has interesting carvings on its four sides: a double-headed monster and a conventional representation of a forest; a group of animals, probably a hunting scene; and on the east side the martyrdom of an early Christian. The carving is vigorous but crude and unlike that on other Norman fonts in Devon. Can it be the work of Saxon craftsmen or even of Saxon date, preserved in this remote place? The church is mainly 14th century, and the oak wagon roof of nave and transepts its outstanding feature. The crossing of diagonal beams has a great central

Puffins, Lundy

boss (a meticulous replica of the original), showing the continuing skill of Devon's carpenters.

South of the village an Iron Age fort on Dumpdon Hill (National Trust), the ramparts enclosing an area of 3 acres, commands the Otter valley above Honiton.

Lydford (2/2C) A village on the north-west border of Dartmoor one mile west of the TAVISTOCK–OKEHAMPTON road (A386) and one of the most interesting places in Devon. In the 9th century it was a town of some size, well-sited on a promontory formed by the river Lyd and a feeder stream. King Alfred made it one of his strongpoints for defence against the Danes, equal in military importance with EXETER and BARNSTAPLE. Parts of the Saxon ramparts across the promontory remain on either side of the road into the village from the north, and the Saxon pattern of lanes and small plots of land has hardly been disturbed. It was still one of only four boroughs in Devon when the Normans erected an early castle, the site probably marked by the earthworks visible south-west of the church. This was superseded a century later by the great keep which still stands close to the Castle Inn. By that time Lydford had lost its military importance and the keep was built as a prison, particularly for those who infringed the harsh Forest and Stannary Laws. It earned a sinister notoriety:

> Oft have I heard of Lydford law
> How in the morn they hang and draw
> And sit in judgement after . . .

Although the parish included the whole of central Dartmoor, some 50,000 acres, the town declined through the Middle Ages. The small 15th-century granite church of St Petrock was obviously built to serve the needs of a diminished community, and its north aisle is a late 19th-century addition. The dedication to St Petrock and the plain Norman tub font are relics of earlier buildings on the site. The church's most interesting features are some medieval glass, the good modern screen (1904) and the tomb outside the south entrance with a lengthy inscription beginning:

> Here lies in horizontal position
> The outside case of
> GEORGE ROUTLEIGH Watchmaker . . .
> Integrity was the mainspring
> And Prudence the regulator
> Of all the actions of his life . . .

and so on with much gentle humour.

A single-arched bridge below the village spans the river Lyd and leads to the entrance to Lydford Gorge (National Trust), one of the most spectacular places in Devon. The Lyd, rushing off the moor, tumbles in waterfalls and whirlpools through a rocky chasm and into a deep, wooded gorge over a mile in length. The canopy of trees closes over it far above. At the lower end the White Lady waterfall splashes down 100 ft into the Lyd. The walk along the gorge is a unique experience.

Lynton and Lynmouth (2/3A) Holiday resorts of very different character on the north coast, one nearly 500 ft up on top of the cliffs and the other where the Lyn rivers reach the sea. They are linked by an 'alpine' road and by a cliff railway opened in 1890 and operated by water ballast tanks.

Lynton was a hamlet until the last half of the 19th century and natives of Lynmouth still sometimes refer to it as 'the village'. The opening of a narrow gauge railway from BARNSTAPLE in 1898 completed its transition into a holiday town. With the exception of the medieval tower of St Mary's Church nearly everything is late Victorian and Edwardian, a totally restored church, a mock Tudor Town Hall and many comfortable hotels. It is not intrinsically a place of beauty but the setting is magnificent, and from it the spectacular coast and hinterland can be explored.

Lynmouth was a fishing village, its harbour built when herring shoals could still be found in the Bristol Channel. It attracted visitors earlier than Lynton, from the time of the Napoleonic Wars. Coleridge and Wordsworth walked over from Somerset at the end of the 18th century and they were followed by Shelley and his ill-fated first wife in 1812. 'This place is beautiful', Shelley wrote, and in spite of growth and a massive rebuilding the setting still impresses. Shut in by the steep, wooded walls of the Lyn valleys, the houses clinging to rocks, Lynmouth was struck by disaster in 1952. Nine inches of rain fell on Exmoor in 24 hours and on the night of 15–16 August, at the height of the holiday season, the swollen rivers tore through the town destroying bridges and power lines, obliterating nearly a hundred buildings, badly damaging the harbour and sweeping cars and caravans into the sea. Thirty-one people died. The town has been rebuilt with suitable precautions against another tragedy and the opportunity taken to widen the bridges and lanes that made road access so difficult. Even the Rhenish tower on the harbour pier, a well-known landmark, was re-erected. It had been built in the 1850s for storage of sea water by a General Rawdon who liked taking salt-water baths in his residence near by.

East of Lynmouth the A39 climbs 1000 ft on its way to the Somerset border. Up this hill the men of Lynmouth with the help of a few horses hauled their lifeboat one wild night in January 1899. Unable to launch from Lynmouth, they took the boat all the way to Porlock Weir in Somerset, launched and stood by a vessel in distress, surely one of the most incredible episodes in the heroic annals of the lifeboat service.

The great bare crown of Foreland Point rises 900 ft from the sea at the east end of Lynmouth Bay, the northernmost tip of Devon. It is safely in National Trust hands and so also is the beauty spot known as Watersmeet where Hoar Oak Water runs into the East Lyn river in a narrow wooded gorge 2½ miles above Lynmouth. Up and down paths on either side of the river lead to it and, although much visited, it is a delightful place with a fishing lodge built c. 1830 in 'cottage orné' style providing refreshment.

Manaton (2/3C) A Dartmoor border village on B3344, 4 miles north-west of BOVEY TRACEY. The buildings along the road are nondescript but the turning off to the church reveals a tranquil, tree-lined green backed by thatched and stone cottages and the lychgate to the churchyard. St Winifred's Church is a 15th-century granite building with a two-storeyed, vaulted south porch. The interior is distinguished by a magnificent screen across nave and both aisles which has been expertly restored (1980–2). Parts of two staircases to the rood loft are visible, one in a projecting turret. Four panels of medieval stained glass remain in the north aisle. In the south aisle modern glass in memory of Esmond Moore Hunt of Foxworthy, aged 17, was designed by the artist Frank Brangwyn who worked as a young man in William Morris's studio. The Church House, a granite and thatched building half in the churchyard, was once an inn, then a poor house, and is now an attractive dwelling.

The parish boundary extends 5 miles into Dartmoor, taking in the large Bronze Age enclosed settlement called Grimspound and the very impressive Hound Tor. From the churchyard a good view is obtained of Bowerman's Nose, a rough pile of fissured granite over 20 ft high on Hayne Down. Local legend says that Bowerman and his hounds were turned into stone for persistently hunting on Sundays. He stands

on Hayne Down and his petrified pack on Hound Tor. Half a mile south of the village on the Bovey Tracey road are Becky Falls, a well-known attraction where the Becky brook tumbles down through thick woodland to join the river Bovey. South-west of the church is Wingstone, a house approached by a beech avenue where John Galsworthy of *Forsyte Saga* fame spent his honeymoon and returned many times as a summer tenant.

Martinhoe (2/3A) A tiny village less than a mile inland from the great hog's-back cliffs of the north coast between COMBE MARTIN and LYNMOUTH, approached by narrow lanes off the A39. The village contains little of interest, but is a good place to leave the car and explore a corner of the Exmoor National Park which is of outstanding beauty. A large group of Bronze Age barrows lies a quarter of a mile eastwards on the way to Woody Bay (National Trust). The bay and its wooded cliffs form one of the most beautiful and unspoiled places in Devon. Apart from marvellous views from the heights, it is worth while going down through the trees to the isolated beach.

North of the village on the Beacon (800 ft) are the remains of a 1st-century AD Roman fortlet, a signal station where for a short period before the conquest of South Wales watch was maintained for raiders crossing the Bristol Channel. A mile to the west the National Trust also owns Heddon's Mouth Cleave, where the little moorland river tumbles through a spectacular, mile-long gorge of wood and scree on its way to the sea.

Good paths lead from the well-known Hunter's Inn to the river mouth and the spectacular towering cliffs.

Marwood (2/2A) An attractive hamlet on a hill 3 miles north-west of BARNSTAPLE. The church of St Michael is a 14th-century cruciform building pleasantly sited above a wooded valley. The north transept was enlarged into an aisle in the 15th century. The screen dated c. 1520 extends only across the aisle and retains part of the beautifully carved loft. Carved bench ends, carved roof ribs and bosses and the 17th-century pulpit are all noteworthy, and also the sundial over the south porch made by John Berry in 1762. He was born in the parish and became a specialist craftsman responsible for many sundials in North Devon. The one at Marwood is one of the best and most elaborate to survive. At some time during the last 100 years it disappeared but was found in the

rectory attic 30 years ago. It shows the signs of the zodiac and purports to indicate the time in Jerusalem and various European cities as well as in a remote hamlet in Devon.

Marwood Hill is a modern house with a fascinating garden of ponds and flowering shrubs created over the last 20 years and open to the public. Northwards from the hamlet a road runs on high ground for nearly 7 miles in a straight line through unbroken farmland to ILFRACOMBE. This follows the line of an ancient ridgeway from the Taw estuary to the north coast.

Mary Tavy (2/2C) A large village 4 miles north of TAVISTOCK on the A386 to OKEHAMPTON. The medieval church, outwardly attractive, was too ruthlessly restored in late Victorian times to be of interest. William Crossing, author of the famous *Guide to Dartmoor*, first published in 1909, is buried in the churchyard. The village's brief importance and prosperity was due to mining. At the end of the 18th century Devon Friendship Mine opened and became the most important producer of copper in the Dartmoor area. Other mines followed, but by the 1870s they were all

Opposite: Woody Bay, Martinhoe (see p. 105)
Below: Royal Oak Inn, Meavy (see p. 108)

becoming unprofitable and the village declined as mining in the area gradually ceased over the next four or five decades. The abandoned workings of Devon Friendship are visible on the east side of the village, 30 acres of jumbled spoil heaps and ruins that give little idea of the vast extent and depth of the underground shafts. Water power for the mine, for pumping and for crushing and stamping the ore, was brought from the river Tavy by a wonderful system of leats. The Reddaford leat still runs from Tavy Cleave for 4 miles round the contours to serve a power station. The leat also served other smaller mines such as Wheal Jewel and Wheal Betsy. The beam engine house of the latter is preserved by the National Trust on the east side of and below the A386 1½ miles north of the village.

Meavy (2/2C) A pleasant village on the south-west border of Dartmoor approached by lanes off the PLYMOUTH–TAVISTOCK road (A386). The church of St Peter has Norman work in the north wall and Norman carving on the chancel arch. The unbuttressed tower may be 13th century, the window, door and pinnacles added when the rest of the church was rebuilt early in the 16th century. Near by on the village green stand the ancient Meavy oak and the village cross on a large

pedestal, restored in 1895. The delightful scene is completed by the Royal Oak Inn abutting on the churchyard and facing south across the green, a long building once the Church House.

South-west of the village where an ancient bridge and ford cross the river Meavy stands Marchant's Cross, a particularly fine example of the trackway and boundary markers of the Dartmoor region. To the north-east lies Burrator Reservoir completed by Plymouth Corporation in 1898. The dam is made of 6-ton granite blocks, quarried and dressed on site, to take the pressure from a thousand million gallons of water which cover 150 acres. The reservoir is fed not only by the river Meavy and its tributary streams but also by some of the water from the old Devonport leat (1793), drawn from the Blackabrook, Cowsic and West Dart rivers high on Dartmoor.

Modbury (2/5A) An ancient market town on the A379 PLYMOUTH–KINGSBRIDGE road, $1\frac{1}{2}$ miles east of the river Erme. The main road runs steeply down one side of a hollow and up the other, a fascinating street of good Georgian buildings, attractive shops and slate-hung houses characteristic of South Ham towns. In the last century the town boasted a dozen inns but only three have survived. The oldest is the half-timbered Exeter Inn, said to date from the 16th century, though much altered since. The White Hart Hotel is a plain double-pedimented building which incorporates the former Georgian Assembly Rooms.

The church of St George stands on the high ground at the west end of the town, its fine 14th-century tower and spire rising to 134 ft, a landmark visible from great distances. The six bells in the tower were cast in 1806 and are one of the best peals in Devon, a source of pride to local people:

> Hark to Modbury bells,
> How they do quiver!
> Better than Ermington bells
> Down by the river

The nave is also mainly 14th century but the rest was reconstructed in the 15th. The church suffered considerable damage during the Civil War, presumably at the hands of the victorious Parliamentary soldiers after a hard-fought skirmish to capture the town in February 1643. The rood screen was torn down and the tombs of the Prideaux family and of the Champernownes

Georgian buildings in Modbury

mutilated. The pulpit is made of panels saved from the rood screen.

The parish boundary north of the town follows a prehistoric ridgeway running north–east from the tidal head of the Erme at Goutsford to the Avon valley. It is worth following this minor road for the fine, contrasting views of the southern bastions of Dartmoor on one side and the fertile South Hams on the other.

Molland (2/3A) A small village north of the Bampton–SOUTH MOLTON road (A361) in the lovely foothills of EXMOOR. The 15th- to 16th-century church of St Mary is of exceptional interest for its unspoiled Georgian interior, the best in Devon. The ceiled roof and the uneven plastered and whitewashed walls form an admirable setting for tall box pews, an impressive pulpit and an unsophisticated 18th-century screen; and good mural monuments to the Courtenays of West Molland add a touch of colour. At Champson, a Tudor farm at the west end of the village, the famous breed of Red North Devon Cattle was perfected by the Quartly family late in the 18th century.

Moretonhampstead (2/3B) A small former market town on the BOVEY TRACEY–Whiddon Down Road (A382). Westward the B3212 crosses Dartmoor to Yelverton and the town is one of the principal 'gateways' to the Moor. It is a pleasant place but without notable buildings, perhaps because of fires in the 19th century. The granite Almshouses (National Trust) in Cross Street are the exception. They have a striking arcade of 11 openings and the date 1637 above the central doorway. Close by stands a tree planted on the site of the legendary 'Dancing Tree', an elm which during the 19th century bore a platform for musicians and dancers. Beneath the tree is the head of a medieval cross. The impressive four-stage tower of the church of St Andrew is early 15th century. The granite building is a spacious example of the moorland type but contains little of note. Many French officers lived in the town during the Napoleonic period, paroled from the crowded prison at PRINCETOWN, and some were buried in the churchyard. Two of their tombstones are preserved in the south porch of the church.

Mortehoe *see* Woolacombe

Morwellham Quay (2/2C) A former riverside port on the Tamar, 4 miles south-west of

Moretonhampstead

TAVISTOCK, brought back to life as a recreational and educational centre of exceptional interest. It is signposted off the Tavistock–Gunnislake road (A390), and coming down the lane through woods to the river it is hard to believe that anything of special importance lies ahead. But the port, at the nearest navigable point to Tavistock, was recorded as early as the 12th century. It seems to have been of moderate importance until the 19th century when the cutting of a canal from Tavistock and the opening of Devon Great Consols mine up-river near Gunnislake brought a brief and hectic heyday which ended about 1900 in total abandonment. The story of these days is well told at the Morwellham Quay Centre by slide shows, by exhibits in the Open Air Museum and by the relics now cherished as fascinating pieces of industrial archaeology. All is available all year round to the visitor: the former Ship Inn where the captains and business men lodged; the lime kilns and timber yard; a ruined school; ore chutes stained by copper sulphate; the stones used to grind manganese; the canal basin and towpath and the mouth of the two-mile tunnel under Morwell Down; and a trip on a mine railway. Perhaps the deserted quays are most evocative of all. A dozen vessels up to 300 tons could moor at one time, to take on copper, arsenic and manganese, to unload timber, limestone and coal during 50 years of frantic activity.

Newton Abbot (2/4C) A large market town at the head of the estuary of the river Teign. Its origins lie back in the 13th century, perhaps earlier, but it was the arrival of the railway in 1846 that turned it into the sprawling, busy town of today. It became an important railway junction, the station and yards catering for two branch lines as well as for the expresses and goods trains between London and KINGSWEAR, PLYMOUTH and, eventually, Cornwall. The station is now half deserted but the decline of the railways has not proved a disaster. The town's position makes it a natural centre of communications; it has attracted many industries and the market and shops continue to draw people from a wide area.

The 19th-century developments ranged from neat terraces of workers' houses to the substantial residences in Courtenay Park and Devon Square, to the Globe Hotel in Courtenay Street, the Hospital and old Workhouse in East Street and the Mackrell Almshouses on the TOTNES road. Development has continued during the present century with new housing and shops, a new market and car parks. Not many old buildings have survived all this but one exception is the 14th-century tower of St Leonard's Church, a solitary symbol of the medieval past at the heart of the town. The rest of this church was demolished in 1836.

Ford House to the east of the railway station is a fine Jacobean mansion (1610) with mullioned and transomed windows and semicircular gables. Inside are some fine plaster ceilings and much carved oak. William of Orange lodged there after landing at BRIXHAM in 1688. The house is now occupied by District Council Offices.

Bradley Manor (National Trust), set in the pleasant valley of the river Lemon at the west edge of the town, is a small 15th-century manor house incorporating some remains of a 12th-century building. Both the great hall and the chapel are notable features. The east front with slate roof, white Gothic gables and oriel windows is particularly attractive. The grounds offer good walking along the mill leat and down the river until it disappears under the town.

Newton St Cyres (2/4B) An attractive village, though divided through the middle by the A377 EXETER–CREDITON road. It is tidy cob and thatch with only a few modern buildings. The Crown & Sceptre Inn, burned down 20 years ago, has been rebuilt in its former style. Newton House, the home of the Quicke family, is a Georgian building rebuilt in 1909. An iron bridge across the main road connects it to the 15th-century church of St Cyriac and St Julitta set picturesquely on a mound. Its reddish volcanic stone was quarried at Posbury near Crediton. The nave arcade is of Beer stone, as in so many Devon churches. Of the monuments to the Northcote and Quicke families the most striking is that to John Northcote (d. 1632). He stands almost as large as life in his top boots, busts of his two wives on either side and his progeny kneeling beneath. More endearing is the small effigy of Sherland Shore who died in the same year at the age of 17, a youth reading a book, elbow on table, cheek propped on hand. The minor road north from the village, crossing the river Creedy on a lovely old bridge, leads to the railway station and the Beer Engine Inn. Real ale is brewed in the cellar of the inn and sold under the names of 'Piston' and 'Rail' ale.

Northam *see* Bideford

North Bovey (2/3C) One of the most pleasing small villages in Devon, $2\frac{1}{2}$ miles south-west of MORETONHAMPSTEAD on a hill above a bend of the river Bovey. Narrow lanes and very narrow bridges over the river have helped to preserve it. The village green is delightful with its oak trees, an ancient granite cross, an upping stock for mounting horses and an old iron pump and a granite basin. Many of the thatched cottages are of 17th-century origin or earlier. Particularly notable is the large building by the churchyard, thought to have been the Church House and now divided into cottages, and the pretty thatched Ring o' Bells Inn, one of the most attractive in the Dartmoor border country.

The church of St John the Baptist is a typical moorland granite building of the 15th century with earlier features. The rood screen has been sadly mutilated but some idea of its former glory can be gathered from the altar in the little Lady chapel, almost certainly made from the missing screen doors. The chancel is the oldest part of the church and this is confirmed by the handsome regilded roof bosses. The heads of a king and of two queens are thought to represent Edward I (died 1307) and his wives Eleanor of Castile and

One of the many thatched cottages in North Bovey

Margaret of France. Another boss shows three rabbits chasing each other, an emblem of the early tinners on Dartmoor.

Less than a mile north-west the Manor House was built in 1907 in Jacobean style for Viscount Hambleden, head of W. H. Smith & Co. It subsequently became a Great Western Railway Hotel with its own golf course and was denationalized a few years ago.

North Molton (2/3A) More of a village than a town, tucked away in the foothills of EXMOOR 3 miles north of the larger and more important SOUTH MOLTON. For centuries it existed, the inhabitants 'poor but healthy' as one chronicler put it, on the wool trade and on mining for iron and copper. When these activities ceased in the 19th century the population was halved and it became a rural village among hills that rise to 1400 ft above sea level 2 miles to the north.

The 15th-century church of All Saints has a massive battlemented and pinnacled tower 100 ft high and a clerestory, uncommon in a Devon parish church. A reasonable restoration in the 19th century has left other features which indicate a substantial and well-furnished 'town' church: the good rood and parclose screens, early 17th-century panelling in the chancel, and a very

fine medieval pulpit with sounding board and trumpeting angel added later. The 17th-century alabaster monument to Sir Amyas Bampfylde is rather impressive. His wife sits at the foot of the recumbent effigy with a book on her knees and their numerous children kneel in the background.

The Bampfyldes (now Lords Poltimore) lived at Court Hall east of the churchyard, a mansion much altered in the 19th century. To the west of the church is Court House, a long two-storeyed Tudor building with some 17th-century windows. The former Church House abuts on the south-east corner of the churchyard, close to the lychgate and the town square. The original Tudor building and two adjoining cottages seem to have been entirely remodelled about 1875 for use as a school, which use continues. The large, three-light, trefoil-headed windows of the façade are an interesting example of Victorian mock-medieval.

Nymet Rowland *see* Lapford

Okehampton (2/2B) A town on the A30 beneath the towering escarpment of northern Dartmoor. The parish church of All Saints stands on a hill a mile west of the town centre and marks the site of the earlier Saxon settlement. The church was gutted by fire in the 19th century and entirely rebuilt except for the 15th-century granite tower.

The Normans created the present town between the East and West Okement rivers and, to overawe it and command the northern route to Cornwall, erected an important castle. The substantial remains (open to the public) stand on a ridge south of the town beside the West Okement, protected to the west by an artificial ditch cut through the ridge. A strong barbican and a long, walled passage lead up to the gatehouse and a narrow bailey with remains of great hall, chapel, lodgings, kitchens. From a mound above the bailey the great double keep dominates all, its western portion 12th century and the oldest part of the ruins. The rest are early 14th century when Hugh Courtenay, Earl of Devon, carried out reconstruction. Two centuries later his successor was beheaded for treason and the castle was ordered to be dismantled.

Apart from the castle the town has no building of any particular merit except for the Town Hall in the main street. This is a splendid three-storeyed 17th-century house converted to its present use in 1821. From the town a long, steep hill leads up to the Moor and gives access, for the energetic, to the Yes Tor–High Willhays ridge. At a little over 2000 ft above sea level this is the highest of Dartmoor's hills.

Okehampton's Museum of Dartmoor Life is open from April to December.

Otterton (2/5C) A large village 2½ miles up the river Otter from the coast, approached by a turning off the Newton Poppleford–Budleigh Salterton road (A376) at Bicton Cross. The tall, brick signpost at the crossroads was put up in 1743 and has biblical texts inscribed on each of the directional plaques.

As you approach the village the old red sandstone tower of St Michael's Church rises attractively above the river. The rest of the church was rebuilt in 1871 and the Victorian interior is extravagantly inappropriate for a Devon village. The Tudor Manor House near by has been adapted for multiple occupation. By the bridge over the river the mill, restored to working order and the wheel driven by water from a wide leat, is a craft centre with shop and restaurant.

Okehampton Castle

Commemorative plaque to Samuel Taylor Coleridge,
Ottery St Mary

Council houses have been built round the village green but on the opposite side of the roadway a row of ancient thatched cottages have varied Georgian doorways. Other buildings of interest in the long street are of cob and thatch, thatch and stone, stone and slate, and one has an enormous central chimney dated 1627.

The gentle Otter river is bounded mainly by red cliffs on the east side but good paths run through the pasture fields on the west bank, upstream to Colaton Raleigh and down to the coast at Budleigh Salterton.

Ottery St Mary (2/5B) A friendly small town of Saxon origin on the river Otter, 12 miles east of EXETER. Some good Georgian houses survive in spite of fires in the 18th and 19th centuries, particularly those on the hill where the church stands.

The large factory by the river is also Georgian and a fine example of an early industrial building.

St Mary's is the grandest parish church in Devon, the result of a 13th-century building being transformed into a superb collegiate church in 1338–42 by the Bishop of Exeter, John de Grandisson. It is not surprising that it looks like a small-scale Exeter Cathedral because Grandisson was at the same time presiding over the completion of the cathedral. He also founded the King's School at Ottery which still flourishes on a new site outside the town. Bishop's Court on the road west of the river to Tipton St John is said to have been one of his country residences.

The church is beautifully maintained and has none of the gloom often associated with medieval buildings. The great size is apparent on entering, though the 14th-century altar screen conceals the ambulatory and Lady chapel which make up the overall length of 180 ft. In the south transept, which serves as a bell tower, a square-faced clock indicates the phases of the moon as well as the hours. The first record of repair was in 1437–8, but it is thought to date from the previous century

Paternoster Row, Ottery St Mary

and is always referred to as 'Bishop Grandisson's clock'. In the nave are two fine canopied tombs of the bishop's brother Sir Otho de Grandisson and his wife Beatrice. The vault bosses of the nave and chancel are equal in merit to those in Exeter Cathedral, particularly those of the bishop himself in full regalia over the crossing and a delightful Virgin and Child in the chancel. The special Christmas stamp for 1974 was based on the latter. In the Lady chapel two finely carved corbels depict the head of the bishop and that of his sister Katharine, Countess of Salisbury. Also in the chapel a gilded wooden eagle, standing on a globe with outstretched wings, was given to the church by Grandisson.

The Reverend John Coleridge was Vicar and Master of the King's School up to his death in 1781. His youngest son, Samuel Taylor Coleridge, baptized in the church on 30 December 1772, was to create the great poems *Kubla Khan* and the *Rime of the Ancient Mariner*. A commemorative plaque on the churchyard wall shows the albatross from the latter. Coleridge recalled the landscape of his youth in a nostalgic Sonnet to the river Otter:

Dear native brook! wild streamlet of the West!
How many various-fated years have past,
What happy and what mournful hours, since last
I skimmed the smooth thin stone along thy breast,
Numbering its light leaps . . .

Less than a mile north-west across the river lies Cadhay, one of the few Tudor country houses surviving in Devon. It is built round a courtyard with entrances through each wing. The north and east wings are the oldest, the staircase in the latter suggesting a date early in the 16th century. The north block contained the great hall, divided into two storeys in the 18th century. The usual long gallery for promenading in bad weather occupied the south block. In the rectangular courtyard four statues in niches over the entrances represent Henry VIII and his three children who succeeded to the throne. The walls of the court have a simple chessboard pattern of alternating flint and sandstone blocks.

The ornate and incongruous font in the parish church is by William Butterfield. He also designed Patteson's Cross, a familiar sight on the

The church of St John, Paignton (see p. 116)

A30 a mile north of the town. This commemorates John Coleridge Patteson, the first Bishop of Melanesia, murdered in 1871. He was born at Feniton Court, north of the main road.

Guy Fawkes is celebrated in the town on the nearest Saturday to 5 November with old-fashioned gusto. Large crowds watch the glittering carnival procession and afterwards the ancient custom of rolling lighted tar barrels

through the packed streets.

East of the town the river valley is bordered by a steep ridge called East Hill. Picnic places have been made among the woodland and a walk to Beacon Hill at the southern end of the ridge gives magnificent views over the lower Otter valley and SIDMOUTH.

Paignton (2/4C) A large resort on Torbay which developed alongside and a little later than TORQUAY. The original village lay half a mile inland, with a small harbour north of Roundham Head, but once the railway arrived in 1859 all the land down to the sea was developed. The streets round the parish church are the oldest part, with cottages going back to the 16th century and Kirkham House to the 14th century.

The church of St John was mainly rebuilt in attractive red sandstone in the 15th century. The south transept (known as the Kirkham Chantry) has a richly carved ceiling and a screen consisting of two canopied tombs linked by an arched doorway. Though small in scale, and the screen sadly mutilated, this is some of the best sculpture of about 1470–90 to survive anywhere in England. The church also contains a finely carved medieval pulpit and a Norman font. Close to the church a much-restored tower is all that remains of the medieval summer palace of the Bishops of Exeter.

The rest of the town is Victorian and later. Something of a phenomenon is Oldway, a mansion of over a hundred rooms used by the local authority for offices and functions. It is said to have been inspired by the palace at Versailles and was built in 1874–1904 for the Singer family of sewing machine fame. Few offices can boast such monumental façades – giant Corinthian columns and pilasters and at the east end a massive colonnade of Ionic columns – or such an extravagant entrance hall and staircase.

On the TOTNES road the Zoological and Botanical Gardens are the largest in Devon and notable for their pleasant and extensive grounds. Animals and birds are given as much space as possible and many types of birds wander freely. The Gardens are run by a charitable trust and the emphasis throughout is on scientific education rather than entertainment, the teaching of young people to care for animals and plants.

Parracombe (2/3A) An attractive village lying below the A39 BARNSTAPLE–ILFRACOMBE road where it curves over the Heddon valley. It is a good starting place for walking the western parts

of EXMOOR, particularly to see the Bronze Age cemetery known as Chapman's Barrows and other prehistoric remains on Parracombe and Challacombe Commons.

The church in the village was built in 1878 and the old parish church of St Petrock, high up beside the main road, threatened with destruction. John Ruskin was among the protesters who helped to save it. The tower and chancel are 13th century, the rest of the fabric a 16th-century reconstruction, but the unrestored 18th-century interior makes it remarkable. Whitewashed walls and ceilings set off a fine Georgian screen and three-decker pulpit, a musicians' gallery and box pews that rise at the west end like seats in a theatre. Even the Georgian hat pegs and wall plaques with admonitory texts have survived so that the visitor steps back over two centuries on entering.

Closer to the village the earthwork known as Holwell Castle is a good example of a small motte-and-bailey castle, one of thousands that sprang up all over England during the century after the Norman Conquest.

Plymouth (2/2C) The largest urban conglomeration in the South West. Since 1900 the city has expanded inland fourfold. The visitor must drive through seemingly endless suburbs to reach the famous Hoe and the remains of the little port that Hawkins and Drake knew.

Occupying the hilly peninsula between the Plym and Tamar rivers, it originated from three separate towns: Plymouth itself on Sutton Harbour; Stonehouse to the west on its own inlet; and Plymouth Dock (later Devonport) on the Hamoaze, the name given to the lower reaches of the Tamar. Plymouth was of little importance until the 16th century when it became the port for innumerable voyages of exploration and colonization, giving its name to 40 places overseas. It also became the chief base for the struggle against Spain. Plymouth Dock developed towards the end of the 17th century, the dockyard founded by William III as a base for the wars against France. Stonehouse lay between the two. By the 19th century the towns overlapped each other and were at last officially united in 1914.

The Hoe, a limestone bluff between the inlets of Sutton Harbour and Millbay, must be one of the finest promenades in the world. On one side lies the city and on the other the Sound stretching out two miles to the great breakwater designed by Sir John Rennie (1794–1874), a mile long and constructed of $4\frac{1}{2}$ million tons of limestone. No

Mural by Robert Lenkiewicz, the Barbican

wonder it took nearly 30 years to build. On the Hoe Drake was playing bowls when news came that the Armada had been sighted:

> He said they must wait their turn, good souls,
>   And stooped and finished the game.

He was a cool customer and the story, recorded within 40 years of the event, gains credence from the probable state of the tide that afternoon. Drake would have known if he could set sail at once or must wait for the tide to ebb to carry his ships out of the Sound.

The Hoe became a public park in 1817 and is properly furnished with a statue of Drake (a copy of Sir Joseph Boehm's statue at TAVISTOCK) and a memorial to the Armada victory. There also are Smeaton's Lighthouse, re-erected in 1882 after 120 years' service on the Eddystone Rocks, and the tall Naval Memorial to the dead of two world wars. At the east end of the Hoe the Marine

Biological Laboratory has a worldwide reputation for research and its fine aquarium is open to the public. Near by the Citadel, built in 1666–70 by Charles II, was defended by 152 guns that could cover the mouth of the Plym (called the Cattewater) and the entrance to Sutton Harbour or, if necessary, overawe the city. Charles was perhaps mindful that 20 years earlier Plymouth had stoutly held out for four years against his father's troops and cannon. The Citadel is still garrisoned, a functional building of bastions and hornworks, barracks, stores, a Governor's House but with a gateway that is a notable example of English Baroque architecture.

North of the Citadel are Sutton Harbour and the area known as the Barbican. Old and new jostle in narrow streets and on the quays: Tudor and 19th-century Custom Houses and a huge modern mural painting by Robert Lenkiewicz; Tudor houses and warehouses and a crowded yacht marina; the fish quay and busy market close to the Mayflower Stone which marks the

Opposite: The Hoe from Smeaton's Lighthouse;
Above: Smeaton's Lighthouse

departure point of the Pilgrim Fathers in 1620. Their names are listed on a board on Island House near by, traditionally where some of them stayed while the *Mayflower* underwent repairs. Behind Island House runs New Street, a winding, cobbled Elizabethan thoroughfare. No. 32 with its jettied timber front is a late 16th-century merchant's house restored in 1926 and well maintained by Plymouth Corporation. Inside visitors can see good 16th-century furniture and the spiral stairs built round a ship's mast. The Corporation owns another interesting merchant's house, No. 33 St Andrew's Street. Its massive limestone walls suggest a mid-16th-century date, the timber front probably added about 1600 when it was occupied by a sea captain and trader called William Parker, Mayor of Plymouth in 1601. The Merchant's House contains a museum of local history and was fortunate to survive the blitzes of the Second World War. Prysten House on the south of St Andrew's churchyard is another miraculous survival, a late 15th-century house and the oldest domestic building in Plymouth. St Andrew's Church purchased and restored it in the belief that it had some ecclesiastical association, but research has shown that it was a medieval merchant's house.

The 15th-century parish church of St Andrew, the largest in Devon, was totally gutted by bombing and the nearby Guildhall extensively damaged. Both have been rebuilt and the impressive new tower of the latter offers a good bird's eye view of the city. The postwar rebuilding included the new shopping centre of Royal Parade, New George Street and Drake's Circus, also the wide Armada Way which leads up to the Hoe. Not everyone approves, but at least it is bold and spacious and it should not be forgotten that after the war the Corporation had also to provide for 20,000 new houses to replace bombed and out-of-date dwellings. Eastwards from the shopping centre stand the ruins of Charles Church. It was a 17th-century building, the only one of its date in Devon until destroyed by bombing. The ruins have been preserved as a memorial of the blitz, a skeleton round which traffic remorselessly circles.

West of the Hoe lie Millbay Docks where the transatlantic liners in their heyday landed passengers. By the 1960s the liners had gone, their place now taken by car ferries to Brittany and Spain which transport far greater numbers of passengers and a substantial commercial traffic. In Millbay Basin the yachts usually assemble for events like the Fastnet, Transatlantic and Round-the-World races.

West of Millbay the next inlet is Stonehouse Creek, dominated by naval buildings: the Royal Naval Hospital, built in 1761 and much enlarged since, the Royal Marine Barracks, and the Royal William Victualling Yard (1826–35) designed by Rennie and covering about 14 acres. The gateway on Cremyll Street has a statue of William IV 13 ft tall to match the vast scale of the complex.

Beyond Stonehouse the Royal Naval Dockyard occupies 2 miles of frontage to the Hamoaze and covers 240 acres. With the closure of Chatham and reductions at Portsmouth, the yard continues in service as the chief base in Britain for the refitting and maintenance of all types of ships. It is the largest single employer of labour in the South West. **Devonport** town is notable for an extraordinary group of buildings by John Foulston (1772–1842). In 1824 Plymouth Dock was granted permission by George IV to change its name to Devonport and Foulston designed the Doric column on its massive plinth which commemorates this event. It was intended to put a statue of the king on the top but funds ran out. Near by at the end of Ker Street the earlier Town Hall (1821) with its Doric columns is a heavy-handed Parthenon; close by is the former Civil & Military Library, an eccentric building in the Egyptian style which became popular after Napoleon's Middle East campaign.

A ring road through the northern parts of the city leads to the Suspension Bridge over the Tamar opened in 1961 and replacing the old ferry to Saltash with its inevitable delays, particularly in the holiday season. Visitors can now cross to Cornwall on payment of a small toll and the population of Cornwall has easy access to Plymouth for its shopping and entertainment. Beside the road bridge, and dwarfed by it, is one of Isambard Kingdom Brunel's masterpieces, the railway bridge opened by Prince Albert in 1859. It was a magnificent feat of engineering and still carries the main line into Cornwall.

Plympton (2/2C) A large urban sprawl on the old EXETER–PLYMOUTH road (A374), incorporated in Plymouth since 1967. Originally it was two ancient towns, St Mary's on the road associated with a rich and important medieval priory and Plympton St Maurice half a mile to the south dependant on the Norman castle. Up to the end of the 13th century it was therefore more important than Plymouth and in 1328 it became a

The dining room, Saltram House.

Saltram House

Stannary town. Silting up of the Plym estuary due to mining activity on Dartmoor began the town's decline while Plymouth prospered.

The Priory was destroyed at the Dissolution (1539) though the early 14th- and 15th-century church of St Mary in its grounds survived. The granite tower, 108 ft high with polygonal pinnacles and large bell openings, is particularly handsome. The south porch of two storeys has an elaborate lierne vault springing from angel corbels. The interior with four aisles is exceptionally wide for a Devon church. A fine east window, a triple sedilia and early 14th-century piscina are notable, also the well-preserved tombs of Richard Strode (d. 1464) and of Sir William Strode (d. 1637).

Of the Norman castle only the motte and fragments of a shell keep remain. South of the castle the main street of Plympton St Maurice is largely unspoiled. The 17th-century Guildhall of slate and granite juts out over the pavement as at Exeter. Nearby the old Grammar School building, also with an arcade, was completed about 1670. Sir Joshua Reynolds was born in the town in 1723 and educated at the Grammar School where his father was headmaster. He was followed to school at intervals by James Northcote RA, by the historical painter Benjamin Haydon

and by Charles Eastlake who became the President of the Royal Academy, 1850–65. It is remarkable that four painters, one of them of the first rank, should be born in a small Devon town within the space of 70 years.

A mile to the south, approached by a road passing over the A38 dual carriageway, is **Saltram House**, the largest and finest mansion in Devon. It was handed to the National Trust with most of its contents in 1957 after being accepted by the Inland Revenue in lieu of estate duty. Apart from traces of its Tudor predecessor, and the fine library and Doric west porch added early in the 19th century, it is an 18th-century building. The Parker family purchased Saltram in 1712 and John Parker built the south and east wings and enlarged the west wing between 1744 and 1750. Twenty years later his son John called in Robert Adam to design the main rooms. The house is full of good furniture, pictures and decorative features, and the dining room and the saloon with every detail planned by Adam are real showpieces. The carpets for these rooms were made at the old AXMINSTER factory, each complementing the ceiling above it. Four of the portraits in the saloon are by 'local boy' Reynolds, a friend of the Parker family and a frequent visitor even when he became the first President of the Royal Academy.

Overleaf: Salcombe from Sharpitor (see p. 125)

The clapper bridge, Postbridge

More portraits by Reynolds adorn other rooms. The diarist and compulsive letter writer Fanny Burney stayed there in 1789 and thought the house 'one of the most magnificent in the kingdom'. Two hundred years later the exquisite taste of the Parker family, and the skill of the artists and craftsmen they employed, are still impressive. The grounds overlooking the Plym estuary, with some fine trees and the usual 'follies', make a worthy setting. Saltram House is open from April to October, the gardens all year round.

Postbridge (2/3C) A straggling hamlet in the middle of Dartmoor on the MORETONHAMP-STEAD–Yelverton road (B3212). Prehistoric man was active in this comparatively sheltered basin from Mesolithic to Bronze Age times. By the 13th century tin mining had spread to the inner moor and medieval farmers had established several 'ancient tenements' close by: Runnage, Pizwell, Hartland and Lower Merripit. It is probable that the famous clapper bridge over the East Dart

river was built at that time so that travellers and packhorse trains could cross dry-shod when the river was in spate. Many clapper bridges have survived on Dartmoor but this is the finest example. According to William Crossing, the locals referred to the old moorland tracks as 'postroads', and a map of 1720 showed the clapper as 'Post stone bridge, 3 arches'. This seems to be the origin of the name of the modern settlement which came into existence when the first turnpike road across the Moor was completed at the end of the 18th century. Today Postbridge is a tourist centre giving access to the heart of Dartmoor.

Powderham Castle *see* Kenton

Princetown (2/2C) At 1400 ft above sea level on an exposed hill, one of the bleakest villages in England. It was the brainchild of Sir Thomas Tyrwhitt, Lord Warden of the Stannaries and Secretary to the Prince of Wales, afterwards George IV. Towards the end of the 18th century he conceived the idea of creating a settlement and a productive farm amid the peat and granite on the slopes of North Hessary Tor. The scheme was near foundering when the renewal of the long war with France in 1803 gave Tyrwhitt a second opportunity. He proposed the building of a prison for captured Frenchmen, to relieve the overcrowded hulks at PLYMOUTH. The building was completed in 1809 and at times held 7000 prisoners. The original impressive entrance still bears the words *Parcere Subjectis* ('Pity the Vanquished'). In 1812 America declared war on England and soon American prisoners joined the French. Between them they built St Michael's Church (1810–15). The east window of the church was inserted in 1910 in memory of the Americans who helped to build the church and 'especially of the 218 brave men who died here on behalf of their country'. The prison was closed when the wars ended and Prince's Town, as Tyrwhitt had grandly named his settlement, faced another crisis. He proposed that the prison should be used for convicts but this idea was not adopted until 1850, long after his death.

Ironically Tyrwhitt's original idea for a farm also eventually materialized: 2000 acres have been won from the moor by the immense labour of convicts to form a model farm. The village continues to live on the prison though visited in the summer by large numbers of tourists, including many Americans. The Plume of Feathers Inn survives from Tyrwhitt's first tiny settlement.

Ringmore (2/5A) An attractive village in the South Hams, set back a mile from the coast between the Erme and Avon estuaries. Good paths lead down to the shores of Bigbury Bay. Many stone buildings with thatched or slate roofs date back hundreds of years, some to the 16th century. The Journey's End Inn claims a 13th-century origin, but is named after R. C. Sherrif's famous play about the First World War which he wrote while staying there.

All Saints Church stands small and picturesque on its mound, the sea visible from the churchyard down a deep combe. The interior was thoroughly restored in the 1860s and is of no interest. Two small, round-headed Norman windows survive in the north transept, but the fabric seems mainly 13th century. The tower, sited on the south side of the nave and its ground floor forming the entrance porch, is of unusual interest. The battlements project on corbels and are more military-looking than decorative. The impression of a fortress rather than a bell tower is enhanced by the windows, mere arrowslits except for two narrow lancets. The tower is capped by a rare 13th-century spire, a funny, stumpy thing yet exactly right for the proportions of the rest of the building.

St Giles in the Wood (2/2A) A small village 2 miles east of GREAT TORRINGTON off the B3227. The church was hopelessly restored in the 19th century but is notable for its monumental brasses. The oldest (1430) is of Alyanora (Elinor) Pollard wearing a wide hat and gracefully folded gown with long, wide sleeves. The brass was carefully restored by experts in 1956 at the instigation of a Canadian descendant of the Pollards. Margaret Rolle (1570) wears the typical ruff, puffed sleeves and spread skirt of an Elizabethan lady. Another brass with heraldic shield and inscription commemorates John Rolle (1591), possibly her husband or son, and finally there is a delightful small brass (1610) in memory of Johanna (Joan) Risdon showing her kneeling on a cushion on a tiled floor. The Risdons lived at Winscott Barton, a mile east of the village, and there Tristram Risdon wrote his historic *Chorographical Description or Survey of Devon*. It took him 25 years (1605–30) but it was not published in full until 1811. He died at Winscott in 1640 and was buried in the chancel of the church.

Salcombe (2/5A) A picturesque resort, the most southerly in Devon, on the west side of the KINGSBRIDGE estuary. It is approached from Kingsbridge along A381. The buildings climb from the waterside in a series of terraces, protected from the north and west by high land and looking out over the superb anchorage and the mouth of the estuary, one of the loveliest views in Devon. When tempests ravage the coast the town sits snugly a mile inland, a natural yachting centre, one of the largest in England. The narrow main street is full of attractive little shops and restaurants. The Museum of Maritime and Local History on Custom House Quay displays aspects of the town's past, and in particular relics of the American troops who trained in the South Hams in 1943–4 for the invasion of Occupied Europe. At Sharpitor House (National Trust) above South Sands, the Overbecks Museum has a room devoted to the clipper schooners that made Salcombe famous in the days of sail. In Sharpitor gardens many subtropical plants – mimosa, agapanthus, palms, bottlebrush and camphor trees – flourish in the mild climate.

Salcombe Castle, otherwise Fort Charles, is a

ruin on the promontory near North Sands. It was one of Henry VIII's forts and in the Civil War the last Royalist stronghold in Devon to surrender (May 1646). The defeated garrison marched out with colours flying after stipulating that the castle should thenceforth be called Fort Charles.

Tennyson visited Salcombe in 1889 to stay with the Devon-born historian J. A. Froude at a Georgian house between North and South Sands. His departure by yacht on a fine Sunday evening, the church bells ringing and the boat passing close to the sandy bar at the estuary mouth, is said to have inspired the poem 'Crossing the Bar' written a few months later.

Saltram House *see* Plympton

Sampford Courtenay (2/3B) An agricultural village on the A3072, 5 miles north-east of OKE-HAMPTON. The main street winds pleasantly between whitewashed cob-and-thatch cottages, widening at the north end where it borders the Church House and the churchyard.

The granite church of St Andrew is a large 15th-century building, outside battlemented and formidable, within all light and spaciousness. The ground slopes from west to east so that the nave is lower than the tower, the chancel built up in 1899 but still a foot lower than the nave. Notable are the Norman font of Purbeck marble, the 16th-century parish chest made from a single piece of oak, wagon roofs with carved bosses and wall plates, and in the south arcade some beautiful Polyphant stone from Cornwall to break the monotony of the granite.

The Church House (*c.* 1500) is a long building of granite rubble with a lateral outside stairway to the upper storey. The murder of a gentleman called William Hellions on these steps on Whit Monday 1549 marked the beginning of the Prayer Book Rebellion in Devon, a protest against the abolition of the Latin Mass.

A mile to the north lies **Honeychurch**, one of the remotest and most unspoiled places in Devon. According to Dr W. G. Hoskins, the distinguished Devon historian, the five farms at Honeychurch recorded in Domesday Book (1086) still exist. The little church of St Mary, 42 ft in length, is also a remarkable survival. The nave and chancel are 12th century, with south porch and west tower added in the 15th. Externally the earlier rubble walling can be seen merging in the later coursed stonework. The interior is delightful with an unusual four-sided tapering 12th-century tub font, plain 15th- and

17th-century benches, an Elizabethan pulpit, all unsophisticated, and unobtrusively restored in 1958.

Shaugh Prior (2/2C) A picturesque village on the south-west border of Dartmoor with fine views across to Cornwall and down the Plym valley to PLYMOUTH Sound. The typical 15th-century granite church of St Edward has a remarkable oak font cover which was found lying in a farm building in 1870 and carefully restored. It is over 8 ft tall, an octagon of two storeys with a conical top surmounted by the figure of a mitred bishop.

At the east end of the village a granite cross, $5\frac{1}{2}$ ft tall and set in a massive socket stone, stands against a field wall. One arm is slightly fractured but it is a good example of a medieval wayside cross.

To the north and west of the village the river Plym rushes down from the moor through a spectacular wooded gorge where Shaugh Bridge, at the meeting of the river Meavy with the Plym, is a deservedly popular beauty spot. Between the rivers the impressive Dewerstone abruptly rises 400 ft, a challenge to rock climbers.

East of the village Shaugh Moor is covered in Bronze Age remains – burials, settlements, and field systems. Surveys and excavations in 1976–80 have recorded as much information as possible before their obliteration by the spread of the china clay quarries near by. These enormous white gougings and mountains have been worked since 1840 and are the main source of the material in Devon.

Shebbear (2/2B) A remote, peaceful village overlooking the upper valley of the river Torridge, reached by lanes running north from the A3072 Holsworthy–HATHERLEIGH road. It is a Saxon village centred round a square. The church of St Michael, mainly early 14th century, has an exceptionally good Norman south door and a carved Elizabethan pulpit.

The Devil's Stone Inn is a well-preserved 17th- to 18th-century hostelry which takes its name from a large boulder lying outside the churchyard on the village green. Like the famous 'blue' stones at Stonehenge, this came from the Preseli (Prescelly) mountains in Pembrokeshire and was probably transported in prehistoric times. Local legend asserts that it was dropped by the Devil and that disaster will overtake the village if it is not turned over on the night of 5 November each year. After a peal of bells the ringers turn the boulder with crowbars and then another peal is rung. This custom dates back for centuries before the Gunpowder Plot of 1605.

Also in the district is the Alscott Farm Museum, open from Easter to September.

Sheepstor (2/2C) A small village on the edge of Dartmoor near Burrator Reservoir (*see* Meavy). It lies below and takes its name from Sheeps Tor (1210 ft), one of the largest and most accessible on the Moor. The climb is worthwhile for the outstanding views from the summit.

The little 16th-century church has the low tower and outsize pinnacles typical of the western border villages. The rood screen was destroyed in 1862 but a copy, based on surviving fragments, erected in 1914. The memorial to Elizabeth Elford (d. 1641) depicts a touching scene: the lady half-reclines on her four-poster, the curtains parted, a baby at her side and three daughters kneeling at the bedside. She was one of the four wives of John Elford of Longstone, the ruined manor house standing close to the reservoir half a mile to the north. In the churchyard are the graves of Sir James Brooke, the white Rajah of Sarawak (d. 1868) and of the nephew who succeeded him. Near the church door a roughly circular slab of granite seems to have been preserved because of the cross-in-a-circle incised on it. It is merely the base of a domestic cheese press with a characteristic 'snout' for draining off the whey.

The striking cross outside the churchyard entrance was restored in 1910 to commemorate the accession of George V. The shaft, with both arms broken off, had previously served as a rubbing post for cattle. Another old cross, also restored, stands in the churchyard where steps lead down to the playing field below. In the field is an iron ring where bulls were tied for baiting, an interesting survival. From the village the walker has easy access to the wealth of prehistoric remains lying north-west of the moorland Plym.

Shute (2/5B) A small village on the B3161 a mile south of its junction with A35 between HONITON and AXMINSTER. The first sight on entering the village is the imposing Tudor gatehouse to Shute Barton (National Trust). Only two wings of the Barton survive. The rest was destroyed at the end of the 18th century, but the remains are of great interest as an early example (about 1380) of an unfortified manor house. It was enlarged in the 15th century and completed with the gatehouse by the Pole family about 1570. The kitchen in the south wing has an enormous fireplace where a whole ox could be roasted. The great hall above it, reached by a newel stair in an external turret, has been divided horizontally so that on the present top floor the magnificent collar beams and curved braces of the original 14th-century roof can be closely studied. The north wing is mainly 15th century and was buttressed externally when the rest of the mansion was demolished. Both inside and out the remains are a fascinating jigsaw of styles over three centuries.

A lane east of the gatehouse leads to St Michael's Church, a 13th-century cruciform building with a central tower, and a north aisle added in the 15th century. The chancel aisle forms the Pole family chapel and contains a monument to William Pole (d. 1741), Master of the Household to Queen Anne. He stands on a pedestal dressed in courtly clothes and holding his wand of office, clearly engaged on mundane affairs. Pevsner pointed out in *The Buildings of England* that it would have graced a public square or garden more properly than a church.

Sidbury (2/5B) A village on the SIDMOUTH–HONITON road (A375) 3 miles inland up the fertile valley of the river Sid. It takes its name from the large Iron Age fort on the prominent spur to the south-west. Many attractive old cottages can be found in the quiet lanes – Bridge Street, Church Street, Green Head – leading off the main road. Some are thatched and of cob on stone footings, others slated.

St Giles and St Peters Church is one of the most interesting in East Devon and its Norman tower and modern spire (1884) dominate the village. The Norman church was altered at different times between 1200 and 1600: Norman, Early English, Decorated and Perpendicular work can be seen inside and out. The tower basement is unusual in having a ribbed vault. Four massive corbels support the ribs, one showing a man apparently carrying the weight of the tower on his shoulders. The 15th-century octagonal font is unique because it has retained its lock. Until about 1550 it was not customary to change the holy water after each baptism and it was kept under lock and key. The west gallery is the main post-medieval feature, built in 1620, extended and the 'marbled' front added in 1754, and again adapted when the present organ was installed in 1941. Most interesting feature of all, to complete the 'story in stone' of medieval architecture, a small Saxon crypt survives under part of the chancel. It was discovered during restoration work and is one of only six known in Britain.

Sidmouth (2/5B) The white buildings of this pleasant resort in East Devon are tucked in between towering red cliffs in the valley of the little river Sid. The small fishing and market town began to attract visitors as a watering place at the end of the 18th century. The long war with France, which prevented the gentry and well-to-do people from travelling on the Continent, contributed to the growth. The population doubled during the first 20 years of the 19th century and houses sprang up by the score. The wealthy built elaborate seaside homes such as the present Woodlands Hotel, with its fancy bargeboarding, in Station Road. Beach House on the Esplanade is another and also the castellated Woolbrook Glen, now the Royal Glen Hotel. The ailing Duke of Kent chose the latter for his residence in the winter of 1819–20, bringing his infant daughter Victoria with him. He caught a chill and died within a month but this did not discourage other

health-seeking visitors. A later royal patron was Victoria's third son, the Duke of Connaught, who visited the town in his old age between the two world wars. The sheltered ornamental gardens at the west end of the front are named after him.

Less elaborate accommodation was provided by terraces and rows of houses such as Elysian Fields, York Terrace on the front, Coburg Terrace, and by smaller 'cottages' in Coburg Road

and many other buildings elsewhere. Fortfield Terrace with its pleasant balconies overlooks the cricket ground which itself dates back to 1820. The double-headed eagle crest on the terrace commemorates occupation of No. 8 by the Grand Duchess Helene of Russia in 1831. Soon afterwards Elizabeth Barrett Browning lived there for a short period, then moved to the detached house in All Saints Road called Cedar Shade. Her father had brought her to Sidmouth hoping that the sea air would help her persistent cough.

The town has nearly 500 'listed' buildings and the centre is full of good Georgian houses and shops too numerous to detail. The parish church of St Nicholas (rebuilt in the 1860s) and All Saints Church (1837–49) are solidly Victorian and contain nothing of interest except the stained glass in the east window of the former, which was given by Queen Victoria in memory of her father. The chancel and east window of the earlier parish church are preserved near by in the curious residence known appropriately as Old Chancel. It was built by a local antiquarian, Peter Orlando Hutchinson, who used everything he could salvage when the old church was demolished. The rest of the house represents his version of various styles of architecture all jumbled together in a manner that defies description – an extraordinary Victorian fantasy.

Although development has spread the town a couple of miles inland, the older part has preserved its early 19th-century character in a remarkable way. The shingle beach, the fine promenade and good shops are particularly attractive to retired people and to holidaymakers who appreciate a modest dignity, an unusual quality for a resort. For one week each year, however, all decorum is cast aside when the International Folk Festival is held, drawing musicians and dancers from all over the world.

Silverton (2/4B) A large, pleasant village on the east side of the Exe valley, 7 miles north of EXETER. It was of early Saxon origin and lies amid fertile 'red' land on the old road over the hills from Exeter to TIVERTON. The route lost its importance when the turnpike along the valley was completed about 1800. As a result the village is largely unspoiled with most modern development confined to the fringes. The three inns and the Church House front the old main road. The last-named is a fine thatched building dating back to the 16th century and unusual in standing away

The Royal Glen Hotel, Sidmouth

from the churchyard. Other old buildings of
different dates make the main street attractive.

The church of St Mary is built of local volcanic
stone and has a sturdy buttressed tower with
battlements and pinnacles. The light and spacious interior, with lofty Beer stone arcades, is
dated to the early 16th century by one of the pillar
capitals. This shows two revolving gridirons,
symbols of the martyrdom of St Lawrence, and
between them the name 'Dobell'. Lawrence
Dobell was the rector in 1519–31 when the wool
trade would have made a rebuilding financially
viable. The wagon roof of the nave is original, the
fine bosses recently renewed and painted.
Unfortunately the Victorians ruthlessly restored
the chancel and destroyed the rood screen. The
door to the rood stairs and the external stair turret
remain. A good west gallery (1734) spans the
whole width of the church, the front panels
recording gifts for the benefit of the poor in the
17th and 18th centuries. Fastened to one of its
fluted, wooden pillars a small alms box is inscribed
with the words 'Pray Remember the Poor'.

Slapton (2/6A) A typical village of the South
Hams, a mile inland from the shore of Start Bay.
The church of St James has a medieval broached
spire and is mainly of the 14th and 15th centuries.
A tower near by, 80 ft high and the most prominent feature of the village, is all that remains of a
chantry founded in 1372 by Sir Guy de Brian, a
trusted soldier and servant of Edward III.

Slapton's main attractions are the Ley, the
largest freshwater lake in Devon, and the great
shingle beach over 2 miles in length along which
the DARTMOUTH to KINGSBRIDGE road runs.
Among interesting plants growing wild on the
beach is seakale. A Slapton gardener in the 18th
century first thought of cultivating it as a vegetable and it became very popular. The granite
obelisk on the beach is a memorial presented by
the United States Army to the people of the South
Hams 'who generously left their homes and their
lands to provide a battle practice area for the
successful assault on Normandy . . .' All signs of
the devastation wrought in 1943–4 have happily
gone, though a Sherman tank at the south end of
the beach serves as another reminder.

The Ley behind the beach, fed by three small
streams, swarms with fish (roach, perch, eel and
pike) and is of special interest to naturalists.
Waterplants, insects, breeding reed and sedge
warblers, wintering flocks of duck, spring

Slapton Ley Nature Reserve

migrants making their landfall and autumn migrants gathering for take-off are the attractions of the Nature Reserve run by the Slapton Ley Field Study Centre. A bird-ringing and observation hut is also maintained by the Devon Bird Watching and Preservation Society. The Field Centre has laid out two nature trails for those who wish to explore the unusual habitat.

South Brent (2/3C) On the old route from EXETER to PLYMOUTH, now bypassed by the new A38 road. It was a large market village taking its name from the 'brant' (steep) hill that rises more than 600 ft above it to the north, one of the chain of prominent heights along the southernmost borders of Dartmoor. The church is dedicated to an important Celtic saint, St Petrock, and has a fine Norman tower at the west end. Originally the tower stood over the crossing of a cruciform church but 14th- and 15th-century rebuilding created a new nave and aisles. The circular font is of red sandstone with three bands of typical Norman decoration: cable, radiating petals, zigzag. The 15th-century building with an impressive porch south-east of the churchyard was the Church House.

William Crossing, of *Guide to Dartmoor* fame, lived at South Brent for many years and from it set out to explore the southern moor in detail. The village continues to be a 'gateway' to the Moor. A narrow road runs two miles up the Avon valley to Shipley Bridge, popular for picnics and as a starting place for walks. The ruined buildings to the west of the bridge were built in the 1840s for the extraction of naptha from peat, an enterprise that failed within a few years. Behind them are remains of ponds and pits for treating china clay, a later enterprise that also lasted only a short time. The line of the tramway over Brent Moor which brought the raw materials to the works – peat from Redlake Mire and clay from near the source of the Bala brook – can still be traced. An easier walk upstream beside the shrunken river leads to the towering dam of the Avon Reservoir, an impressive feat of engineering that has nevertheless destroyed a beautiful moorland valley. On the hill south-west of the reservoir are the remains of a large Bronze Age settlement known as Riders Rings, two stone-walled enclosures and the foundations of more than 30 buildings.

South Molton (2/3A) A busy market town, dating from Saxon times, on the Taunton–BARNSTAPLE road (A361). It has attracted some light industries without losing its agricultural impor-

tance and rural character. Through traffic to the north coast resorts is a problem that will be solved when a proposed relief road is completed. Broad Street, the well-preserved town square, lies off the through road and has many good 19th-century buildings, such as the Market Hall (1863) and at the west end the substantial Post Office (1888). The square's main feature is the earlier Town Hall (1743), a handsome Georgian building, its well-proportioned front carried out over the pavement and surmounted by a clock tower. Also pleasing on an island site at the east end is the chemist's shop known as Medical Hall with an iron veranda on four Ionic columns.

A pathway from the square leads to St Mary Magdalene Church, a 15th-century building with a tall, severe west tower. The church was enlarged and restored in the 19th century and the clerestory added. The 15th-century pulpit and the font are good examples of medieval stone carving.

Quince Honey Farm on the road to Barnstaple has a large indoor apiary where bees can be watched at their labours and the whole process of honey making is demonstrated and explained in detail.

South Tawton (2/3B) A small village in the Dartmoor foothills, a mile north of the A30 between Whiddon Down and OKEHAMPTON. The parish extends to 11,000 acres and includes the village of South Zeal and a large part of north-east Dartmoor. The Church House by the churchyard gate is remarkable, a granite, barn-like structure with thatched roof and medieval windows. It stands on sloping ground and a few steps lead up to the entrance door over which the double, external stairs to the first floor form a porch. Repairs to the building were recorded in the 16th century but it is at least a century earlier.

The 15th-century granite church of St Andrew with a handsome west tower stands on a mound above the centre of the village. The tall nave piers are of Beer stone, the wagon roof and bosses original. The oak pulpit has inlaid panels showing three of the Evangelists – for some reason St John is not represented – and is a superb example of early 18th-century craftsmanship. In the north chancel aisle the dignified effigy of John Wykes (d. 1592) has its feet resting not on a heraldilc beast or cushion but on a sturdy duck. In the Lady chapel the memorial to Robert Burgoyne and his wife (1651) is also curious, their small kneeling figures in stone above a slate slab incised with figures of their ten children, one in a shroud

The Church House, South Tawton

and one in a cradle.

For several generations the Burgoynes lived at **South Zeal** half a mile to the south. Their substantial house of early 16th-century date with mullioned windows and a splendid porch is now the deservedly well-known Oxenham Arms Hotel. In one of its back rooms a prehistoric standing stone, too deeply embedded to be removed, was incorporated in the structure. South Zeal lay on the old road from EXETER to Okehampton and is a good example of a small medieval town, its houses on either side of a wide street with long, narrow lots running back behind them. The chapel of St Mary in the middle of the street, looking quaintly medieval, was rebuilt in 1713. Beside it stands the impressive medieval Market Cross on an enormous pedestal, a reminder of the cattle markets that for centuries were held in the street.

South Zeal *see* South Tawton

Spreyton (2/3B) A small village in the hills north of Dartmoor, little visited but well known because of Uncle Tom Cobley, immortalized in Devon's national anthem, 'Widecombe Fair'. He was a yeoman of Spreyton parish and set off from the village with his companions, all local men,

for the famous ride across Dartmoor to WIDECOMBE IN THE MOOR. He died in 1794 and was buried in the churchyard of St Michael's close to the south porch, but in an unmarked grave. The pleasant village inn is naturally called the Tom Cobley.

The church, approached along a lovely avenue of lime trees first planted in 1802, has considerable character. The massive oak door has to be heaved open. The fine wagon roof is particularly notable in the chancel, where a long Latin inscription on rafters and purlins records the names of benefactors and of the vicar, Henry le Maygne, 'who caused me to be built AD 1431'. Stained glass inserted in 1889 fills the original east window. The rood stairs are well preserved in the north wall and a fragment of the original screen lies against the tower wall. An eight-sided Norman font wedged against a nave pillar has primitive but meaningful carvings on the pedestal: the Tree of Life, Eve, Our Lady crowned, the Wheel of Life, a skull and crossbones, figures of a man and a woman who may have been the donors. The bowl of another font, a simple slab with a drain hole, is preserved in the north aisle and is said to be Saxon.

Staverton (2/3C) A small village 2 miles north of TOTNES. The setting on the slopes of the Dart Valley is delightful. The tower of St Paul's

Above: The chapel of St Mary, South Zeal (see p. 133)   *Opposite: St James, Swimbridge (see p. 136)*

Church is plain 13th-century without buttresses and battered at the base. The rest of the fabric is mainly early 14th century, with a two-storey, battlemented south porch and the octagonal granite piers of the aisle arcades decorated with simple leaves and flowers. The windows have all been renewed, with the exception of one in the chancel with original star-shaped tracery at the top. The quite impressive rood screen is also a reconstruction carried out at the end of the 19th century. The old Sea Trout Inn may have been the Church House. The village is best approached by turning off A384 at Huxham's Cross and driving over the narrow, six-arched Staverton Bridge (1413). It has pointed buttresses on both sides between the depressed arches and is one of the finest medieval bridges in Devon. Close by is a station on the Dart Valley Railway Company's line (*see* Buckfast).

Stockland (2/5B) A most attractive village in the valley of the river Yarty, 5 miles north-east of HONITON. The buildings are all of stone with thatched or slate roofs except for the new Vicarage – how could this have been permitted? The King's Arms Inn is a notable stone and thatched 16th-century building. South-west of the churchyard are some cottages which may be even older, and a most interesting thatched farmhouse dated 1602.

The church of St Michael, a 14th-century rebuilding in dressed flint and Ham stone, enlarged and altered in the 15th century and restored in the 1870s, was also originally thatched and the slate roof substituted only about 200 years ago. The tower is nearly 100 ft tall, graceful and conspicuous, the arch and jambs of the west door decorated with fruit and leaves. The 15th-century north aisle, buttressed, battlemented and with a projecting rood stair turret, presents an impressive façade to the village. Unusually the north door forms the main entrance and inside the nave arch in line with it has a wider span than the others, a nice touch.

A mile and a half south-west on Stockland Hill is Stockland Great Castle, an Iron Age fort cut by a minor road. The southern half is merely defined by field hedges, but the single rampart of the northern half survives, rising to 40 ft in places. The fort was one of many built on their eastern frontier by the Celtic tribe of the Dumnonii (their name, much modified by Saxon tongues, lives on in the name of the county). Also on Stockland Hill is a tall, slender mast that beams TV programmes to a large area.

Stokenham (2/6A) A village beside the A379 KINGSBRIDGE–DARTMOUTH road, a mile before it reaches the coast at Torcross. It has some attractive old cottages of local slate and thatch and a remarkably large church of 15th- and early 16th-century date. This also is built of the local slaty stone and towers impressively above the main road. The 16th-century Perpendicular windows and nave piers are of usual types, but gain much from the church's setting and its spacious interior. The 15th-century rood screen extends across the whole width of the church, an early example and of rather simpler design than the exuberant and luxurious screens that came later. The former Church House, now an inn, lies below the churchyard.

Torcross is a small resort on the edge of Start Bay with only the pebble beach between the houses and the sea. An old slate quarry in the cliffs to the south, on National Trust land, is worth a visit. Lanes running south from Stokenham lead to Beesands, a charming fishing village; to Hallsands where an older village was damaged by a series of storms and finally overwhelmed in 1917; and to Start Point with its precipitous cliffs and lighthouse, built in 1836 and nearly 100 ft tall. The scenery of the whole area is striking and Start Point is a good place for observing birds on migration.

Swimbridge (2/3A) A village on the A361 SOUTH MOLTON–BARNSTAPLE road. It has some old cottages and Georgian houses, but the main attraction is the large and exceptionally interesting church of St James. The tower and lead spire rise to 90 ft and are both dated 1310; the spire is one of only three of medieval date in North Devon. The rest of the church is 15th century, restored not too drastically in the 1880s. The interior furnishings are lavish for a village church. The font is an unusual example of the late 15th century: lead encased in oak panelling and surmounted by an elaborate cover and richly decorated canopy. The stone pulpit of the same date is shaped like a wineglass but the stem ends in a square base. It is beautifully ornamented and retains traces of colouring and gilding. The figures on it, once named on the scrolls in their hands, are St Paul (with sword), St Peter (with key) and three doctors of the Church, Saints Augustine, Ambrose and Jerome. The chief feature of the interior is the restored rood screen which stretches the full width of the church.

The ceilure above the rood is part of the original fine wagon roof, but the rood figures

The inn sign at Swimbridge

are modern (1956).

The Reverend Jack Russell, the famous hunting parson and breeder of the terriers named after him, was vicar of St James for 46 years (1833–80). Feats of endurance in the hunting field, sustained into old age, were combined with a simple devotion to his parishioners. When he died at the age of 87 they flocked to his funeral. His tomb lies at the east end of the churchyard. In his day six inns flourished in the village. Only one survives, the former New Inn which changed its name to The Jack Russell in 1962.

Tavistock (2/2C) A pleasant, well-planned town on the PLYMOUTH–OKEHAMPTON road (A386). One of the attractions is the river Tavy, fresh from the heights of Dartmoor, running through it and crossed by two 18th-century bridges. In the past a Stannary town for medieval tinners, then a centre for the wool trade and then for copper mining, Tavistock has always been and continues to be the centre of a large agricultural area stretching from Dartmoor to the Tamar. The original small Saxon settlement by the river grew into a town under the influence of the Benedictine abbey which was founded in the 10th century and became the wealthiest and most important in Devon. It was destroyed after the Dissolution (1539), though a few remains can be found in the area between the river and the parish church. The most substantial are the oddly named Betty Grimball's tower, which was a 15th-century gatehouse; another tower and length of walling beside the river; the dining hall for the sick now used as a Nonconformist chapel; and the main Abbey Gateway in Bedford Square, restored by John Foulston in 1824.

After the Dissolution the lands passed to the Russells, later Dukes of Bedford. The parish church, with its unusual dedication to St Eustace, continued to serve the community. It is a 14th-century building rebuilt and enlarged a hundred years later and has an impressive east end of three gables and three five-light windows facing Bedford Square. Stained glass in the north aisle window is by William Morris, and the alabaster monument to Sir John Glanville (d. 1600) and his wife in the Lady chapel is also of quality. He was born in the town and became the first mere attorney to attain the judicial bench.

The town's other church, St Mary Magdalene, stands large and conspicuous half a mile south-

west of Bedford Square. It was built for Francis, 7th Duke of Bedford, in 1865–7 to serve the mining community he had housed in model cottages along the road to Yelverton. These formed part of the extensive rebuilding of the town during the copper boom in the Tamar and Tavy valleys in the first 70 years of the 19th century. Greenish volcanic stone from the Hurdwick Quarry 1½ miles to the north was used and the centrepiece was Bedford Square with the imposing, castellated civic buildings and the statue of the 7th Duke. He looks down the fine, broad thoroughfare of Plymouth Road which he also created. At the other end is the vigorous statue by Joseph Boehm (1883) of Sir Francis Drake, of which a replica stands on Plymouth Hoe. Drake was a Tavistock man, though the actual house of his birth has not been identified with certainty. In the Plymouth Road is the Bedford Hotel, an early Georgian house which became an inn and was remodelled about 1820. The ballroom of the original house makes a rather splendid dining room.

Another result of the copper boom was the construction of the canal to MORWELLHAM QUAY on the Tamar. The 2-mile stretch of towpath from the town basin to the mouth of the tunnel under Morwell Down makes a delightful walk. Later came the railway and the disused viaduct towering over the houses north-west of Bedford Square recalls the engineers and navvies who drove the line through this hilly countryside.

Tawstock (2/2A) A small thatched village with some attractive buildings a mile south of BARNSTAPLE and reached by lanes off the A377 or A39. Tawstock Court belonged to the Bourchiers, created Earls of Bath in 1536. Their house was destroyed by fire in 1787 and rebuilt by Sir Bourchier Wrey, one of their successors, as a castellated 'Gothick' mansion. Of the earlier building only the fine Gatehouse (1574) survives.

The church of St Peter stands east of the village in a beautiful parkland setting above the Taw valley. It is mainly a 14th-century building with a tall central tower, not common in Devon. It is also remarkable for the monuments crowding the interior. Nearly four pages in Nikolaus Pevsner's *The Buildings of England* are devoted to this small country church.

The oldest monument is in the chancel, a 14th-century oak effigy of an unknown lady. Within

Previous page: The derelict railway viaduct, near Tavistock

the altar rails the tomb of the 3rd Earl of Bath (d. 1623) and his wife is all colour and magnificence. Both are shown lying in their robes and he wears his coronet. In the south chancel aisle the black and white marble tomb (c. 1680) of the 5th Earl has a huge base with four obelisks at the corners and four squatting dogs supporting a bulging sarcophagus. Near by are two notable sculptures, one a life-size standing figure in white marble of Rachel, Countess of Bath (d. 1680), the other the effigy and grandiose tomb of Frances, Lady Fitzwarren (erected 1589) which has been much praised for its beauty.

The church contains many other monuments and other good things, the fine plaster ceilings of the transepts, medieval glass in the north transept window and the open wagon roof of the south chancel aisle (1540). The carved and canopied manorial pew is an unusual survival. Over the south door the elaborate sundial dated 1757 is by John Berry (*see* Marwood) and bears the motto 'Watch and pray Time steals away'.

Teignmouth (2/4C) A south coast port and holiday resort 11 miles from EXETER on A379. As a trading port it was twice burned by the French (in 1347 and 1690) and suffered badly in the Second World War from tip-and-run raids (228 houses destroyed and 2000 damaged). In spite of these disasters it is still a port from which the valuable ball or potter's clay quarried in the Teign valley is exported to many European countries. Boatbuilding also continues and the town is fortunate in not being wholly dependant on holiday trade.

The resort developed in the second half of the 18th century and Fanny Burney came three times, bathing from a machine pushed into the sea by two sturdy women. In 1802 Jane Austen visited Teignmouth, and in the spring of 1818 John Keats. He enjoyed the countryside and the Devon Maids:

> Where be you going, you Devon Maid?
> And what have ye there in the basket?
> Ye tight little fairy, just fresh from the dairy,
> Will ye give me some cream if I ask it? –

but complained with good humour about the Devon weather – 'it is a splashy, rainy, misty, snowy, foggy, haily, floody, muddy, slipshod county'. No. 20 Northumberland Place, a white Georgian house, bears a plaque stating that he stayed there. Other good late Georgian and early Victorian buildings exist, particularly the handsome Den Crescent (1826) along the front, but set well back from the promenade, and in the adjoining streets. Bitton House (now Council Offices) is Regency, once the home of Sir Edward Pellew, 1st Viscount Exmouth, a renowned naval officer during the Republican and Napoleonic Wars and after. The pleasant gardens with views across the river are open to the public. The town continued to be a fashionable watering place until the arrival of the railway in 1846, when its appeal began to widen and it became the popular resort of today.

Thorverton (2/4B) An attractive agricultural village amid the red, fertile soil of the Exe valley 5 miles north of EXETER. It has many old thatched buildings of cob and of the local stone which was quarried from medieval times at Raddon, a mile to the west. Abbotsford next to the Bell Inn, Bridge House with its butcher's shop, Post Office House and the Dolphin Hotel are all good examples, also the long building abutting on to the south side of the churchyard, which is almost certainly the former Church House dating from the 15th century. The streets are wide with channelled water running through them to join the brook, known to the inhabitants as 'the Jordan', which flows through the village. Mains water was not available until 1939 and up to then wells provided drinking water.

The church of St Thomas Becket has a typical late 15th-century tower, window tracery and tall Beer stone arcades. The oldest part, and the outstanding feature, is the south porch with blind arcading on both sides and interesting bosses on the stone vault.

Throwleigh (2/3B) A granite village on the north-eastern border of Dartmoor, 2 miles south-west of Whiddon Down on A30 along narrow lanes. The centre of the village with its attractive thatched and granite buildings – the Barton, the former Royal Oak Inn and particularly the fine Church House by the lychgate to the churchyard – is delightful. The church of St Mary the Virgin is a typical moorland building in a beautiful setting. It was rebuilt in the 15th century, and the north aisle added in the 16th century. The main features are the south chancel door, unusually large and well decorated for a priest's entrance; the pulpit made up of pieces from the vanished rood screen; and a good 15th-century font. Over the south porch door the sundial is dated 1663 and inscribed *Vivat Carolus Secondus* and with various Latin puns. It was only placed there in 1914 after being found in an Exeter junk shop. It was made in Devon by W. Hake but for which

church or house is not known. The village cross is set in an ancient socket stone, but the short octagonal shaft and cross were made locally and erected in 1897 to mark Queen Victoria's Diamond Jubilee.

Thurlestone (2/5A) A village 4 miles south-west of KINGSBRIDGE on a long ridge running inland from Bigbury Bay. Its name is derived from the holed (Old English *thyrel*) rock offshore, already a landmark in Saxon times. With a mild climate, golf course, good beaches and other amenities the village is always in danger of being swamped by tourism but this has not yet happened. The mainly agricultural community survives alongside holiday homes and a handful of hotels. Old cottages make the main street attractive notwithstanding modern building on the south-east slopes. The beaches are far enough away to need their own car parks and ice cream stalls.

The church of All Saints stands high at the south end of the village next to ancient farm buildings. It has a fine Norman font made, like others in the South Hams, of red sandstone. The earliest part of the building is the north wall of the chancel with 13th-century lancet windows. The rest is 15th century or later. The Dartmoor granite pillars between the nave and south aisle are notable, also the late 16th-century south porch where the boss of the crossbeams is carved with a Tudor rose. Two interesting 17th-century memorials in the Lady chapel contrast with a simple 20th-century wall tablet to Sir Courtenay Ilbert on the north wall of the nave, designed by the sculptress Kathleen Scott, widow of Robert Falcon Scott and later Lady Kennet. The robust church tower has tall, set-back buttresses and a stair turret rising above the battlements. By the 19th century the tower had become tilted towards the east, due to the foundations settling unevenly, and the upper stage was dismantled and rebuilt vertically. This causes a slightly bent profile when it is viewed from north or south.

Tiverton (2/4B) A busy market town in the Exe valley, the centre of a wide agricultural district, its economy balanced by a large textile factory. It developed as a wool town at the end of the 15th century and within a hundred years became the most important in Devon, maintaining this position until the trade itself declined. Some of the almshouses given by the wealthy merchants remain, John Greenway's in Gold Street with its Tudor chapel (1529), Waldron's in Well Brook Street west of the Exe (1579) and Slee's in St Peter

Street (1610). Another merchant, Peter Blundell, founded the great school that still bears his name. Near the bridge over the river Loman Old Blundells's buildings (National Trust) were converted to dwellings in the 1880s when the school moved to its present site outside the town on A373. R. D. Blackmore was educated at Old Blundells and describes life there in the opening chapter of *Lorna Doone*.

The merchant John Greenway also gave the splendid south porch and south chapel (1517) of St Peter's Church which have one of the most lavish façades of any parish church. The fine red sandstone tower of St Peter's with its eight pinnacles is also striking, but the rest of the structure was rebuilt in the 1850s. Brass figures of John Greenway and his wife survived this, also the tombs of John Waldron and George Slee, and two good paintings: an *Adoration of the Magi* by Caspar de Crayer, a contemporary of Rubens, and *St Peter released from Prison* by Richard Cosway (1742–1821), a native of the town.

The other church in the town centre, St George's in Fore Street, is a fine Georgian building consecrated in 1733. Many good Georgian houses can be seen in the main streets, such as the brick Bridge House by the Exe and Bampton House in the street of the same name, all built after a devastating fire in 1731. One earlier merchant's house that survived the fire stands at the south end of St Peter's Street close to Slee's almshouses.

The Tiverton Museum, housed in an old school building in St Andrews's Street, is excellent. One of its exhibits is displayed beside the A373 near the former railway station: the tank engine which used to draw the 'Tivy Bumper', the train that ran between the town and Tiverton Junction on the main Taunton–EXETER line.

The Castle, once of considerable importance, was dismantled at the end of the Civil War (1645) and is a private residence. An imposing gatehouse and corner towers of the 14th century remain.'

The textile factory west of the Exe was founded by John Heathcoat in 1816 after he had been driven south from Loughborough by the machine-wrecking Luddites. His grandson and heir, John Heathcoat-Amory, built Knightshayes Court (National Trust), the large mansion on the hill $1\frac{1}{2}$ miles north of the town. He employed the architect William Burges, widely known for his work at Cardiff Castle, but much of the interior decoration was eventually done by

The south porch of St Peter's Church, Tiverton

The yew hedge, Knightshayes Court

J. D. Crace. The hall is a good example of Burges's exuberant style and the National Trust has uncovered and restored many of Crace's painted ceilings and wall decorations. The 25 acres of lovely gardens include a yew hedge cut to represent hounds chasing a fox. The magnificent parkland extends to 200 acres and all was given to the Trust by Sir John Heathcoat-Amory (d. 1972), grandson of the builder. Knightshayes Court is open to the public from April to October. Sir John's widow lives in part of the house and is perhaps better known by her maiden name of Joyce Wethered, the finest British woman golfer of all time. Her sporting medals are displayed in the house.

East of the town the disused Grand Western Canal, designated as a Country Park, runs to HALBERTON and the Somerset border. Trips by horse-drawn barge leave from the basin in summer and the towpath provides wonderful walks through the countryside.

Topsham (2/4B) An ancient port on the Exe estuary, administratively part of EXETER but still retaining its individual character. It lies on the peninsula where the river Clyst converges on the Exe, the waterfront and the old streets safe from through traffic. The historic buildings are so numerous that the whole town is designated a Conservation Area. Although the fishing fleet is no more, salmon netting greatly reduced and hardly any cargo boats use the Quay, the town continues to flourish. The estuary is full of moorings for sailing boats and cabin cruisers of all kinds, shipyards build and maintain them, and the maritime importance has changed rather than ceased. The narrow streets, the narrower side streets and alleyways should be explored at leisure to appreciate the town's special charm.

At the north end of the waterfront (Ferry Road leading into Underway) the house called Furlong was a sail loft and carpenter's shop for a large shipbuilding yard. A slipway for launching and the figurehead of a man-of-war on the corner of the building remain from the past. On the opposite side of the road Follett Lodge was the birthplace of Sir William Webb Follett in 1798, the youngest man ever to become Attorney-General. The Passage Inn is one of the town's many fascinating pubs, with a terrace by the waterside for watching the tide ebb and flow. The Topsham Sailing Club, founded 1888, occupies the adjoining premises. Further on are Nail Cellars and Nail House, once a factory where large ship's nails were made, and opposite is the house called Wixels, a former sail loft standing on its own quay. Beyond the churchyard wall are a shipyard and the Quay, and south from the latter runs The Strand – warehouses converted to houses and garages and beyond them Shell House (c. 1600), named from the large scallop shell in the canopy over the doorway. The excellent Topsham Museum is housed at No. 25. Nearly every building in The Strand is worth looking at. The most prominent are the gabled merchants' houses built of Dutch bricks brought back as ballast when the port thrived on trade with the Low Countries from the 16th to 18th centuries.

Fore Street, the main thoroughfare parallel to Ferry Road and Underway, is also full of historic buildings including the Salutation Inn (1726) with its portico and the handsome Georgian Globe Hotel. The town's oldest inn, The Bridge Inn by the river Clyst, dates from the 16th century.

St Margaret's Church, on the cliff between Fore Street and Underway, was rebuilt in 1876–8 except for the medieval tower. It contains a Norman font and a monument to Admiral Sir John Duckworth (d. 1817), showing in relief one of the numerous naval battles in which he took part, but nothing else of interest. From the churchyard the view at evening over the river to the reed beds, canal and marshes, and beyond to the Haldon Hills, is spectacular. A passenger ferry crosses the river from near the Passage Inn and there is good walking along the canal bank up to Countess Wear and Exeter, or down to Turf and along the sea wall to Powderham. The area is noted for the variety of its birdlife, ranging through the seasons from wintering avocets and brent geese to breeding reed buntings, sedge warblers and sparrowhawks.

Torbryan (2/3C) A pleasant hamlet west of the NEWTON ABBOT–TOTNES road (A381) reached through the village of Ipplepen and on a minor road to nowhere. It is worth visiting for the beautiful grouping of Holy Trinity Church, the Church House and the handful of cottages. The 15th-century church tower is impressively tall and simple, the south porch has a lovely fan vault and the interior is spacious and nearly all of a piece. The rood screen stretches across the nave and both aisles. The pulpit is made of the parts of the screen that formerly encased the nave piers. Georgian box pews cover original 15th-century oak benches. The Church House, said to be contemporary with the church, is a long building of rubble masonry with a slate roof, though originally thatched. Inside is some good panelling and a large open fireplace. By crouching in the hearth and looking up the chimney, you can see a patch of sky far above as though through a telescope.

Torcross *see* Stokenham

Torquay (2/4C) The largest and best-known resort in Devon, beautifully situated on the hills at the north end of Torbay. The medieval hamlet of Tor Quay changed little until the Fleet began to use the bay during the wars with France (1793–1815) and officers and their families sought accommodation ashore. The upper classes, prevented from travelling on the Continent by the wars, followed and were soon praising the sheltered position and mild, healthy climate. Tennyson stayed in 1838 and thought it 'the loveliest sea-village in England' and he was followed by many other eminent Victorians. The population trebled even before the railway arrived in 1848 to stimulate further growth. Today the town extends 4 miles inland but at heart remains thoroughly Victorian, the terraces and gabled villas, the alleyways and tree-lined drives always under threat but so far surviving in spite of the planners' fondness for tower blocks, shopping precincts and suburban housing.

Kent's Cavern on the Babbacombe road was explored in the 19th century. The bones of extinct animals (cave bear, cave lion and sabre-toothed cat) and evidence of occupation by man at least 30,000 years ago, perhaps earlier, were found. It is one of the oldest inhabited sites in Britain, now well-lit and easy of access.

At the west end of the town Torre Abbey was

Overleaf: The Pavilion, Torquay

founded in 1196. The principal remains of the medieval buildings are the Abbot's tower, a 14th-century gatehouse and the splendid 'Spanish' tithe barn, so called from having served as a prison for Armada captives. The present Torre Abbey mansion facing the sea was built by the Cary family early in the 18th century and is used by Torbay Corporation as a museum and art gallery. The extensive gardens are one of the many attractive open spaces in the town.

For admirers of Victorian church architecture the town provides a feast, nearly every architect of note being represented: Anthony Salvin, Arthur Bloomfield, Sir George Gilbert Scott and Sir Charles Nicholson. St John's Church, conspicuous on a shelf of the cliff above the harbour, was the work of G. E. Street who designed the Law Courts in London. It contains stained glass by Morris & Co to designs by Edward Burne-Jones who also painted the chancel. All Saints at Babbacombe is by William Butterfield and All Saints, Bamfylde Road, by J. L. Pearson. The latter does contain a Norman font carved with interesting figures including a harp player and a man with a dog. St Saviour, north-east of Torre Abbey, was a medieval church drastically restored in 1849, though some interesting monuments survive: the fine Renaissance tomb of Thomas Cary (d. 1567), a brass of John Gifford (d. 1581) and his Cary wife, and the reclining alabaster effigy of Thomas Ridgeway in armour (1604).

On the town's western fringe, only a mile inland and reached along a wooded lane where horse-drawn carriages transport the visitor in summer, the village of **Cockington** is a surprise. The thatched cottages and famous forge seem almost too perfect, but the Council deserves credit for preserving the village so close to the built-up area. The 15th-century church of St George and St Mary, built of red sandstone, is in keeping. Cockington Court was an Elizabethan mansion remodelled in the 18th century. Only the Drum Inn is modern (1934), successfully designed by Sir Edwin Lutyens with thatched roof and bold chimney stacks to harmonize with the lovely setting.

Totnes (2/3C) A historic town on a hill at the head of the navigable Dart, already a borough in Saxon times. With its many important medieval and later buildings it is like a small-scale EXETER.

Fore Street, climbing up from the river, begins with the good-looking Seven Stars Hotel (c. 1825) and contains many 16th-, 17th-century and Georgian buildings. No. 70 is an Elizabethan house occupied by the local museum and reference library. East Gate astride the roadway, though rebuilt in the 16th century, marks the line of the medieval town walls which can be traced to right and left. Beyond it the narrow High Street continues the climb through the old town. It is lined with Elizabethan and Georgian buildings, and particularly notable are the Butterwalk and Poultrywalk where slate-hung or painted upper storeys project over the pavements on colonnades of wooden, cast-iron and granite pillars.

Set back from the High Street the parish church of St Mary, rebuilt in the 15th century, is a magnificent red sandstone structure with a conspicuous tower rising high above the town. The main feature of the interior is the beautiful screen of Beer stone (1459–60), deliberately planned to rival that of the Lady Chapel in Exeter Cathedral, an indication of the town's pride and wealth at the time. This runs across the church with parclose screens at right angles to it on both sides of the chancel. The rood loft was taken down when George Gilbert Scott restored the church in 1862 but the elaborate rood stairs survive in the north chancel.

To the north of the churchyard the Guildhall seems modest in comparison. It was built on part of the site of Totnes Priory in the 16th century. The council chamber has a fine plaster ceiling dated 1624. Loggias and slate-hung gables and upper walls make it a most pictuesque building.

The castle, which is open all year, is the best example of a Norman motte and bailey in Devon, the motte large, over 50 ft high and projecting inside the town wall to overawe the citizens. It stands on a rock but was mainly man-made in the 11th century. The circular shell keep on the summit is reached by a curving stairway, but originally access would have been by a straight flight of steps against the wall to the west. The keep replaced earlier wooden structures and is itself a rebuilding early in the 14th century. Stairs in the 6 ft-thick wall lead to the wall walk and the well-preserved battlements. The bailey is also large, horseshoe in plan and marked out by a deep, steep-sided ditch. A stone curtain wall, of which a section remains on the west side, was probably erected round it when the stone keep was built.

The graceful bridge over the river was built by Devon-born Charles Fowler in 1826. From a quay below the bridge steamers in summer depart for DARTMOUTH, passing through some of the loveliest river scenery in England.

Ugborough (2/3C) A large village built round a square 1 mile south of A38 between SOUTH BRENT and Ivybridge. The church of St Peter stands above the square inside a prehistoric earthwork. From this elevation the granite tower and long, battlemented north façade completely dominate the village and the tower seems to beckon further afield, to Ugborough Beacon and Butterdon Hill 2 miles to the north where the parish rises dramatically to over 1000 ft up on the edge of Dartmoor.

The church was consecrated early in the 14th century and enlarged in the 16th. It has a Norman font of red sandstone, like others in the South Hams, and a 17th-century stone pulpit. The large wooden bosses of the north aisle roof are beautifully carved, and include a sow with eight piglets, symbol of St Brannoc (*see* Braunton). The screen has been mutilated but is notable for the wainscoting of 32 painted panels of the Annunciation, the Assumption of the Virgin and other events of the Church's calendar. The parclose screens are of open wooden tracery and are simple yet refined. An unusual brass of an unknown lady in the north transept is not flat but in low relief and dated by the lady's costume to *c.* 1500.

Walkhampton (2/2C) A pleasant village on the south-west edge of Dartmoor, half a mile north of the PRINCETOWN–Yelverton road (B3212) and half a mile south of the medieval Huckworthy Bridge over the river Walkham. The village and the bridge were on the ancient trackway between the two greatest monastic houses in Devon, Plympton Priory and Tavistock Abbey. North of the bridge a tall cross on Huckworthy Common marked where a branch turned off to Sampford Spiney, which belonged to the priory.

The church and Church House stand by themselves on a hill north-east of the village. The large granite tower of the church, a well-known landmark, dwarfs the rest of the small 15th-century building. The Church House on the east boundary of the churchyard is the usual long building, in this instance of granite rubble with a slate roof. Above the central doorway is a stone inscribed '1698', probably the date of restoration of a much older building.

A path down the left bank of the river passes the rubble heaps and other remains of Wheal George and Walkhampton Consols, two small copper mines that were worked in the middle of the 19th century. An attractive walk up the east side of the Walkham valley, mostly through woodlands, leads to Merrivale Bridge on B3357.

Welcombe (2/1A) A scattered village in unspoiled country close to the Atlantic coast a mile north of the Cornish border. The former blacksmith's forge is now a picturesque inn. The church, like several in Cornwall, is dedicated to the 6th-century St Nectan, and another common Cornish feature is the holy well near by. The building was originally a chapel dating back to Norman times and only became the parish church in 1508 when transepts were added. The Norman font is plain and the low west tower, also early in date, unbuttressed and with small round-headed bell openings. The rood screen has tall panels in groups of four with carving of early 14th-century date, the oldest screen to survive in Devon, though the cornice is later. The Jacobean lectern is also something of a rarity.

North-west of the church the road descends to a stream and follows it down a gorge to the small beach at Welcombe Mouth. On each side the cliffs rise to 300 ft and long ridges of jagged rock run out into the sea like arms waiting to embrace any ship storm-driven on to this formidable coast.

West Putford (2/1B) A small agricultural village in the upper valley of the river Torridge, reached by lanes off the A388 BIDEFORD–Holsworthy road. The soil is clay and loam, hard to work, and the village typical of the remote area where the infant Torridge seems no more than a stream. The church in its wooded churchyard is one of the best in North Devon, an early 14th-century building of nave, chancel and north transept with uneven plastered walls, all left undisturbed in Victorian times. The west tower, unbuttressed and with stumpy pinnacles, may be a little later in date. The Norman tub font is unusual for its lack of ornament, only a cable girdle round the waist, and for standing on the tiled floor without any base. Much of the chancel is floored with medieval Barnstaple tiles. The pulpit and communion rails with twisted balusters are both 18th century. The exceptionally peaceful and unspoiled character of village and church constitute the main attraction.

Westward Ho! *see* Bideford

Whimple (2/4B) A village north-east of EXETER, a mile from the crossroads known as 'Hand and Pen' on A30. The name is Celtic and means 'white pool', and a settlement existed early in Saxon times. The square is busy and attractive with its thatched Post Office and a channelled stream

Above: A thatched cottage in Cockington (see p. 148)

Opposite: Fore Street, Totnes (see p. 148)

flowing through it.

The church of St Mary, except for the 15th-century tower, was thoroughly restored and partly rebuilt in 1845. The rood screen had already been removed (1777) but eight painted panels from it had been used as steps for a Georgian three-decker pulpit. The pulpit in turn was demolished but the panels saved. They are incorporated in the modern belfry screen at the west end of the nave. They depict a king, believed to be Henry VI, and seven saints including local girl St Sidwella, martyred near Exeter in AD 740.

The village is surrounded by good farmland and by extensive apple orchards which are a fine sight when laden with blossom or fruit. Huge letters beside some of them proclaim that they are WHITEWAY'S CYDER ORCHARDS. These signs were put up many years ago to catch the eye of travellers on the Waterloo–Exeter trains which still pass through the village. Whiteway's factory, north of the railway line, now makes fortified wines and soft drinks as well as the cider that made it famous.

Widecombe in the Moor (2/3C) The best known of Dartmoor villages; visitors arrive in their thousands during the summer months and in September for the famous fair:

Tam Pearce, Tam Pearce, lend me thy grey mare
All along, down along, out along lee,
For I want vor to go awver to Widecombe Fair . . .

Uncle Tom Cobley and his companions travelled 14 miles over the Moor to attend the annual gathering, a mixture of business and festivity. The village sign on the green depicts them and near by are the cafés and souvenir shops that cater for today's visitors.

The setting of the village is beautiful, the granite church and buildings clustered in the green valley of the East Webburn river and surrounded by small, irregular enclosures that edge up to the high moorland. The centre of the village is particularly attractive with the Church House (National Trust) and Glebe House, both 16th-century buildings, and St Pancras Church. The Church House is the most spectacular in Devon, well built of granite and along the front a cobbled loggia with seven monolithic granite posts. A double flight of lateral steps at the rear leads to the upper storey. The church is known as the 'Cathedral of the Moor', a long, rather low 14th-century building with a magnificent tower over 100 ft high, impressive and graceful too. Tablets in the church record in doggerel verse the

disaster that occurred on Sunday 21 October 1638 during afternoon service. William Crossing in his *Guide to Dartmoor* puts it simply: 'a sudden darkness fell, and speedily a terrific thunderstorm broke over the building doing considerable damage. Four persons were killed and sixty-two injured either by lightning or falling masonry, large stones being hurled from the tower into the body of the church . . .' In the superstitious 17th century the disaster was naturally attributed to a visitation by the Devil who, it was reported, had been seen earlier in the day riding a black horse and breathing fire in the neighbouring hamlet of Poundsgate.

Widworthy (2/5B) Half a mile south of Wilmington on the AXMINSTER–HONITON road (A35T) the church stands on a mound in the lovely valley of the Umborne brook. Widworthy is a parish of scattered houses and farms. Only three dwellings can be seen from the churchyard: a modern bungalow on the hill to the west; an attractive 18th-century house with three gables, once the rectory, across fields to the south-east; and adjoining the churchyard Widworthy Barton, a well-preserved Elizabethan manor house with large mullioned windows. The parish spreads southwards between the Offwell and Umborne brooks with narrow lanes leading to isolated farms, undisturbed countryside where only cars and the machinery of modern agriculture intrude.

St Cuthbert's Church is a small cruciform building, erected mainly in the 14th century to replace an earlier structure. The transepts were added about 1500 and the south porch later in the 16th century. It is full of monuments, the oldest illegible. Those to the Marwood family in the transepts are good examples of 18th- and 19th-century memorial sculpture, but out of all proportion to the size of the church. In the north transept the effigy of a knight, partly in chain and partly in plate armour, is thought to be Sir William Prouz (d. 1329) whose three daughters built the church as a memorial to him. A plain marble tablet in the nave reveals that William John Tucker was rector in this peaceful spot for no less than 62 years. On the opposite wall a bust and tablet commemorate Thomas White, Steward to the Marwoods, who died in 1838. The date of his death is in different lettering from the rest of the inscription and it is apparent that the tablet was prepared during his lifetime and the date inserted afterwards. Outside the south porch, beside the modern sundial, is a good example of a simple sundial scratched on the church wall.

Woodbury (2/4B) A large village 4 miles south-east of EXETER on B3179. New housing estates have not unduly disturbed the older part of the village. The medieval church of St Swithin, finely sited, the battlemented tower with its tapering buttresses very noble, was disastrously restored in the 1860s though it is now well furnished and maintained. The 15th-century font of Beer stone and the Jacobean pulpit and altar rails survived the restoration, also the many floor slabs from the 16th century onwards, one with the touching epitaph:

> He first deceased
> Shee for a little tryed
> To live without him
> Liked it not and dyed

The colourful set of kneelers were embroidered by members of the congregation from the beautiful and meticulous pictures in *The Concise British Flora*, first published in 1965, by the Reverend Keble Martin who lived in the village towards the end of his life.

A mile south-east of the village Woodbury Common occupies part of the sand and pebble ridge that stretches from EXMOUTH nearly to OTTERY ST MARY. The name Woodbury Common is loosely applied to include neighbouring commons – and the whole uncultivated area is good walking and riding country, with wonderful views over the Exe estuary on one side and the Otter valley and the sea on the other. Several Bronze Age barrows are marked by clumps of trees but those at the Four Firs crossroads and to the east along B3179 are the result of 19th-century attempts at landscaping. Woodbury Castle, from which the village takes its name, is an Iron Age fort on a commanding site. It is a favourite picnic place, the steep double ramparts divided by a ditch forming a natural playground.

Woolacombe (2/2A) A small north coast resort reached by the B3343 from Mullacott Cross on the BARNSTAPLE–ILFRACOMBE road (A361). It developed in Edwardian times and is well known for its 2-mile stretch of pale yellow sands backed by dunes and the steep slopes of Woolacombe Down (National Trust).

Less than a mile to the north lies the pleasant old village of **Mortehoe** with its inn and small, unrestored church of St Mary Magdalene. The church is a most interesting cruciform building of the early 14th century with Norman doorways, a splendid 15th-century wagon roof and good carved bench ends of the 16th century inserted when the short north aisle was added. The table tomb in the south transept with the incised figure of a priest is thought to be of Sir William de Tracey, Rector, who died in 1322 and was probably responsible for rebuilding the Norman church.

Woolacombe beach lies between two prominent headlands, both National Trust. Baggy Point to the south has spectacular cliffs of sandstone and shale out of which the sea has worn a huge cave known as Baggy Hole. Morte Point to the north is a fearsome place with reefs of sharp slate running out into the sea that ripped the bottom out of many ships in the days of sail.

CORNWALL

Above: The Devil's Frying Pan, near Cadgwith *(see p. 168)*

Previous page: St Mawes Castle (see p. 208)

Cornwall Gazetteer

Altarnun (1/5B) A village to the south-west of LAUNCESTON on the edge of BODMIN MOOR. The street of stone cottages runs down a hillside and at the bottom an ancient hump-backed bridge over a stream leads to the 15th-century church known as the 'Cathedral of the Moor' from its impressive tower, one of the tallest in Cornwall. It is dedicated to St Nonna, mother of St David of Wales, and is built of moorstone (surface granite). The bases, columns and capitals of the aisle arcades are each fashioned out of one piece of stone. Unusual features are wagon-roofed porches to both north and south aisles, 17th-century communion rails that extend across the whole church, and a large Norman font carved with bearded faces and rosettes. The 16th-century bench ends, 79 in all, are outstanding. Apart from such usual subjects as the instruments of the Passion and the village idiot, one depicts a man playing a fiddle, another a bagpipe.

In the churchyard are some slate memorials by the sculptor Nevill Northey Burnard (1818–78), born in the village. As a young man he also carved the bust of John Wesley (Wesley's cottage can be seen at Trewint) over the door of the Meeting House by the stream, but it is his seraphs and trumpeting cherubs on slate in numerous churchyards that have earned him the lasting affection of Cornishmen. His tragic life has inspired some moving verses by the present-day Cornish poet, Charles Causley.

Annet *see* Scilly, Isles of

Antony (1/6C) A village on the A374 west of Torpoint where a car ferry crosses the Hamoaze to and from Devonport. The 13th-century church of St James, with slate tower and the aisles added in the following centuries, is notable for the memorial to Margery Arundell (1420). The large brass is set in marble and shows the lady in a horned headdress and ample gown of the period. This is one of the best and earliest of Cornish brasses. The church also contains monuments to the Carew family including the antiquary Richard Carew, famous for his delightful *Survey of Cornwall* (1602).

The Carews lived at Antony House, closer to Torpoint, from the late 15th century onwards.

The present mansion (National Trust) was built by Sir William Carew in 1710–21 in classical style, the finest early Georgian building in Cornwall. The silver-grey stone was brought by sea from the Pentewan quarry near MEVAGISSEY. The main front is a superbly proportioned composition, the central block linked by brick walls to pavilions on either side and the pleasing courtyard enclosed by stone walls and pillars. It is strange that the name of the architect responsible for such a masterwork was not recorded. Inside the rooms are panelled in oak or pine and exhibit furniture, china, books, tapestries and paintings. Many articles are contemporary with the mansion, but some panelling and furniture is preserved from an earlier Tudor house. Family portraits up to modern times include one of Richard Carew (painted 1586) and one of Sir Alexander Carew, Governor for Parliament of Drake's Island in Plymouth Harbour during the Civil War, but executed for disloyalty in 1644. At some stage the portrait was cut out of its frame and later stitched back in do-it-yourself fashion. The extensive, beautifully landscaped grounds of the house run down to the river Lynher. The house is open from April to October.

Bedruthan Steps (1/4B) A famous beach on the Atlantic coast 5 miles north of NEWQUAY. The 'Steps' are volcanic rocks detached by erosion from the cliff. Depending on the tide, the waves lash them or clean sand provides a pleasant walk round them.

The National Trust has a car park near by and maintains the precarious stairs cut in the cliff that give access to the beach. One rock is called 'Queen Bess' and another 'The Samaritan' after a ship wrecked offshore in 1846. Its cargo of textiles was looted by the local people who nicknamed the wreck 'the Good Samaritan'. The remains of an Iron Age promontory fort called Redcliffe Castle stand on the cliffs above the Steps close to the Coastal Path.

Bodmin (1/4B) The county town occupies a central position 12 miles from both north and south coasts, and halfway between LAUNCESTON

Overleaf: Bedruthan Steps

and TRURO on the A30. It only wrested the title
from Launceston in 1838 and therefore the Assize
Court, the massive walls and gateway of the
former gaol, the former market and many houses
are rather dull Victorian. Its importance went
back much further, to the establishment of a
priory in the 10th century, the Shrine of St
Petrock, one of the most prominent of the Celtic
saints. Only negligible fragments of the priory
remain but the fine parish church, the largest in
Cornwall, is dedicated to St Petrock. It was
rebuilt in the 15th century and restored in the
19th. Some Norman work can be seen in the
lower stages of the tower and the exceptionally
fine Norman font, a large bowl supported on five
shafts and richly carved, survives. Between the
chancel and the north aisle the tomb of Thomas
Vivian, one of the last priors, is of grey marble
and of black stone from Catacleuse Point near
PADSTOW (1533). It was brought from the priory
church after the Dissolution and is one of the
most splendid Renaissance memorials in
Cornwall.

In the south aisle the ivory Bodmin Casket,
almost certainly of Spanish origin, is reputed to
have held the bones of St Petrock when they were
recovered in 1177 after being stolen. In the
churchyard are the ruins of a 14th-century chapel
and slate memorials by the Cornish sculptor
Burnard (*see* Altarnun).

The Beacon above the town gives wide views
over north and central Cornwall. The 144 ft
obelisk on the summit was erected in 1856–7 in
memory of Lieutenant-General Sir Walter
Raleigh Gilbert (1785–1853), a distinguished
soldier of the Indian Army. Other military memories are contained in the Duke of Cornwall's
Light Infantry Regimental Museum in The
Keep in the town.

Castle Canyke south-east of the town was an
Iron Age Fort on the important prehistoric route
across the peninsula from the Camel estuary to
FOWEY. Traders between Brittany, Wales and
Ireland had used the route since early Bronze Age
times to avoid the dangerous passage round
Land's End.

At Nanstallon, due west of the town, a rectangular earthwork is the remains of a Roman fort
with barracks for 500 cavalry and infantry. It was
one of a series built down the spine of the south-
west peninsula to guard river crossings, in this
instance the Camel, and was abandoned in
approximately AD 75.

Granite rocks, Bodmin Moor (see p. 162)

Bodmin Moor (1/4B) A granite highland comprising about 80 square miles of rough grazing broken by tors, marshes, plantations, reservoirs and enclosed fields. The A30 (T) road from LAUNCESTON to BODMIN cuts through the middle and in the hamlet of Bolventor, halfway between the two towns, is the Jamaica Inn which gave its name to Daphne du Maurier's tale of smuggling and mayhem. It was built in the 18th century as a coaching inn when the first road was constructed across the moor. It ceased to be an inn when coaching gave way to rail travel, but was reborn to meet the motorist's needs. Though much altered, the wild situation makes it a place where legends of skulduggery are easy to believe.

The northern moor, bleak and treeless, rises to its highest points (and to the highest points in Cornwall) at Rough Tor (1311 ft), which belongs to the National Trust, and 1377 ft at Brown Willy. From both the Atlantic and the English Channel are visible. On the former stands a memorial to the men of the 43rd Wessex Division who fell in the Second World War. Close by a group of Bronze Age hut circles and enclosures are a good example of many scattered over the moor. South of the tor lies the important Fernacre stone circle, the largest on the moor with more than three dozen small standing stones. To the west, towards the vast china clay works at Stannon, are Bronze Age barrows and another stone circle. The easiest approach to this interesting area is from Camelford along a minor road known as Jubilee Drive and then on foot to the tors.

Also on the northern moor, between Hawkstor and the old china clay works south-west of Bolventor, the Stripple Stones are a Neolithic henge monument consisting of a roughly circular bank and ditch. Inside is a circle of granite blocks, some fallen, which may have been added in Early Bronze Age times.

Two lanes from Bolventor cross the southern moor. One passes Dozmary Pool, a large natural tarn, the source of many legends. It was supposed bottomless until it dried out one hot summer. Some like to believe that King Arthur's last battle took place on the surrounding moor and that the shallow pool is the resting place of the sword Excalibur. Another legend tells of Tregeagle, the unjust steward, who is forever condemned to empty the pool using a limpet shell with a hole in it. The lane goes on south to the new reservoir at Colliford and to ST NEOT.

The other lane provides a delightful drive or walk down the valley of the river Fowey to the beauty spot known as Golitha Falls. East of the lane the Siblyback Lake Reservoir submerges a pleasant moorland valley but seeks to compensate by providing for canoeing, sailing and windsurfing as well as angling and birdwatching. East of the Siblyback Lake Reservoir in the area of Craddock Moor, and around Stowe's Hill and Caradon Hill, are the relics of dozens of copper mines that flourished in the 19th century. An older monument is the Longstone standing beside the road from Redgate to Minions, over 9 ft tall and one of the most impressive of Cornwall's medieval crosses. The area also has important prehistoric sites: the crumbled ramparts of an Iron Age Fort on Stowe's Hill and near Minions the Hurlers, three Bronze Age stone circles in a row made of shaped rather than undressed stones. The name perpetuates the legend of their origin: men playing the ancient Cornish game of hurling (*see* St Columb Major) on a Sunday were turned to stone. Five hundred yards to the north lies Rillaton Barrow, a large cairn with a burial kist where a beautiful ribbed and handled gold beaker, now in the British Museum, was found. North again is an older and natural phenomenon, the celebrated Cheesewring, a top-heavy stack of deeply fissured granite.

Boscastle (1/5A) A small stone and slate village on the Atlantic coast with a picturesque, landlocked harbour. For a long time it served as a port for LAUNCESTON. Records go back to the 14th century and the curving, inner breakwater which Sir Richard Grenville built in 1584 replaced older works. The 19th-century outer breakwater was blown up by a drifting mine during the Second World War and has been rebuilt – no mean task – by the National Trust. Sailing ships were towed through the narrow, winding entrance with cargoes of coal and limestone, and took on board manganese ore, grain and Delabole slate. The harbour and the headlands of Willapark and Penally Point on either side of the entrance belong to the National Trust. From the roadbridge over the Valency stream good paths lead out to the headlands.

Of Bottreaux Castle, which gave the village its name, only a mound remains. Thomas Hardy (*see also* St Juliot) called the village Castle Boterel in *A Pair of Blue Eyes*, one of his earlier novels (1873). Many years later he revisited the scenes of his courtship of Emma Gifford and recalled an incident in the fine poem 'At Castle Boterel'.

Boscastle

Breage (1/2C) A pleasant village on the north side of the HELSTON–PENZANCE road (A394), a mile and a half from the shore of Mount's Bay. Two hundred years ago the inhabitants were mainly tin miners and had a reputation for looting ships wrecked in the bay. The 15th-century church stands on a mound and a pause at the south door gives a striking view of Mount's Bay and of the coastline down to Lizard Point. The head of a Saxon cross near by in the churchyard is the only one made of sandstone known in Cornwall. The church is large by Cornish standards with a fine buttressed and pinnacled tower of three stages. A 3rd-century Roman milestone is preserved in the north aisle, part of the evidence for the extraction of tin under imperial control. The most interesting features of the church are the wall paintings of saints in the north aisle executed c. 1470, particularly the sturdy St Christopher carrying the infant Jesus and the Warnings to Sabbath Breakers. Other paintings can be seen in the south aisle.

A mile and a half north-west of the village Tregonning Hill, reached by lanes and footpaths, is a good viewpoint and of particular interest because of the importance of the china clay industry. There in the 18th century William Cookworthy, a Devon-born chemist and Quaker preacher, made the first discovery of kaolin or china clay in England. The mining history of the district is commemorated by the engine house and chimney at Wheal Prosper (National Trust) and the ruins of Wheal Trewavas, both 2 miles south-west of the village on the Coastal Path.

Bryher *see* Scilly, Isles of

Bude (1/6A) The northernmost resort on the Atlantic coast, mainly Edwardian in character. It differs from other resorts in facing not towards the sea but across a wide combe where the river Neet flows through a gap in the cliffs. The sands by the river mouth are delightful, and surfing and bathing are safe except at low water. Beside the river runs the Bude Canal constructed 1819–24 to carry sea sand to inland farms, but abandoned when the railway arrived in the 1890s. A 2-mile stretch from the sea lock remains navigable and is used for recreational purposes. The Bude Town Museum with much information about shipwrecks occupies the old forge by the canal.

The ancient town of **Stratton** is almost joined to Bude and the parish church of St Andrew

Right: Widemouth Bay, near Bude
Overleaf: Fisherman's cottages, Cadgwith (see p. 169)

served both places until a new church was built at Bude in 1835. Stratton has some good Georgian houses in its narrow streets. St Andrew's Church is mainly 14th century, with a south aisle added in the 15th century and the tall tower with its set-back buttresses probably a little later. The font is Norman, plain and circular. Memorials include a damaged effigy of a cross-legged knight, probably Sir Ranulph Blanchminster (*c.* 1348), and a fine brass of Sir John Arundell of TRERICE (1495–1561) and his wives and numerous children. In the churchyard casualties of both sides were buried in unmarked graves after the valour of Cornish Royalists had defeated the Parliamentarians at the Battle of Stratton (1643). The site of the battle is 1 mile north of the town on Stamford Hill where Iron Age earthworks occupied by the Parliamentary forces are still visible.

A mile south-east of Stratton in a wooded valley is **Launcells**. Its church, dedicated to St Swithin, is a gem unharmed by Victorian restorers and in a beautiful setting. Inside are an early Norman font with cable mouldings, 15th-century Barnstaple tiles in the chancel, a faded Tudor wall painting and, most notable of all, over 60 carved bench ends. They are the best set in Cornwall and render symbolically scenes from the life of Christ: e.g. wine and bread on a table represent the Last Supper. Near the church is St Swithin's Well approached by a little bridge over the stream running down the valley to join the river Neet. This is one of a hundred streams or springs in Cornwall sacred from the first years of Christianity here and probably having an earlier, pagan significance.

Cadgwith (1/2C) A picturesque fishing village 2½ miles north-east of Lizard Point. It is approached off the HELSTON–LIZARD road (A3083), the last half mile down steep, narrow lanes. Fishermen's cottages, an inn and a small chapel occupy a natural break in the formidable cliffs. Many of the cottages are built of the local serpentine stone (*see* Lizard Peninsula). On this dangerous coast both the village and Lizard Point had lifeboat stations, but since 1960 a single station has operated from Kilcobben Cove roughly halfway between the two. The National Trust owns the cliffs on both sides of the village. To the south is the curious rock formation known as the Devil's Frying Pan where the roof of a large cave has fallen in leaving a great pit spanned by an arch of hard rock, the waves thundering 200 ft below.

High on the cliffs to the north stands a hut where the 'huer' kept watch for the pilchard shoals on which the livelihood of the village once depended. By the end of the First World War, for some unaccountable reason, the shoals had ceased to come to the Cornish coasts.

Calstock (1/6B) A former port on the river Tamar, well-known for the railway viaduct of concrete blocks completed in 1907 that towers over the river and the deserted quays. The coming of the railway killed the port which had handled granite for centuries, and paper, bricks and copper during the 19th century. Only

Cotehele House, near Calstock

trippers from Plymouth and an occasional small boat now use the quays.

It is an attractive town, the streets steep and the houses climbing terrace by terrace from the riverside, among them the 16th-century Boot Inn and the Wesleyan Chapel. The mainly 15th-century church of St Andrew stands higher still, away from the town, and commands wonderful views over the Tamar valley. In the churchyard are many carved slate memorials to victims of accidents in nearby mines. All along the road to Gunnislake abundant remains bear witness to the intense activity in the 19th century: a cutting for a mine railway, ruined buildings and stacks, spoil heaps.

The industrial landscape contrasts with the beautiful woods and gardens to the west of the town at **Cotehele House** (National Trust). The estate belonged to the Edgcumbe family from the 14th century. In 1947 this was the first historic house to pass to the National Trust after being accepted by the Treasury in satisfaction of estate duty. Parts of a 14th-century house survive in the great granite building begun by Sir Richard Edgcumbe in 1486 and completed by his son Piers in 1539. The only later addition was the north-west tower in 1627 and soon afterwards the house ceased to be the family's chief residence. Though

only used occasionally, the building was well maintained and the family's armour and weapons, the nationally important 17th-century tapestries and the magnificent furniture were all left undisturbed. The combination of an un-altered Tudor mansion and fittings that have never left it gives Cotehele a unique atmosphere. The house is open to the public from April to October.

The beautiful gardens – subtropical trees and plants and a medieval dovecot – descend steeply to the river where a path along the bank goes up to Calstock or down to Cotehele Quay. At the latter the last surviving Tamar barge, the *Shamrock*, built in 1899 and painstakingly restored, is docked and forms part of a National Maritime Museum display on the shipping and trade of the river. Above the quay the estate corn mill has also been restored to full working order with two waterwheels, a forge, a wheelwright's shop and tools and a cider press.

Also in the grounds the 'Chapel on the Cliff' stands 70 ft above the Tamar, a small 15th-century building dedicated to St George and St Thomas Becket. It was built by Sir Richard Edgcumbe in gratitude for his escape from Richard III's adherents after he had declared allegiance to the future Henry VII in 1485. Closely pursued, he threw his cap with a stone in it into the river and his enemies assumed he had leaped to his death. He lived to fight at Bosworth Field, to be knighted by King Henry and to begin the building of the most impressive Tudor mansion in Cornwall.

Camborne-Redruth (1/2B) The two towns con-stitute the largest urban concentration in Corn-wall, sprawling for 5 miles along the old London to PENZANCE road. Formerly rivals, except against outsiders, they are now one ad-ministratively and both bypassed by the new A30(T) road. They have little of architectural interest but for those interested in mining and engineering the area offers much.

Towards the end of the 19th century hundreds of mines were in operation close by and factories turned out the engines, safety fuses and other equipment to keep them, and mines all over Cornwall and the world, functioning. In Hol-man's Museum in Camborne and the Tolgus Tin Stream Museum in Redruth some of the history of these activities is preserved. At Pool, swal-lowed up between the two towns, the National Trust has taken over a winding engine built at Holman's in 1887 and a beam pumping engine

built by Harvey & Co of Hayle (1892). Ruined mine buildings clutter the landscape on all sides. By early 1986 only two mines were still operating but the celebrated Camborne School of Mines (moved to new buildings in Redruth in the 1970s) continues to export its mining technology throughout the world. William Bickford, inven-tor of the safety fuse which saved many lives in the mines, came from Tuckingmill in Camborne. There is a fine statue of the great inventor Richard Trevithick, perfector of the beam engine among other achievements, in Camborne. Known as 'the Cornish Giant', he holds a model of his steam locomotive in one huge hand. He was born in 1771 at Penponds in Camborne and the family cottage there is in the care of the National Trust.

The Wesleyan Church in the main street of Redruth, built in 1826, is a simple but majestic version of the many smaller Methodist chapels throughout Cornwall. John Wesley visited Redruth and Camborne many times and gained many followers among the miners. In 1743 he spoke for the first time at **Gwennap Pit**, 1 mile east of Redruth in the hamlet of Busveal. The pit is an amphitheatre formed from an old mine working and capable of holding a large number of people. The circular rows of seats were cut after Wesley's time; his congregations generally stood when he preached in the open air. Since 1807 a service to commemorate his achievements has been held in the pit every Whit Monday. A Museum of Cornish Methodism opened near by a few years ago.

Apart from the disused mines, an outstanding feature of the area is the granite boss of Carn Brea (pronounced Bray) 1 mile south-west of Redruth, one of the great places of Cornwall not only for its fascinating views but for its long archaeological record. The hill rises to 738 ft, the escarpment steep on the north side. It should be approached over the easier southern slope from the hamlet of Carnkie. Excavations revealed a large, walled Neolithic settlement up on the eastern summit, the earliest of its kind in England. Occupation in the Iron Age followed, spread over a larger area. Later a medieval castle was built on the eastern summit, the surviving ruins disfigured by Vic-torian cladding. Mining in the 18th and 19th centuries, possibly earlier, has eaten into the southern slopes. In 1836 the Basset monument was erected on the central summit, the highest part, a memorial to Lord de Dunstanville of Tehidy, formerly Sir Francis Basset (1757–1835), a benevolent landowner who had done much to promote the welfare of the miners. The roots of West Cornwall seem to grow from this rough, bleak hill with its views of abandoned mines and small fields, the railway line and the coaching road to Penzance, the packed buildings of the two towns and 4 miles away the Atlantic Ocean.

Cardinham (1/5B) A typical inland parish on the south-west edge of BODMIN MOOR. The tiny churchtown merely forms a centre for scattered hamlets like Millpool, Welltown, Fletcher's Bridge and the group of houses down by the river Cardinham. It is also typical in the visible relics of long occupation by man starting with inscribed stones of the 6th or early 7th century AD. Two can be found at the crossroads near Welltown and one in the churchyard has the inscription, in Latin, 'Rancori the son of Mesgi', though it does not necessarily mark a grave. Also in the churchyard is a fine 10th-century cross, 8½ ft tall and with the characteristic four-holed head, the shaft inscribed and decorated.

The 15th-century church of St Meubred has a noble granite tower. The interior, little restored, contains a late Norman font, fine wagon roofs and bench ends and, most notable, an early brass with the full-length figure of Thomas Awmarle (c. 1400). The Normans built one of their motte-and-bailey castles down by the river soon after the Conquest. It fell into disuse in the 14th century and only earthworks remain, and traces of a keep on the mound.

Come-to-Good (1/3C) A hamlet 3 miles south of TRURO, reached by turning off the Truro–FALMOUTH road (A39) at Carnon Downs. It is noted for the simple Quaker Meeting House built in 1710 and still in use, a most attractive thatched and whitewashed building. The stables under the same roof were necessary in pre-motoring days when Friends rode considerable distances to attend meetings in spite of persecution. The name is misleading, a corruption of the descriptive Cornish *Cwm-ty-quite*, 'the house of the combe in the woods'.

Crackington Haven (1/5A) One of the most spectacular places on the wild Atlantic coast, reached by turning off the A39(T) BUDE–Camelford road at Wainhouse Corner. A cluster of houses, the village shop and the inn lie between cliffs rising

The Quaker Meeting House, Come-to-Good

over 400 ft above the sea. The formidable rocks are of alternating strata of whitish granite and darker volcanic stone. It is hard to believe that cargo boats beached or moored against the rocks in the 18th and 19th centuries, bringing coal from South Wales and loading sea sand and slate. A gated road leads south to Trevigue Farm (National Trust – car park) for High Cliff, at over 700 ft the highest point of the magnificent Cornish coastline.

North-east and high above the haven stands **St Gennys** Church, isolated in a superb setting. St Gennys was a Celtic saint who came from Wales to establish his 'cell' in this remote spot and a Norman church followed. The lower stages of the tower and the chancel survive from Norman times, but the setting is paramount – and the unforgettable views along the coast and inland over typical small-field farmland to the edge of BODMIN MOOR.

Delabole (1/5B) A village in North Cornwall spread out for nearly 2 miles along the B3314 west of Camelford. It is famous for its slate quarry, a great hole nearly 1½ miles in circumference and 500 ft deep. Visitors are welcomed to view this phenomenon and the nearby Slate Museum, which is open April to September. Slate has been extracted since the 15th century and by 1602 the 'hole' was a notable feature recorded in Richard Carew's *Survey of Cornwall*. The slate is bluish and of high quality. For centuries it was used for roofing and flooring in the South West, and was exported to Belgium and the Netherlands in large quantities from Port Gaverne, Port Isaac and BOSCASTLE until the railway arrived. Many gravestones and memorials of Delabole slate can be found in Cornwall, some notable ones carved by Burnard (*see* Altarnum). Powdered slate from the quarry is now used in the manufacture of plastics, cosmetics and paint.

Falmouth (1/3C) The largest town in Cornwall until CAMBORNE and REDRUTH combined to claim the distinction. It has two faces: the port with its quays, dockyard and yachting centre looking out to the magnificent anchorage of Carrick Roads; and, turning its back on those activities, the holiday resort facing the open sea. The latter developed with the coming of the railway (1863) and the mild climate attracts visitors all year round. It has all the amenities of a first-class resort enhanced by its beautiful position on Falmouth Bay, and by the tropical trees and plants that flourish in the parks and gardens.

The port is the best in Cornwall and Carrick Roads one of the largest and finest open anchorages in the world. It developed late, TRURO and Penryn being the main ports using the river Fal until Henry VIII built castles at St Mawes and at Pendennis Point to protect the mouth of the river. Thereafter, under the influence of the Killigrew family, the port developed and eventually supplanted its rivals. The Killigrew monument was erected in Grove Place in 1737 to commemorate them and across the road stands Arwenack House where they lived, though little remains of their large Tudor mansion. The growth of the port was marked by the building of King Charles the Martyr Church in 1662–4, much altered and restored since but retaining the granite pillars with plaster Ionic capitals of its arcades and its unusual rectangular tower. Few other 17th-century buildings of any note have survived, and only some brick houses in Arwenack Street of the 18th century. The handsome Custom House, the Synagogue in Vernon Place, the Polytechnic Arts Centre in Church Street and many of the town's terraces are early 19th century.

Castle Drive (a one-way road) runs out from the town to encircle Pendennis Point and gives wonderful views of the port and anchorage on the way out, and of the resort and bay on the way back. On Pendennis Point is the important Maritime Rescue Centre, opened by HRH Prince Charles in 1981, which coordinates all search and rescue operations round the coastline of Britain.

In a commanding position on the headland **Pendennis Castle** is one of the best survivors of the chain of forts for artillery built by Henry VIII against the threat of attacks from France. The outer curtain wall with its angular bastions was added later in the 16th century. The inner castle consists of a 16-sided rampart protecting a round keep with its characteristic low profile and immensely thick walls. A drawbridge at first-floor level gives access to the firing platform, octagonal in shape with eight splayed embrasures for guns and ammunition. Open to the public throughout the year, it is all in immaculate order and worth visiting if only for the all-round views of town, river, sea and coastline.

Fowey (1/4C) An ancient port and most attractive town approached along B3269, a turning off the A390 LOSTWITHIEL–St AUSTELL road. The busy, whitened quays and jetties from which china clay is exported are fortunately half a mile up-river from the town. The cargo boats that come to collect the clay are merely passing spectacles from the town's waterfront, narrow streets and higgledy-piggledy buildings that look across the beautiful harbour to POLRUAN and the woods of Bodinnick falling to the water's edge.

The commercial importance of the town in medieval times derived from its situation on the trade route from the Continent to Ireland which ran overland to the Camel estuary on the north coast. It is therefore not surprising to find the parish church dedicated to a 7th-century Irish saint, Finbarr. The church tower is a particularly fine one – tapering, set-back buttresses almost reaching to the decorated battlements and bold pinnacles – and the clerestory is unusual for Cornwall and odd in itself, the windows not over the nave arches but above the spandrels between them. Other notable features of the mainly 14th-century building are the finely carved Norman font, a Jacobean pulpit and the 16th- and 17th-century Rashleigh memorials.

The Rashleighs lived at Menabilly south-east of the town, later the home for many years of Daphne du Maurier. She put some of its history in *The King's General* and called it 'Manderley' in her very popular *Rebecca*. The Rashleighs' town house is now the Ship Inn at the bottom of Lostwithiel Street, a 15th-century structure rebuilt in Tudor times and masked by a late 19th-century façade. In Fore Street the Lugger Inn is a 17th-century building also refronted. Next to it the Noah's Ark Museum occupies the oldest house in the town; another museum is in Trafalgar Square in the medieval Town Hall, rebuilt in Georgian times. Many other 16th- to 18th-century buildings can be found in the winding streets of the old part of the town.

Along the Esplanade stands the house called The Haven; a plaque records that it was the home for more than 50 years of the novelist and Cornishman Sir Arthur Quiller-Couch (1863–1944). A frequent visitor was his friend Kenneth Grahame and the river Fowey is said to have inspired his classic children's book *The Wind in the Willows*. The Esplanade continues south to Readypenny Beach and beyond is the harbour entrance and the ruins of Henry VIII's St Catherine's Castle on land given to the National Trust as a memorial for the men of Fowey killed in the First World War.

A mile north-west of the town an interesting 6th-century inscribed stone moved from Castle Dore (*see* Golant) stands 7 ft tall beside the B3269. The first word of the vertical Latin inscription is not now clear but it was said to read 'here lies Drustans, the son of Cunomorous'. Many believe that this refers to that early Cornish hero, Sir Tristram of Lyonesse, immortalized in several medieval romances.

Golant (1/4B) A quiet riverside village 2 miles north of Fowey and reached by a turning off B3269. The small 15th-century church of St Samson stands high above it, a building consecrated in 1509 but containing later box pews and a pulpit made of medieval bench ends, one of which depicts the 6th-century Welsh saint himself. The ancient holy well is sited beside the south porch.

To the west of the village abutting on the B3269 is Castle Dore, a small circular Iron Age fort with double ramparts and ditches. Excavation has shown two periods of use, *c.* 150 BC–AD 100 and then in the 6th century AD. Traces of two large rectangular buildings in the interior were found and dated to the second period. These, and the inscribed stone moved from the fort or near by (*see* Fowey), tend to support the tradition that Castle Dore was the palace of King Mark, husband of the beautiful Iseult and uncle or perhaps father of Sir Tristram.

Gulval (1/2B) A small, tranquil village on the north-east outskirts of PENZANCE amid fertile soil where the earliest flowers on the mainland are grown. The churchyard is full of hydrangeas, palms, yuccas and other subtropical plants. The church of St Gulval retains its tower (1440) but was otherwise partly rebuilt and partly restored in 1892. The parish stretches northward into the granite heights of the Penwith or Land's End peninsula where the Iron Age fort of Castle-an-Dinas, three stone ramparts and three ditches, occupies a hill over 750 ft above sea level west of the Penzance–ST IVES road (B3311). The views from the summit, where the tower inside the fort is a *c.* 1800 folly, stretch over Mount's Bay and most of West Cornwall.

Half a mile west of the hill, reached by the turning off B3311 at Badger's Cross, is the Iron Age village of Chysauster. It continued to be occupied in Roman times and was only abandoned in the 3rd century AD. Eight houses, their rooms grouped round open courtyards and with garden plots, line a street. To the east lies a Celtic field system and to the south a ruined *fogou*, a stone-lined trench covered with stone slabs and soil, peculiar to West Cornwall. They were probably food stores comparable to cellars and icehouses in later times. The best surviving example is at Carn Euny (*see* Sancreed).

Gunwalloe Church Cove (1/2C) A popular sandy beach (National Trust) on the west coast of the LIZARD PENINSULA reached from HELSTON by the A3083 and then by a minor road that ends on the north side of the cove. Among the sandhills is St Winwalloe's Church protected from the sea by a cliff. St Winwalloe was a 6th-century Breton abbot. The 15th-century church has an earlier detached tower of slate with a pyramidal roof built into the cliff and a Norman font (restored) to indicate the existence of older buildings in this remote place. The most interesting feature of the church are two panels saved from the 15th-century rood screen, beautifully carved tracery above painted panels of the Apostles. The detached tower contains three pre-Reformation bells with Latin inscriptions, one translated as:

> All people cheer
> When me they hear.

The crews of sailing ships driven by southwesterly gales against this inhospitable shore had little to cheer about when the bells tolled to summon the scattered inhabitants to the wreck.

Gweek (1/2C) A pleasant village at the head of the westernmost creek of the Helford river. It became a port for HELSTON in the 13th century but the harbour is silted up and only a few small boats now come so far up-river. The older cottages are attractive and a clapper bridge, probably of medieval origin, has been retained as a footpath beside one of the later road bridges. The Seal Sanctuary, a short walk down river, cares for injured animals found along the coast, many of them young seals washed off the breeding ledges by storms. Three pools on the hillside above the river provide for some permanent residents at the Sanctuary and for those that, after treatment in the 'hospital', will be returned to the sea.

Gwennap Pit *see* Camborne-Redruth

Gwithian (1/2B) A village 3 miles north-east of Hayle on the B3301. Standing aloof from the holiday development close to the beach, it has attractive old cottages, a cob-walled Methodist chapel (1810) and St Gothian's Church. Only the low 15th-century tower remains of the medieval church, the rest was rebuilt in 1866. Several shipwrecked people are buried here.

Opposite: Slabs covering the water channel to No. 4, Chysauster Iron Age village, near Gulval
Right: Frenchman's Creek, near Helford

Between the village and St Ives Bay lie the 'towans', huge dunes of wind-blown sand which run for 3 miles down to the mouth of the river Hayle. Surfing and waterskiing are popular but the lighthouse on Godrevy Island to the north is a reminder that the bay can be dangerous when the winds blow. Many ships were wrecked about Godrevy Point before the light was lit in 1859, hence the graves in the churchyard. Between the village and Godrevy Point the aptly named Red river reaches the sea stained with tin waste from mines about CAMBORNE. Buried under the 'towans' are an important prehistoric settlement and also the 7th- or 8th-century Oratory, predecessor of the village church, of the Irish martyr St Gothian.

Helford (1/2C) A delightful village set snugly along a creek on the south side of the Helford estuary. It is reached from the GWEEK–St Keverne road (B3293) by minor roads through Manaccan, and in summer by passenger ferry across the river from Helford Passage. Visitors' vehicles are barred from the single narrow street in the holiday season but a car park is provided on the approach road. Near the ferry point the old Shipwrights Arms serves Cornish pasties in paper bags. In this way they retain their heat but can be held in the hand and eaten in the traditional manner without knife or fork. Half a mile west is the lovely Frenchman's Creek made famous by Daphne du Maurier's novel of that name. The National Trust owns the east bank and the access is near the farm at Kestle, signposted off the road to Manaccan. A delightful path goes down through the woods beside the creek to the main river where the banks and broad, tidal waters are strikingly beautiful and a paradise for yachtsmen.

Helston (1/2C) Twelve miles east of PENZANCE on the A394, the 'quaint old Cornish town' of the well-known song holds its Furry (Fair) Dance on 8 May each year. Pairs of children and formally dressed adult couples dance through the main streets and in and out of the houses to an age-old tune. Legend says the dance celebrates St Michael's victory over the Devil for possession of the town. In the 18th century learned men invented a Roman origin and called it the dance of Flora, the goddess of flowers, hence the modern name of 'Floral Dance' and the song popularized by the Australian baritone Peter Dawson.

A Saxon market town, and later one of the Stannary towns where tin was weighed and stamped before sale, it was also a port until the river Cober became blocked in the 13th century and the town had to open a new harbour at GWEEK. It is still a market town, its pleasing main streets lined with many listed Georgian buildings, though the Market Hall in the centre is early Victorian. The Angel Hotel, formerly the town house of the Godolphin family, is in part 16th century. St Michael's Church, built by the Earl of Godolphin in 1751–61, has a striking exterior and inside a gallery on three sides supported by iron columns and a good plaster ceiling in the chancel.

Two miles south is Loe Bar, sands and a shingle bank blocking the river Cober's outlet to Mount's Bay and forming Loe Pool, the largest expanse of freshwater in Cornwall. Good paths run along the edge of Loe Pool (National Trust). On the cliff south-east of Loe Bar is a monument to Henry Trengrouse (1772–1854) of Helston. In 1807 he witnessed the wreck of the frigate *Anson* on the Bar with the loss of a hundred lives. He devoted the rest of his life to perfecting, and getting the Government to accept, the life-saving rocket that has since saved thousands of lives.

Isles of Scilly *see* Scilly, Isles of

Laneast *see* St Clether

Lanhydrock House (1/5B) The great house stands about 2 miles south-east of BODMIN in magnificent parkland and woodland sweeping down to the river Fowey. A fine avenue of beeches and sycamores, originally planted in 1648, leads up to the 17th-century gatehouse and large courtyard. The Robartes family built the house between 1642 and 1651 but much of it was

Right: Lanhydrock House
Overleaf: Lizard Point

devastated by fire in 1881. It was rebuilt on the original plan within the next four years, a splendid Victorian mansion with important 17th-century features which passed to the National Trust in 1953. The south and west wings are a labyrinth of rooms which give a vivid impression of life in a wealthy Victorian and Edwardian household with large numbers of servants.

The north wing survived the 1881 fire and contains the outstanding room of the house, the 116 ft long gallery on the first floor, well lit by large mullioned windows. The plaster ceiling stretches the whole length of the room and has pendants and twisting ribs, the main panels depicting scenes from the Old Testament and subsidiary panels birds and beasts. It is a masterpiece of the plasterer's art and almost certainly the work of the Abbott family of North Devon, known for many fine ceilings and overmantels in the region. The house is open to the public from April to October.

Formal gardens (open all year) around the house and the church of St Hyderoc crammed up against it complete the lovely setting. The church is of little interest but in the churchyard the carved shaft of a Saxon cross is a relic of the days when St Petrock's Priory at Bodmin farmed the estate.

Launcells *see* Bude

Launceston (1/6B) A hilltop town on the A30(T) close to the Devon border and known as 'the gateway to Cornwall'. William the Conqueror's half-brother Robert of Mortain chose it for the site of the castle from which he ruled Cornwall. The town grew round the castle and continued to be the administrative centre of the county until 1838, when improved roads encouraged a move to the rather more centrally placed BODMIN.

In spite of this loss of status Launceston is still the 'pretty town' visited by the topographer John Norden in 1584. Good buildings of 16th- to 18th-century date survive in High Street, Church Street, Angel Hill and the thoroughfares that led to the medieval town gates, of which only one remains. Castle Street is conspicuous for a number of good Georgian houses, among them Lawrence House of 1753 (National Trust) which contains the excellent town museum and some notable plaster ceilings.

St Thomas's, the older of the town's two churches, has the largest Norman font of more than a hundred in Cornwall but the building was much restored in 1874. More interesting is St Mary Magdalene, a granite building of 1511–24 (except for the 14th-century tower) and little altered. It was built by a local landowner, Sir Henry Trecarrel, after the loss of his wife and a son, and is remarkable for the profusion of carving which covers nearly every part of the exterior. Below the ornamented battlements a Latin inscription runs round the building above crowded panels of roses, thistles, palm trees, heraldic lilies and coats of arms. At the east end the fine chancel window is surmounted by the Royal Arms and beneath the window in a niche is the recumbent figure of the Magdalene guarded by angels. Not before or since has intractable granite been decoratively carved on quite such a scale.

The castle ruins provide a good example of an early motte and bailey later embellished with stone walls and a keep. Most of the bailey is a public park with remains of north and south gatehouses and short stretches of the curtain wall. The north gatehouse was at one time used as a prison and numbered George Fox, founder of the Society of Friends, among its inmates. Public executions took place in the bailey until 1821. An inner gatehouse protected the long flight of steps that leads up the south side of the very high motte, a natural mound scarped to make the slope steeper. On the motte an oval shell keep was erected early in the 13th century, the wall 12 ft thick and the ramparts reached by two staircases in the wall. Later in the 13th century a circular tower twice the height of the shell keep was built inside it, an unusual arrangement that nevertheless resembles the remodelling in the previous century of the great shell keep at Windsor Castle.

Lizard Peninsula (1/2C) Designated an Area of Outstanding Natural Beauty, it is approached through GWEEK or HELSTON and two roads (A3083 and B3293) drive down the plateau to Lizard village and St Keverne respectively. The flat heathland and cliffs are important botanically for many rare plants, including Cornish heather (*Erica vagans*) which mingles in profusion with commoner species like gorse and bog rush. A Nature Reserve run by the Cornwall Naturalists' Trust has been established on Predannack Downs to ensure that the rarities will survive.

The peninsula is also important geologically for its mixed sedimentary and igneous rocks dominated by the rare serpentine, commonly though not exclusively dull green in colour and much mottled and veined. It can best be seen in all its natural forms on the cliffs at Kynance Cove. It often contains flaws and has not been greatly valued for building – though used for some of the cottages at CADGWITH and the low church tower at Landewednack, a pretty village near Lizard Point, where the serpentine alternates with lighter blocks of granite. But the stone has found its way into homes the length and breadth of England and overseas in the form of ashtrays, paperweights and other ornaments and souvenirs made in Lizard village and sold in innumerable gift shops, a flourishing local industry for more than a century.

Lizard village is entirely devoted to the tourist trade and the Point, the southernmost tip of mainland Britain, attracts many visitors. Stretching out from it are long reefs of granite and serpentine, dangerous at all times and particularly when the south-westerly gales blow. The disused lifeboat station tucked below the cliffs was replaced by a new station 2 miles to the northeast in 1960 after saving some 600 lives in a century of service. On the cliff top the flat lighthouse (1751) originally had two lights, but one was dismantled during alterations in 1903 when a single more powerful light was installed. A coal-burning light, put up by Sir John Killigrew early in the 17th century, ceased operating when opposed by Trinity House – and by the local inhabitants, who feared that fewer wrecks would badly affect their 'hereditary' claims to salvage. Today the emphasis is all on rescue. From the important Culdrose Airfield towards HELSTON the Royal Naval Air Service conducts its 'search and rescue' operations. Helicopters, which have added a new dimension to rescue work, are always on standby to cooperate with coastguards, police and lifeboats in plucking people to safety from the sea or the cliffs and ferrying the injured to hospital.

The Lizard Peninsula has also been important in the development of radio communications. A granite monument on the cliffs owned by the National Trust near MULLION commemorates the experiments carried out by Guglielmo Marconi which resulted in the first transmission across the Atlantic (1901) and other important developments. Only 3 miles away on Goonhilly Downs, among the wild flowers and prehistoric hut foundations and barrows, the bowl-shaped scanners of the Post Office Earth Station track satellites through space.

See also Gunwalloe Church Cove; Helford.

Looe (1/5C) A resort on the south coast 12 miles from the Tamar and reached by roads from the Saltash Bridge or the Torpoint ferry. It is a place of character, attractively strung out on both sides of the long harbour at the mouth of the Looe river. Originally two towns, East and West Looe, linked by a bridge built in 1411 and replaced in the 19th century, they were not united until the 1880s. Both were fishing and trading ports. Today the fishing is supplemented by the holiday trade: cruises to FOWEY and POLPERRO and out to Looe island, once a haunt of smugglers and now a privately run bird sanctuary. The town is also the centre for shark fishing in the English Channel. Sharks caught in local waters can be seen in the Aquarium on East Looe quay.

The main street of East Looe runs parallel to the quay and has many ancient buildings and picturesque side lanes. The 16th-century Guildhall is a museum which preserves the stocks, pillory and many other relics of the town's history. In Lower Street a Cornish Folk Museum, open in the summer season, occupies an old fish cellar. The 16th-century Fisherman's Arms is an inn of character matched in West Looe by the Jolly Sailors Inn, mainly 17th century but dating back to the 15th.

The Looe churches illustrate a typical Cornish feature: the development of the towns late in medieval times and away from the original oratories or chapels founded by the Celtic saints and later rebuilt and enlarged. The mother church of West Looe, a 13th- to 15th-century building, lies nearly 2 miles westward at Talland. The small church of St Nicholas on the quay was a medieval chapel which, after use for civil purposes, only became the parish church in the 19th century.

The mother church of East Looe was St Martin-by-Looe half a mile out of the town on the B3253. It has a good Norman doorway, 13th-century windows and fabric, and a tower of the 14th and 15th centuries with diagonal buttresses. In the 1850s the 13th-century chapel of St Mary near the town beach was rebuilt and became the present parish church.

Lostwithiel (1/5B) An ancient town on the Liskeard to ST AUSTELL road (A390) where it crosses the Fowey. It was important in medieval times as a port and a Stannary town where tin was assayed and taxed before being sold and exported. With the silting up of the river, contributed to by the waste from tin mining upstream, the town gradually declined. Today it is a touring centre and visited by many anglers for the river's salmon and trout.

The five-arched bridge over the Fowey was

built in the 15th century and is still in use, preserved by the construction of a modern bridge upstream to carry the main road. The arcaded Guildhall in Fore Street (1740) is a museum displaying the town's regalia and copies of its charters dating back to 1189. The Municipal offices near the Guildhall and the old Grammar School in Queen Street are late 18th-century buildings, and most of the streets have some good Georgian houses. A curiosity is the 17th-century tablet on the corner of the former Malt House recording that 'Walter Kendal founded this house and hath a lease for 3000 years which has beginning Sept 29 1652'.

St Bartholomew's Church is notable for its 14th-century octagonal spire, one of only six in Cornwall, boldly contrived on top of the earlier tower with its lancet windows. The nave and aisles are also 14th century, the octagonal columns without capitals and one of Cornwall's four clerestories above. The east window is particularly fine, and the early 14th-century font outstanding for its size and the spirited carvings on the bowl.

A mile north of the town **Restormel Castle** stands on a promontory above the beautiful river valley, a superb place for a picnic. The castle is open to the public throughout the year. The great shell keep, 30 ft high, has been immaculately kept by successive state departments. The keep is surrounded by an enormous ditch, the slopes yellow in spring with primroses. The bailey to the west has disappeared. The position is so immensely strong that the keep was not built on the usual mound and the layout of the 13th-century domestic buildings inside it is remarkably clear.

Luxulyan (1/4B) A remote hilltop village 4 miles north-west of ST AUSTELL, reached by lanes off the road to BODMIN (A391) or to LOSTWITHIEL (A390). It has some handsome granite cottages and the church of St Cyriac and St Julitta is all grey granite blocks, the tower severe without buttresses or pinnacles. A Saxon cross stands beside the tower and a holy well near by. Fragments of 16th-century glass remain in the west tower window and the south porch has a striking vault.

From the village the Par–NEWQUAY railway line winds down a thickly wooded valley towards Par Station. Spanning the valley the Treffrey viaduct, 100 ft high and over 200 yd long, is an outstanding piece of industrial archaeology. It is not a railway viaduct but an earlier structure

(1839–42) built by the industrial tycoon Joseph Thomas Treffry. He built it for a tramway to transport the products of his mines and quarries down to the port he had created at Par. It also served as an aqueduct taking water to work the mine engines. The climb to the top is well worth the effort. Below the viaduct paths lead down the valley, a beautiful walk at all times through oak and alder woods but best when the massed bluebells are out.

Madron (1/1B) A village 2 miles north-west of the centre of PENZANCE on B3312. The buildings are mostly granite set among glasshouses and fields of broccoli and potatoes. The 14th- and 15th-century church of St Madern (Madron) was the mother church of Penzance and its Norman font a relic of a building which existed long before the town. In the south aisle the 17th-century brass to John Clies, Mayor of Penzance, shows the church's continuing status. The holy well of St Madron is a mile north of the village with a roofless but interesting baptistery near by. The water was said to cure cripples and the well traditionally visited on May Day by maidens to wish for a happy marriage.

South-west of the village the garden at Trengwainton (National Trust; open Wednesday to Saturday from March to October) is one of the best in the county. It was created from 1926 onwards by Sir Edward Bolitho of the well-known banking family who still occupy the house. The large shrub garden contains many rare types of rhododendron and a walled garden has plants not grown elsewhere in England.

The parish extends northwards to the moorlands where the ruined chimney and engine house of Ding Dong mine form a prominent landmark. North-west from it stands the 8 ft tall Mens Scryfa (written stone) with a vertical inscription 'Riolobran son of Cunoval', one of the most impressive of its kind, probably of the 6th century, its position on the bare moor a mystery. It is easily accessible from the side road which crosses the moors from Madron to MORVAH and so also are the important prehistoric sites in the parish. Lanyon Quoit (National Trust) is beside the road, the massive capstone and three uprights of a 3rd millennium BC chambered tomb which was originally at the north end of, and covered by, a mound 30 yd long. Similar remains of another tomb lie 2 miles north-east, high on Mulfra Hill. At Bodrifty to the west are remains

Trengwainton House, Madron

of an Iron Age village of eight huts subsequently enclosed by a wall to contain cattle. The hut platforms were levelled by cutting into the hillside and the largest hut was built on earlier Bronze Age foundations. Occupation went on into Roman times. Traces of Iron Age fields can be seen on the hillside above the village. Westward again is the Nine Maidens Bronze Age stone circle, 6 standing stones and 5 fallen surviving from a probable 22, and a stone in the centre. South-west of this are the curious relics known as Men-an-tol (stone of the hole), two short stone pillars and in line between them a slab pierced by a circular hole. Perhaps the stones are the remains of a chambered tomb with a porthole entrance, but evidence is lacking. Traditionally children were passed through the hole as a cure for rickets.

Marazion (1/2B) A village 2 miles east of PENZANCE on the A394. The name means 'little market' and it originated as a mainland trading post for the priory on St Michael's Mount, a third of a mile offshore. Through traffic makes it difficult to appreciate the long, main street, its inns and good Victorian buildings such as the Methodist Chapel (1862).

St Michael's Mount, a granite island some 21 acres in extent, is one of the great sites of England, as romantic as its counterpart off the coast of Normandy. Two Saxon crosses bear witness to an early religious foundation and the medieval priory lasted in one form or another until appropriated by the Crown at the Dissolution (1539), when the monastic buildings became a 'castle' occupied by a Governor. In the 17th century the Crown sold it and after passing through the hands of Robert Cecil, Earl of Salisbury, and the Basset family, it was purchased in 1659 by the St Aubyns who live there still. They were raised to the peerage as Lords St Levan in 1887 and the 3rd Lord gave the island to the National Trust in 1954.

The buildings (open to the public on most days throughout the year) are dominated by the tower of the chapel, a 14th-century building much restored but remarkable for its position on the highest point of the island, 200 ft above the sea. Under the St Aubyns the 'castle' evolved into a stately home where the trappings of 18th- and 19th-century gentility contrast with the rugged, gale-torn setting. The walls and roof of the Chevy Chase room are the main survivals from medieval

Right: Men-an-tol (stone of the hole)
Overleaf: St Michael's Mount

times, with the notable plaster frieze added in the 17th century. The Blue Drawing rooms were created in the 1750s in the ruins of the Lady Chapel, delightful 'Strawberry Hill' Gothick in style and furnished with pieces made by local craftsmen in imitation of Chippendale. The battlemented south-east wing, rising sheer above the cliff and with the living rooms above the bedrooms to give the loftiest view, was designed in the 19th century by the architect, Piers St Aubyn, a cousin of the 1st Lord Levan. The fine furniture, silver and paintings include a self-portrait by John Opie (1761–1807), painted when he was only seventeen. He was born near ST AGNES. Among other paintings by him at the Mount is a portrait of the famous fishwife, Dolly Pentreath, of MOUSEHOLE.

Mevagissey (1/4C) A famous fishing port on the south coast, 5 miles south of ST AUSTELL on the B3273. Pilchards were once the mainstay of its economy, thousands of tons a year being caught, cured and exported to Italy or sold to the Royal Navy, whose seamen called them 'Mevagissey Ducks'. The harbour and the old town on the north side are still attractive but overcrowded in summer and many new houses and boarding houses occupy the hillside above.

The church of St Peter is a 13th-century cruciform building on a Saxon and Norman site. A north aisle was added in the 16th century, built of Pentewan stone from the historic quarries a mile or so to the north. A 19th-century restoration respected the Norman font and the elaborate memorial (1617) to Otwell Hill and his wife, the inscription beginning

Stock Lancashier, Birth London, Cornwall gave
to Otwell Hill Inhabitance and Grave . . .

By the 17th century at least one 'foreigner' had discovered this still unspoiled hinterland.

Morvah (1/1B) A hamlet 3 miles north-east of ST JUST IN PENWITH on the B3306. The modest church tower is 14th century, the rest rebuilt in 1828. Once the focus of considerable mining activity – remains can be seen from the road – the parish is interesting today for two prehistoric sites on the moorland 1 mile south of the church. Chun Quoit is one of the most striking of the 3rd millenium BC chambered tombs in Penwith with a 12 ft square capstone supported on four uprights. It was originally sited at the centre of a round barrow 35 ft in diameter. Some 300 yd to the east on the same ridge is Chun Castle, an Iron

Age fort of more than usual interest. It consists of two nearly circular ramparts faced with granite blocks, the entrances staggered to hamper an assault. Excavation revealed construction in the 3rd to 2nd century BC and evidence of tin and iron smelting as late as the 5th or 6th century AD, a long period of use. The 'Pulpits' on the main ramparts are 19th-century adaptations for Methodist preachers to conduct open air services.

Morwenstow (1/6A) On the Atlantic coast in North Cornwall, bordering on Devon, a parish of scattered hamlets and farms, the church, vicarage and an old farmhouse forming an isolated group half a mile from the cliff edge. It is inescapably associated with the name of Robert Stephen Hawker, vicar from 1834 until his death in 1875, who devoted himself to this remote parish with courage, energy and some eccentricity. He built the vicarage at his own expense, with chimneys imitating the towers of different churches where he had lived before coming to Morwenstow, and the large kitchen chimney representing his mother's tomb.

His church of St Morwenna retains more Norman work than is usual in Cornwall: part of the north arcade, the south door (though moved and altered when the south aisle was added) and an early font. Of the Norman carving the vigorous heads of men and beasts are particularly notable. The open wagon roofs also are well preserved and in the chancel a medieval wall painting represents St Morwenna. In these surroundings Hawker reintroduced the Harvest Thanksgiving service, so appropriate for his agricultural parish.

As a poet and writer he is best remembered for one of his *Cornish Ballads*, the stirring 'Song of the Western Men':

And have they fixed the where and when?
And shall Trelawny die?
Here's twenty thousand Cornish men
Will know the reason why!

which has become a national anthem for the Cornish. Above all he is remembered for his efforts to change the traditional attitude to wrecks by striving to save the crews of the ships that foundered so frequently below the terrible cliffs and, if that was not possible, to give the dead Christian burial. Many victims lie in the churchyard, including the crew of the brig *Caledonia* wrecked in 1842, the grave marked by the ship's figurehead. From the churchyard gate

St Morwenna, Morwenstow

Above: The grave of Joseph Crapp, Mylor

language recording his gifts for repairs to the church and for building the almshouses that still adjoin the churchyard. A granite obelisk in the churchyard wall commemorates Dolly Pentreath (died 1777), the Mousehole fishwife whose portrait by John Opie hangs in St Michael's Mount (*see* Marazion). Traditionally she was the last person who never used English, speaking and swearing only in Cornish. The memorial was erected in the 19th century by Prince Louis Lucien Bonaparte, a nephew of Napoleon and something of a philologist.

a path leads through National Trust land to the cliffs and to the hut, built by Hawker of driftwood, where he often sat and smoked and contemplated the Atlantic.

Mousehole (1/1C) An attractive fishing village 2 miles south of Penzance. Narrow approach roads have helped to preserve the picturesque buildings that cluster round the small harbour and in the winding streets and alleys. Among them are the pleasant Ship Inn and the 16th-century former manor house in Keigwin Street with its large porch of granite columns which survived a devastating raid by some Spanish ships in 1595. On Ragannis Hill a pioneer sanctuary for injured sea birds was started privately by the Yglesias sisters in the 1920s and happily continues as an RSPCA hospital. To the north near Penlee Point the lifeboat station has the steepest slipway of any in England; the boat is crewed by men from Mousehole and NEWLYN. In December 1981 the boat, launched in appalling conditions to aid a stricken vessel, was lost with all its crew, all Mousehole men.

The parish church stands high above the village in the hamlet of Paul. It was badly damaged in the 1595 raid. A memorial to Captain Stephen Hutchens (1709) has an epitaph in the Cornish

Right: Fishing Boats, Newlyn Harbour

Mullion (1/2C) A village on the LIZARD PENIN-SULA reached by the A3083 from HELSTON and then along the B3296 to the churchtown and Mullion Cove. The mainly 15th-century church of St Melaine is notable for its early 16th-century bench ends and for the use of local serpentine stone with granite in the construction of its tower. The delightful Mullion Cove (National Trust) lies a mile south-west on a beautiful stretch of the coast. The neat little 19th-century harbour is tucked in between rocky cliffs with a sandy beach exposed at low tide. It looks a secure haven but

gives little protection when south-westerly gales sweep across Mount's Bay and the sea breaks over the piers. Mullion Island also belongs to the National Trust and is run by the Cornwall Naturalists' Trust as a Reserve for breeding sea birds.

Mylor (1/3C) Once a small dockyard, now a yachting centre, at the entrance to a creek of the river Fal. Lanes off the TRURO–FALMOUTH road (A39) lead to the hamlet, or it can be approached by good footpaths from Flushing (connected to

Falmouth by ferry) across fields or along the edge of the river. The church of St Melor, beautifully sited near the water, has two Norman doorways and an attractive 15th-century entrance to the south porch. Beside the porch stands a round-headed cross, 10½ ft tall and the largest of its kind in Cornwall. It was 'discovered' in the 19th century, upside down and propping up the church's south wall. When erected in its present position the bottom of the shaft was buried 7 ft deep, which may have reduced the original visible height by 2 or 3 ft, but in any event it is an impressive Christian monument of the 10th century.

Newlyn (1/1B) On the shores of Mount's Bay, cheek by jowl with PENZANCE, the most important fishing port and market in Cornwall. A small harbour was built in the 15th century, and in 1884–94 the long jetties that reach out to enclose some 40 acres of sea. Old houses and cottages rise on terraces overlooking the harbour, the sail lofts and fish cellars converted to other uses, the streets narrow and crooked. Daily auctions of the catch from trawlers and inshore boats take place in the market buildings on the quay.

A hundred years ago the artist Stanhope Forbes went to Newlyn and painted fish being sold on the beach. He stayed for the rest of his life and became a leading member of the 'Newlyn School', artists in revolt against studio painting who worked mainly out of doors and in the fishermen's cottages to leave a remarkable record of a vanished way of life. Early in this century other artists who were to achieve distinction discovered what one of their number, Frank Brangwyn, described as the 'unbelievable light' which made western Cornwall so attractive to them. Lamorna Birch, Alfred Munnings, Harold Knight and his more famous wife Laura all painted at Newlyn. Already the town had been provided with the fine Art Gallery in New Road, the gift in 1895 of the Cornish-born journalist and philanthropist Passmore Edwards (1823–1911). Many artists continue to live in the area and show their work at the gallery along with the permanent exhibition of paintings, sculpture and pottery.

Newquay (1/3B) The largest resort on the north coast. The superb position and sandy beaches form the background for every holiday activity from bowls and golf to surfing and deep-sea shark fishing. Good cliff walks, caves to explore, leisure gardens, a zoo and an aquarium are other attractions for the visitor. Yet for centuries it was a modest fishing village sheltering to the east of Towan Head. The whitewashed walls and stumpy tower of the Huer's House near the Atlantic Hotel is a relic of the days when watch was kept for the pilchard shoals. The name 'huer' derives from the cry of 'hevva! hevva!', meaning a shoal of fish, which alerted the fishermen. Only after the railway arrived in 1875, crossing the river Gannel on a fine viaduct, did the village develop into the present popular resort and centre for exploring the rest of the county. The Gothic-style church of St Michael, a large building prominent on the slope of Mount Wise, was not built until 1909–11.

Many prehistoric sites were destroyed during development but Bronze Age burials survive on Pentire Point East and in the open space called Barrowfield on the clifftop north-east of Tolcarne Beach. Half a mile up the coast is Trevelgue Head with two large barrows and one of the best examples of an Iron Age promontory fort. The remains of six sets of ramparts and ditches run across the head from cliff to cliff. Excavation revealed a bronze-smelting site and huts occupied through Iron Age and Roman times.

North Hill (1/6B) A largely unspoiled village on a hillside above the river Lynher, looking across to the eastern edge of BODMIN MOOR. It is 7 miles south-west of LAUNCESTON off the road to Liskeard (B3254). The 15th-century church of St Torney is a handsome granite structure and the interior spacious and well maintained with its original ceiled wagon roofs. The 17th-century memorials are remarkable. The earlier ones are of slate: Henry Spoure (1603), Thomas and Jane Vincent with their 15 children (1606) and Richard Spoure (1653). These are dwarfed by the tall, elaborate wall monument to another Henry Spoure (1688), his sister and their parents. It is one of the finest in Cornwall, still Jacobean in style with classical columns and a flamboyant pediment and coloured coat of arms. The parents kneel on cushions, facing each other across a small prayer desk, and the dutiful Henry and his sister stand gracefully posed in niches behind them. The detailed portrayal of late Stuart costume is coloured with realistic restraint.

Padstow (1/4B) An ancient port on the Camel estuary reached from Wadebridge along the A389 which fortunately does not penetrate to the old part of the town. The name is a corruption of Petrockstow, its origins going back at least to the

6th century AD when the best-known of the Celtic saints, St Petrock, landed from Wales and founded an important monastery. Even after the monastery was removed in the 10th century to BODMIN the town's importance continued because of its position on the main route from Ireland to the Continent. Eventually the sand built up on the Doom bar across the mouth of the river, hundreds of ships were wrecked on it and access became so difficult that trade declined. The town is now a shopping centre for a wide area and a holiday resort. The beautiful but unruly estuary provides excitement for experienced sailors, and for bird watchers good views of terns, grebes, duck and divers. The course of the abandoned railway line to Wadebridge, crossing Little Petherick creek on a long, curved bridge, makes an excellent 6-mile walk along the edge of the estuary.

The old part of the town has retained much of its compact medieval and Elizabethan character. Granite and slate-hung cottages line the narrow streets and alleys that slope steeply to the attractive harbour and waterfront. On the north quay is the 15th-century Merchants Guild House, and on the south quay the 16th-century Raleigh's Court House where Sir Walter's agents collected dues when he was Lord Warden of the Stannaries. In 'up-town', as the natives call it, rises the tower of St Petrock's Church. The spacious interior is mainly 13th–14th century with an amusing bench end of a fox in a pulpit preaching to geese. Seventeenth-century memorials commemorate the Prideaux family who came to live at Place on the edge of 'up-town' in Tudor times and are still there. The beautifully carved 15th-century font, of dark stone from Catacleuse 3 miles to the west, was said to confer immunity from the gallows, however great a villain the child became. The legend died in 1787 when a man called Elliot, who had been baptized in the font, was hanged.

On May Day the town welcomes summer with a robust celebration that makes no concessions to visitors. For hours on end a 'Hobby Hoss' and a man with a club called 'the Teaser' prance and dance through streets decked with flags and greenery. Musicians and singers accompany them and everyone sings the choruses:

> Unite, all unite! Let us all unite!
> For summer is acome today –
> And whither we are going, let us all unite
> On the merry morning of May . . .

At times the 'Hoss' bumps into women or girls in the crowd, or takes one momentarily under its

Egyptian House, Penzance

sailcloth cape, enacting a fertility rite going back to pagan times.

Pendennis Castle *see* Falmouth

Penzance (1/1B) The westernmost resort in England, cooler than London in summer, far warmer in winter, and beautifully situated on Mount's Bay. The earliest flowers and vegetables on the mainland are grown in the district and the town has always been a market as well as a port. For 150 years it was the mining centre of the Penwith peninsula. Raiding Spaniards sacked it in 1595 and, for its loyalty to King Charles, Parliamentary soldiery ravaged it at the end of the Civil War. The growth of the modern town began with the construction of a turnpike road from 'up-country' late in the 18th century and its development as a resort followed the coming of the railway in 1859.

The London–Land's End road (A30) constitutes the main thoroughfare of Market Jew Street and Alverton Street. At their junction the former marketplace is occupied by the classical, domed Market House (1837) and in front of it stands a statue of the town's most famous son, Sir Humphry Davy (1778–1829). Knighted for his services to chemistry, he is best remembered for the invention of the safety lamp which saved hundreds of lives wherever coal was mined.

Chapel Street, winding down from Market House to the harbour, was the old main street and makes a delightful stroll. Many good Georgian and Regency buildings contrast with the extraordinary Egyptian House (c. 1835 – Landmark Trust). On its façade, fantastic rather than Egyptian, the Royal Arms seem incongruous. More in keeping with the town's spirit are The Turks Head, dating from the 13th century and only partly burned by the Spaniards, and the Admiral Benbow with a pirate sprawled on the roof looking out to sea.

Further down, Chapel House is a fine Georgian building and nearly opposite is No. 25 where a prosperous merchant of the town, Thomas Branwell, lived in his later years. Of his 11 children Maria, born in 1783, was to die far away among the Yorkshire moors, mother of the three Brontë sisters. Did Cornish imagination play some part in the creation of their novels? At the end of the street stands St Mary's Church built in 1832–5, its tower a landmark for returning seamen, and below it the Customs House and the harbour.

From the harbour Battery Road leads to the magnificent promenade that stretches for a mile to NEWLYN with views over the whole sweep of the bay, from Penlee Point and St Michael's Mount near at hand to Lizard Point 20 miles away. Gardens are a feature of the resort: St Anthony Gardens in Battery Road and along the front Alexander Grounds, the Penlee Memorial Park of 15 acres (Penlee House contains the Penzance and District Museum) and the Bolitho gardens next to the beach. Best of all are the secluded Morrab gardens, a short distance from the front in an area of attractive terraces characteristic of the town.

Polperro (1/5C) One of the most picturesque of all the small fishing villages on the south coast, reached from LOOE along the A387. It occupies a steep, winding gorge between rocky cliffs and

Below: The Shell House, Polperro
Opposite: The ruined chapel on Roche Rock
(see p. 196)

wooded hillsides, the old slate cottages rising one on top of the other, many with characteristic outside staircases where people lived above the cellars for storing salted fish. The Shell House in Warren Street is a good example, its exterior fantastically decorated with shells by a fisherman, not to please visitors but for his own enjoyment. All the lanes converge on the harbour which is protected by two jetties. The narrow, oblique entrance to the inner harbour can be blocked by timber baulks when gales threaten the anchored vessels. Early in the 19th century 30 boats inside were destroyed in a single storm. The channel to the open sea, only 50 yd wide between the dark rocks, makes a difficult landfall for strangers.

In the 18th century the village was notorious for smuggling. Everyone played their part and the old cottages were good hiding places for contraband. The Smugglers' Museum near the inner harbour recalls those days. Today even fishing is secondary to the holiday trade.

Cars are banned from the centre of Polperro.

Polruan (1/4C) Across the mouth of the river Fowey from FOWEY town, a typical small Cornish port of steep, narrow streets running down to the quay. It is unsuitable for cars and the approach is through tortuous lanes leading south-west off the B3359 road to POLPERRO. A car park at the top of the village provides wonderful views of the estuary. A walk down Fore Street leads to the Lugger Inn and the 'penny' passenger ferry across the river to Fowey town.

The village's churchtown was Lanteglos, over a mile north-east above the wooded creek of Pont Pill. The 14th-century church of St Willow was carefully restored in the 19th century but retains many unusual features. The aisles are extended to embrace the west tower, the nave arcades have round arches and piers of Pentewan stone, aisle windows have four lights not three, and the fine 13th-century font has a base of Purbeck marble.

Polruan is essentially 'walking country', and not only the town itself and the Coastal Path to Polperro. A good walk, mostly on National Trust land, goes along the south side of Pont Pill to the head of the creek where the Trust has rebuilt the quays and operates an interesting water-powered sawmill. Across a footbridge the path turns back along the north side of the creek to Penleath Point where a granite pillar commemorates Sir Arthur Quiller-Couch (see Fowey). The path continues to Bodinnick and its car ferry. The walk can be rounded off by crossing to Fowey, walking along the waterfront and returning to Polruan by the passenger ferry.

Porthcurno see St Levan

Probus (1/3B) A village 5 miles north-east of TRURO on the A390. The church, mainly 15th century and restored in 1851, is renowned for its granite tower built in 1520–30 and the tallest in Cornwall ($123\frac{1}{2}$ ft). Superb carving and the Somerset-type arrangement of string courses, windows, battlements and pinnacles make this superior to any other tower in the county.

On the main road east of the village the County Demonstration Garden supplies an admirable advisory service. Six and half acres are laid out in plots to demonstrate what shrubs and plants can be grown on different soils, also vegetable and fruit plots, a small arboretum and a nature trail for wild flowers. The site formed part of the Trewithen estate and a little further along the road the 25-acre garden at Trewithen itself is one of the finest in the county and is open from March to September. Its creator, Mr George Johnson, was an authority on Asiatic magnolias of which every available kind is grown together with rare camellias and rhododendrons.

Redruth see Camborne-Redruth

Restormel Castle see Lostwithiel

Roche (1/4B) A clay-mining village on the B3274, 5 miles north-west of ST AUSTELL and just south of the A30(T). The church of St Gonand was rebuilt twice in the 19th century but retains its medieval tower. The fine Norman pillared font is decorated with angels' heads, entwined snakes and lilies. Less than half a mile south-east beside the road to Bugle is Roche Rock, a 100 ft high lump of black tourmaline rising spectacularly from the plain. On top St Gonand, traditionally a leper, is said to have had his cell. The present ruins on the rock comprise a tiny chapel and a cell beneath it dated about 1400. Like others on the top of rocks the chapel is dedicated to St Michael the Archangel. The building is reached by clambering over the outcrop and up one steep ladder to the cell and then another to the chapel. The sheer physical effort of erecting the building in medieval times remains a marvel. The view from the chapel contrasts the great spread of china clay workings to the south and east with marsh, rough grassland and stone walls to north and west.

St Enedoc, near Rock

Rock (1/4B) A resort on the Camel estuary opposite PADSTOW with sandy beaches and easy access to those at Daymer Bay and Polzeath to the north. Rock is a good centre for sailing with its own training school, and among its sand dunes is one of the most interesting natural golf links in England. The links are named after the Celtic St Enodoc whose little church lies romantically among them. At one time it was buried by blown sand and could only be entered through the roof. In 1863–4 the sand was cleared away and the building restored. It has a low tower and a stumpy spire raised in the 13th century over the north transept of a basically Norman church.

Sir John Betjeman, Poet Laureate 1972–84 and author of the first Shell Guide to Cornwall in 1934, is buried in the churchyard among the tamarisk hedges. He knew the district well from childhood and wrote of it affectionately in several poems: 'Trebetherick', 'Seaside Golf', 'Greenaway' and, particularly, 'Sunday Afternoon Service at St Enodoc's'. Also in the churchyard, with its lovely view down to and across the estuary, lie many unknown shipwrecked sailors. The church bell came from an Italian ship, the *Immaculata*, wrecked off Greenaway in 1875.

St Agnes (1/3B) A former mining village close to the north coast, reached from the A30(T) between BODMIN and REDRUTH along the B3277. Modern houses have been built but the terraces of miners' cottages and the steep streets remain, one of the latter enjoying the name of Stippy Stappy Lane. Though now occupied by business people working in Redruth or Truro, or adapted for summer letting, the cottages retain much of their character. The nearest beach is Trevaunance Cove north of the village. A harbour to handle the output of the tin mines was built there with great difficulty in 1793 but the storms of the last 50 years have swept all away.

St Agnes Beacon (625 ft) belongs to the National Trust and rises west of the village overlooking scores of ruined mines and half of Cornwall. Some Bronze Age barrows among the furze suggest that prehistoric man also streamed for tin in the valleys below the hill. To the north-west is St Agnes Head where fulmars and guillemots nest, and kittiwakes in large numbers. Glimpses may be caught of grey seals, which breed in the caves around Portreath a few miles to the south-west, and of lizards and shy adders. The clifftop is a natural rock garden bright with flowers in spring and summer: vetches, thrift, samphire, sea campion and sky-blue squill.

Above: Castle-an-Dinas Iron Age fort (see p. 201)

South of St Agnes Head are the ruins of Wheal Coates (National Trust). The pumping engine house and chimney are on the cliff 200 ft above the sea, and further up the winding and stamping engine houses. Silent and isolated amid beautiful coastal scenery, the buildings have shed for ever the bustle and harshness of their active days (c. 1860–90).

In a lane off the B3285 north-east of the village is Harmony Cot, the thatched and whitewashed cottage where John Opie RA (1761–1807) was born, the son of a carpenter. He went to London and painted many society portraits and historical pictures – 500 have been catalogued – and became known in fashionable society as 'the Cornish Wonder'. He was buried in the crypt of St Paul's Cathedral beside another West Countryman, Sir Joshua Reynolds. Examples of his work can be seen at St Michael's Mount (*see* Marazion) and in the County Museum and Art Gallery at TRURO.

St Agnes (island) *see* Scilly, Isles of

Opposite: The ruins of the Wheal Coates tin mine

St Austell (1/4B) A large town for Cornwall, centre of the china clay industry. The quarries and pyramids of waste stretch north and west creating a 'moon landscape' of uncompromising greyness and aridity. Wheal Martyn at Carthew on A391 is an old clayworks restored as an open air museum devoted to the history of the industry. The small market and mining town expanded and prospered when the extraction of china clay began in the second half of the 18th century. Today it is also a busy shopping centre with a large pedestrian precinct.

Only the old churchtown serves as a reminder of the remoter past. The parish church of Holy Trinity has one of the finest towers in Cornwall (1478–87), notable for the severe but decorative figures in niches on all four sides.

Four bands of ornamentation on the upper stage, battlements and pinnacles complete the impression of symmetry and strength. The granite tower is faced with Pentewan stone from the famous quarries 3 miles to the south. The whole of the exterior is attractive with battlemented aisles and a two-storey south porch. The interior is less so, all smartened up to serve a large town rather than a modest one. It is mainly of the

15th century, with some 13th-century features, and contains an interesting pillar piscina and a font carved with faces and dragons, both Norman.

St Buryan (1/1B) A village in the Penwith peninsula, 4 miles south-west of PENZANCE on the B3283. The houses and cottages are built round, and are entirely dominated by, the church standing in a raised, enclosed churchyard. The ground has been gradually built up by successive burials over many centuries. The four-stage 14th-century tower is 92 ft tall and a landmark all over the parish and beyond. The interior of six bays in nave and both aisles is unusually large for a remote parish. The reason is that from the 13th century at least it was an important collegiate church. Before then it may have been a Celtic monastic site whose status was confirmed rather than created by a charter of King Athelstan in about AD 930. A 10th-century crosshead carved with a crucified figure stands in the churchyard. The main feature of the interior, the early 16th-century rood screen across nave and aisles, renewed in the 19th century, is thought to have been the work of Devon craftsmen sent down by the Bishop of Exeter. A litany desk incorporates some 15th-century bench ends, one of a mermaid – the sea is barely two miles away.

A path leads north from the village to the Bronze Age stone circle at Boscawen-un, the largest in the Penwith peninsula, with 19 regularly spaced small blocks and a tall leaning pillar in the centre. It is a true circle laid out using a thong from a central point. No astronomical significance is apparent. South-east of the village beside the B3315 is another good circle, the Merry Maidens turned to stone for dancing on a Sunday. The stones are about 4 ft high, all carefully selected natural blocks. About 400 yd north-east two standing stones are known as the Pipers, musicians turned to stone as they fled from the dancing. Both stand over 13 ft above ground and are aligned on the centre of the circle. The nature of the ceremonies held at such sites is not known.

St Cleer (1/5B) An ancient village 2 miles north of Liskeard on the southern edge of BODMIN MOOR. Development since the Second World War has turned it into a small town in all but name. The 15th-century church has a fine tower and one doorway remaining from the earlier Norman building. The chapel over the saint's holy well beside the village street is also 15th century, restored in 1864 and one of the best of its type.

Less than 1 mile north-west on the Redgate–Minions road (B3360) stands the famous Doniert Stone which is two stones, one the base for a cross inscribed, in Latin, 'Doniert has asked (prayers) for his soul', and beside it a cross shaft, both with interlaced decoration. The inscription is thought to refer to King Dumgarth of Cornwall who was drowned in the river Fowey in about AD 870.

North-east of the village in a field is an earlier relic, the striking remains of a chambered tomb known as Trethevy Quoit. The huge capstone and uprights were originally buried under an oval mound 130 ft long. Many similar tombs exist in the Penwith peninsula and have been dated to the third millenium BC. Trethevy is a particularly impressive example and the only one known in East Cornwall.

St Clether (1/5B) A tiny, charming village 8 miles west of LAUNCESTON in the Inny valley, reached by turnings off the A395. The church was rebuilt in 1865 and retains only a Norman font, some Norman columns and a 15th-century tower from medieval times. Of exceptional interest is the saint's holy well 500 yd to the north-west, all by itself in an unspoiled setting above the river. Water from the canopied well flows beneath the stone altar of the chapel, a 15th-century building carefully restored and the largest of its type in Cornwall. Little imagination is needed to picture the saint leading a hermit's life in this beautiful spot and persuading the natives to accept baptism.

A mile and a half to the east, **Laneast** is another tiny village on the slopes above the Inny river. Some of the Norman fabric of the church, a Norman font and the lower 14th-century stages of the tower survived the 15th century reconstruction. A good rood screen, and wagon roofs in south porch and south aisle, are matched by the fine set of restored 15th-century bench ends. The building over the holy well to the south-east is 16th century. Both villages are to be savoured for their remoteness, though only a mile or so off a main road, and Laneast for a church never grossly tampered with for over 500 years.

St Columb Major (1/4B) A small town 6 miles east of NEWQUAY, bypassed by the A39(T) Wadebridge–TRURO road. The granite and slate buildings occupy a hilltop, their grey severity mellowed by the setting above the beautiful Lanherne valley running westward to the sea. The town's fame is athletic. Polkinghorne, a great exponent of Cornish wrestling, ended his days there as landlord of the Red Lion Inn where a plaque commemorates him. And the ancient Cornish game of hurling is still played in the streets on Shrove Tuesday and on the Saturday 11 days later. Hurling is possibly a medieval or Tudor predecessor of rugby, a robust, handling game, the wooden ball covered in silver and the goals some 2 miles apart. Hundreds of men on each side struggle to carry the ball through their own goal. The windows of houses and shops in the main street are wisely boarded up for the occasion.

Dozens of prehistoric barrows are scattered over the downs to the north and on the east side of A39 are the Nine Maidens, the remains of an early Bronze Age stone row. It is the only one known in Cornwall, though over 60 survive on Dartmoor. Only six stones, about 5 ft high, remain upright, three others having been broken in recent times. Less than half a mile to the north is a single block known as the Magi stone close to a round barrow, both of which may be connected with the alignment.

Two miles south-east of the town on Castle Downs, at 700 ft above sea level, is the circular Iron Age fort of Castle-an-Dinas, three massive stone ramparts enclosing 6 acres. It is worth climbing the path to the gorse-covered summit for the views, particularly over the other-world landscape of the china clay works to the south.

St Gennys *see* Crackington Haven

St Germans (1/6C) A most interesting small town on the river Tiddy a few miles west of the Tamar Bridge and reached along the A38(T) and B3249. Where the road slopes down to the town are Sir William Moyle's Almshouses built in 1538 and carefully restored 30 years ago. They form a picturesque group with six projecting gables supported on tall, stone pillars covering a loggia on the ground floor and a balcony above reached by an outside staircase. The town is full of other good buildings.

It was an important place in Saxon times and for a brief period (994–1050) the seat of the Bishops of Cornwall. Thereafter Cornwall was included in the diocese of Exeter until the present diocese of TRURO was formed in 1876. The Normans established a large Augustinian priory at St Germans so that the church is of monastic origin, unusual for Cornwall. The north aisle and east end of the Norman church have gone but it is still a lofty and spacious building. The west front is the most impressive example of Norman archi-

tecture in the county. A magnificent doorway of seven receding arches is set between two square towers, the solid harmony broken only by the 13th-century octagonal lantern on top of the northern tower. This was a showpiece entrance to what must have been by far the largest church west of the Tamar. The nave and south aisle display many styles from the Norman down to the north transept added in 1803, and the good stained glass in the east window from the Morris workshop (1896). Pevsner (*Buildings of England*) considered the memorial by John Rysbrack to Edward Eliot (1722) the most ambitious 18th-century monument in Cornwall.

The Eliot family (later Earls of St Germans) bought the Priory after the Dissolution and have lived at Port Eliot ever since. The house incorporates parts of the medieval buildings but is mainly 19th century. Sir John Eliot (1592–1632) was the great Cornishman who defied Charles I and died imprisoned in the Tower of London, a martyr in the cause of parliamentary liberty.

Below the town the river is spanned by a 13-arch viaduct, one of the many, mostly by Isambard Kingdom Brunel, which had to be built to carry the main railway line from Saltash through to Truro. A good path goes up the right bank of the river to Tideford on the A38.

St Ives (1/2B) A fishing port and market town on the north coast which developed into a popular resort in the last half of the 19th century. Fine beaches on either side of St Ives Head (also known as the Island) proved an asset when the railway brought large numbers of visitors. The town has also attracted many artists, notably the world-famous pottery designer Bernard Leach and the sculptress Barbara Hepworth, who gave many examples of her work to the museum in Barnoon Hill which is named after her. St Ives also has the Barnes Cinematograph Museum, situated in Fore Street.

The older houses climb the hill above the harbour with its main pier built by John Smeaton in 1767–70 and since lengthened. The early 15th-century parish church stands close to the small West Pier and is dedicated to St Ia, traditionally an Irish missionary of the 5th century. The fine tower of four stages has pinnacles projecting on corbels, an uncommon feature. An outer south aisle was added *c.* 1500 so that the east end is very wide with four gables, an impressive sight from the water with the tower rising behind. The granite font is also unusual with lions on the circular base and stylized angels with shields at the corners of the bowl. The Lady chapel has a *Madonna and Child* by Barbara Hepworth. Close to the church is the lifeboat station with a fine record of service since the first boat was launched in 1840.

Two and a half miles south is Trencrom Hill (National Trust), the summit 500 ft above sea level and giving wonderful views over West Cornwall and down to the Lizard. It forms a superb site for a small Iron Age fort, a single rampart incorporating natural outcrops of rock and enclosing about 1 acre. Inside were traces of nearly a score of hut circles, and surface finds of pottery dated occupation to the 2nd century BC. Paths from Carbis Bay make a pleasant 2-mile walk across country to the hill.

St Juliot (1/5A) The church stands in an isolated position in the beautiful and unspoiled Valency valley 2 miles inland from BOSCASTLE. Much of the lower valley is owned by the National Trust

and offers good woodland walking. The small 15th-century church fell into disrepair in the 19th century and in 1870 Thomas Hardy, still working as an architect, was sent to carry out a survey. He stayed at the St Juliot Rectory, welcomed by the rector's sister-in-law Emma Gifford, with whom he fell in love. He returned to supervise the restoration and to continue his courtship which ended with their marriage in 1874. After his wife's death in 1912 Hardy made a pilgrimage to St Juliot and erected a memorial tablet to her in the church:

> There it stands, though alas, what a little of her
> Shows in its cold white look . . .

After Hardy's death in 1928 a memorial to him was also placed in the church. He never forgot his early impressions of the wild Cornish coast,

Below: St Ives
Opposite: The lighthouse, St Ives

Above: St Just in Roseland

so different from his native Dorset, and the 'Lyonesse' of his imagination appears again and again in memorable poems of his later years.

St Just in Penwith (1/1B) At the end of the A3071 from PENZANCE: the dour miners' cottages and other granite buildings epitomize the wind-swept ruggedness of the Land's End peninsula. Its appearance has no doubt contributed to keep tourism and other forms of commerce within reasonable bounds. All around are abandoned mines, perhaps the most spectacular being on the coast at Botallack to the north. Two ruined engine houses perch on the rocks high above the Atlantic surf. The workings extended out under the sea bed and copper, tin and arsenic were extracted until the mine closed in 1914. It is a good place to savour the hard and dangerous life of the Cornish miner. Prehistoric man also left many relics of his presence in the area, notably the stone circle (originally two) at Tregeseal and the important Bronze Age cairn at Carn Gluze on the clifftop to the west.

In the town by the clock tower a curious shallow amphitheatre called Plen-an-gwary, the 'playing place', was once used for performances of the medieval miracle plays. It is a protected monument. The large Methodist chapel (c. 1830) can hold a thousand people and shows the continuing influence of John Wesley among the mining community.

The 15th-century church is a solid granite structure looking well able to withstand the Atlantic gales for another 500 years. Two medieval paintings on the north wall of the aisle – the Warning to Sabbath Breakers and St George – have been carefully restored. The east window of the aisle has unusual tracery imitating palm trees. That St Just was an ancient Christian site is shown by the Saxon crosshead carved with Christ crucified in the churchyard, and by the earlier inscribed stone inside the church (5th or 6th century). The latter has the early Christian monogram (Chi-Rho) on one side and on the other a vertical inscription *Selus ic iacit* (Selus lies here).

St Just in Roseland (1/3C) A hamlet on the peninsula east of the Fal estuary, a region of sheltered, wooded creeks and valleys reached by A3078 through Tregony. Beside one of the creeks stands the simple 13th- to 15th-century church of St Just, its lychgate level with the top of the tower

Opposite: St Juliot's Church (see p. 202)

Overleaf: The Tregeseal stone circle

and the steep churchyard full of flowering shrubs – Chilean myrtle and fire bush, palms, fuchias, magnolias. Few churches anywhere have such a superb setting but clumsy restoration in the 19th century stripped the interior and filled it with heavy Victorian pews. Only the 15th-century font and a fine brass of a priest (c. 1520) survive of the older furnishings.

St Just is also the parish church for **St Mawes**, the attractive harbour and yachting centre 1½ miles to the south at the mouth of the Percuil river. The port developed below the castle built by Henry VIII in 1540–3. A fort for artillery rather than a true castle, it is different in plan but complementary to Pendennis Castle on the other side of the entrance to Carrick Roads at FALMOUTH. It consists of a massive round tower and on three sides lobed bastions facing over the water, the central one lower and larger than the other two. Though not so elaborate as contemporary castles at Deal and Walmer in Kent, it was a formidable fortress with guns able to fire in a wide arc from four different levels. No invading force ever attempted to sail into Carrick Roads and the guns were never fired. They remain in place today as clean and new as the day they left the foundry more than 400 years ago. The castle is open to visitors throughout the year.

St Levan (1/1C) Three miles south-east of Land's End, at the end of a minor road off the B3315 from PENZANCE, the churchtown occupies a tranquil, sheltered position, its church tucked into a hillside. In the valley below a stream runs down a few hundred yards to the cliff edge and the small, sandy beach of Porthchapel (Chapel Cove) named from the ruined baptistery of St Levan's Well on the cliff. The well water is still used for baptisms.

The mainly 13th- to 15th-century church has a two-storey tower, unbuttressed but pinnacled, and inside are a Norman font with typical restrained ornamentation and the panelling of an early 16th-century rood screen carved with symbols of the Passion. Some of the old bench ends are unusual, depicting pairs of fish, eagles and clowns and one of St James as a pilgrim. In the churchyard a fine Saxon cross stands not far from the communal grave of the crew of the *Khyber* of Liverpool, a grain ship which foundered in 1905 at Porth Loe a mile to the west.

East of the churchtown is **Porthcurno** and its seashell beach where many submarine cables came ashore, including the first to reach England across the Atlantic. High above the beach is the well-known Minack Theatre, the stage and rows of seats cut out of the sloping cliff and behind the stage a sheer drop to the sea. It opened in 1932, appropriately with a production of *The Tempest*. No other open air theatre in England has quite such a magnificent backcloth of sea and sky.

St Martin's *see* Scilly, Isles of

St Mary's *see* Scilly, Isles of

St Mawes *see* St Just in Roseland

St Mawgan in Pydar (1/2C) A charming village in the wooded Lanherne valley, 4 miles north-east of NEWQUAY. In the churchyard a board in the shape of the stern of a ship's lifeboat marks the resting place of nine men and a boy 'drifted ashore in a boat, frozen to death, at Tregurrian beach in this Parish on Sunday 13th Decr MDCCCXLVI', a moving reminder of the dangers of the Atlantic coast 2 miles away:

> From Padstow Point to Lundy Light
> A watery grave by day and night

The church was restored and partly rebuilt in 1860–1 but retains a 13th- and 15th-century tower. Notable are the brasses, mainly 16th-century memorials to members of the Arundell family. They formerly lived at the nearby manor house of Lanherne which has been a convent since 1794. Inside its main entrance stands an elaborate Saxon cross, richly decorated on all sides and with a mutilated Christ crucified on the four-holed head. It is probably of 10th-century date and originally stood beside the holy well of St Gwinear, a few miles south-west of CAMBORNE. From the village one of the best of inland walks goes up the valley through beautiful woods and can be continued to ST COLUMB MAJOR.

St Michael's Mount *see* Marazion

St Neot (1/5B) A village in a beautiful, wooded valley on the southern edge of BODMIN MOOR, approached by lanes off the A38(T) Liskeard–BODMIN road. The mainly 15th-century church with its older tower dominates the granite and slate cottages and is famous for its 15th- and early 16th-century stained glass. This was restored in 1826–9 but much of the original glass remains. In quality and profusion it has few rivals in any other parish church in England.

The largest window, at the east end of the south aisle, tells the story of the Creation, the Fall, the Murder of Abel and God commanding

Noah to build the Ark. The next aisle window continues the story of Noah. Other windows commemorate local families and their patron saints. Of particular interest are those showing the life of St Neot himself, a dwarf of whom little is known beyond the endearing legends recorded here in exquisite detail. The saint's holy well is 300 yd from the church by the river. In the churchyard the remains of five old crosses include a shaft carved on all four sides with interlaced patterns, one of the best examples in Cornwall.

Less than a mile down river is Carnglaze, a disused slate quarry open to the public in summer. A high-grade roofing slate was hacked out of the hillside west of the river for at least two centuries leaving two enormous caverns on different levels, the lower one containing pools of translucent water.

St Tudy (1/5B) A typical granite village on the north-west borders of BODMIN MOOR, built round its church and churchyard. It lies off the Camelford to BODMIN road (B3266). The large 15th-century church preserves its Norman font of Purbeck marble and in the south porch a Saxon tombstone of the type known as a 'coped stone', hog's-back in shape. It is one of only four in Cornwall and they are also rare elsewhere in England. The church is remarkable for its many monuments, the best a 16th-century memorial, of Delabole slate finely worked in high relief, to the Nicholls family. The parents and their four daughters all kneel with heraldic shields above them. The unmarried state of the third daughter is indicated by her girdle and headdress, and by her shield with its bare dexter side. The monument to Antony Nicholls (1659) is more conventional with limestone figures on grey marble. Outside on the church wall a slate slab commemorates Charles Bligh (died 1770), the grandfather of Admiral William Bligh, of *Bounty* fame, who was born at Tinten in the parish in 1754.

Samson *see* Scilly, Isles of

Sancreed (1/1B) A small village on the windswept Penwith peninsula 1 mile north of the A30 between PENZANCE and Land's End. The 15th-century granite church is small and low, seeming to crouch in its exposed position. It has good wagon roofs and humorous carvings on its rood screen: a clown blowing a trumpet, an owl, a goat among thistles, perhaps the work of a local carpenter mocking the triumph of Roman ritual over the Celtic. In the churchyard are two fine Saxon

crosses, one possibly an earlier inscribed stone re-used.

The parish is notable for its prehistoric monuments. Close to the main road the Blind Fiddler is a standing stone put up at least 3000 years before the Celtic saints arrived. At Brane, south-west of the village, is the best example in Penwith of a chambered tomb of the type known as 'entrance graves' (*see* Scilly Isles). The round barrow is still over 6 ft high with a diameter of 20 ft marked by a kerb of large stones. On the hilltop to the north-east is the circular Iron Age fort of Caer Brane, perhaps on the site of a Neolithic camp, and below it the interesting remains of Carn Euny Iron Age village. Excavation has shown that this was occupied from about 500 BC through to Roman times. Its *fogou* (a trench roofed over with stone slabs and soil) is the best preserved in Cornwall, the stone-walled passage 65 ft long and leading off it an unusual round, corbelled chamber, perhaps a grain silo.

Scilly, Isles of (1/1A) Twenty-eight miles south-west of Land's End the last outcrops of granite form a rugged archipelago of five inhabited islands and more than a hundred others. Their occupation in prehistoric times is evidenced by a bewildering number of remains: settlements, field boundaries, standing stones, chambered tombs and a few promontory forts of the Iron Age. Today they are attractive for their peaceful and uncrowded beaches and mild climate, for the grey seals that breed on uninhabited islands and for the unrivalled variety of sea and migrant birds. When a rare species is sighted, some blown across the Atlantic by contrary winds, the *Scillonian III* sails from PENZANCE with many dedicated birdwatchers aboard. The islands can also be reached from Penzance by helicopter.

St Mary's is the principal island and its airport and harbour at Hugh Town the main link with the outside world. In Church Street, Hugh Town, the Isles of Scilly Museum offers a good introduction to local history and prehistory. The town occupies the neck of land between the main part of the island and the Garrison peninsula, fortified in the 16th century to counter the Spanish threat. The Garrison is entered through an impressive gateway (1742) and higher up is Star Castle (now a hotel) built 1593–4 in the shape of an eight-pointed star. A good walk round the peninsula to the various gun emplacements gives fine views of the other islands and of spectacular skies when the sun goes down beyond the Atlantic.

The Abbey Gardens, Tresco

A coastal path round the rest of the island leads to many beaches and to curious rock formations best seen at Peninnis Head and Porth Hellick Bay. At the latter a massive boulder is a memorial to Admiral Sir Cloudesley Shovell and a reminder of the most disastrous of the islands' many wrecks. In October 1707 the Admiral's flagship the *Association* and three other warships foundered on the Western Rocks with the loss of

The inter-islands ferry

2000 men. The Admiral's body, washed ashore and buried at Porth Hellick, was later removed to Westminster Abbey.

On Porth Hellick Down above the bay are a group of five chambered tombs, one of them carefully preserved and a fine example of the 50 entrance graves scattered among the islands. Under a round barrow a slightly curved passage 3 ft wide leads into a burial chamber of roughly the same width. This type of chambered tomb is peculiar to the islands, West Cornwall and south-east Ireland. Other good examples are at Innisidgen and Bant's Carn in the north of the island. Near the latter are the remains of an Iron Age village.

Hugh Town Quay dates back to the 16th century and was twice extended in the 19th century. From it open motorboats run regularly to the other islands.

Tresco has 16th- and 17th-century fortifications and prehistoric relics but the world-famous Abbey Gardens are its main feature, on the site of a medieval Benedictine priory of which only two arches and some walling remain. They were begun by Augustus Smith, a Hertfordshire land-owner who leased the islands from the Duchy of Cornwall in 1834. A nucleus of plants from Kew

was gradually expanded by specimens acquired from all over the tropics and the southern hemisphere. Carefully protected from gales by windbreaks, thousands of trees, shrubs and plants exhibit a tropical profusion very different from the more formal gardens of the mainland. Among the gardens the Valhalla Museum, also started by Augustus Smith, is a collection of figureheads and other articles salvaged from ships wrecked on the islands. They recall the famous prayer of Parson Troutbeck in the 18th century: 'Dear God, we pray not that wrecks should happen but if it be Thy Will that they do, we pray Thee to let them be for the benefit of Thy poor people of Scilly.'

Bryher has the remains of at least eight entrance graves and also of interest are the prehistoric stone hedges which appear at low tide on the sandy beach running south of the Quay. These show how the land has subsided since Bronze Age times when the island was joined to Tresco. Similar hedges exist on uninhabited **Samson** to the south, a real 'desert island' popular for its unspoiled beaches.

St Martin's supports three small communities and offers a similar combination of bathing beaches and prehistoric relics.

St Agnes is the smallest and most westerly of the inhabited isles. The disused lighthouse (1680) was one of the earliest in Britain and is an attractive whitewashed building still serving as a daymark. The pleasant 19th-century church was built to replace one claimed by the sea. The nearby islet of Gugh can be reached across a sandbar and has a linear prehistoric cemetery and a good example of a standing stone known as 'the Old Man of Gugh', the most westerly of the hundreds of similar stones found all over England and Scotland. St Agnes is particularly popular

Figureheads in the Valhalla Museum, Tresco

The Neptune Steps, the Abbey Gardens, Tresco

with birdwatchers and half a mile to the west lies **Annet**, a sea bird sanctuary where landing is not allowed during the breeding season. Colonies of great and lesser black-backed gulls, puffins, fulmars, guillemots, razorbills and kittiwakes can be observed from a boat. Elusive Manx shearwaters and storm petrels also breed on the island.

Stratton *see* Bude

Tintagel (1/5A) A visitors' honeypot north-west of Camelford on the B3263, but also a place of special historic and scenic interest. A path from the village leads to the headland with its black cliffs rising 250 ft sheer from the Atlantic and only a low, narrow isthmus, much eroded since medieval times, connecting it to the mainland. On the 'island' are the remains of an important early Christian site, possibly a Celtic monastery of the late 5th century. In the 12th century a castle was built on the 'island' and rebuilt a hundred years later with a strong gatehouse and two narrow wards on the mainland. The remains are fragmentary, the wild beauty of the setting unsurpassed. Modern steps down and up enable visitors to cross to the 'island' and muse on the legends that this was the birthplace and court of King Arthur or the castle of King Mark to which Tristram brought Iseult from Ireland. The legends, self-contradictory and totally lacking any archaeological or historic corroboration, were popularized in the 19th century by the poems of Tennyson, Matthew Arnold and Swinburne and have drawn tourists in increasing numbers since.

The church also stands away from the village in an exposed position close to the cliffs. Norman windows, masonry, the south door and the cruciform plan have survived alterations later in medieval times. The battlemented west tower of three short, tapered stages is built as solid and plain as a castle keep. In the church are preserved a Norman font, an early 15th-century brass and a 4th-century milestone, one of five in Cornwall regarded as evidence of tin extraction in Roman times.

The village, full of Arthurian contrivances, has one notable building, the Old Post Office (National Trust), open from April to October. Part of it was used as a Post Office from 1844 to 1892, hence its name, but it is an early 15th-

Trelissick gardens and the water tower

century slate manor house and a rare example of a medieval domestic building.

A mile east of the village are Rocky Valley and St Nectan's Glen, exciting walking for the energetic. A path from the hamlet of Bossiney on the road to BOSCASTLE leads to the thickly wooded glen and upstream to a 40 ft waterfall where St Nectan reputedly had his cell and was buried in the kieve or basin below the fall. The stream winds down the glen to the Boscastle road and into Rocky Valley, a deep, rugged gorge half a mile long. At the bottom the water plunges direct from the rocks into the sea: a wild, memorable spot.

Trelissick (1/3C) Splendid gardens, woodlands and park (National Trust) 4 miles south of TRURO, on either side of the B3289 where it runs down to the King Harry car ferry across the river Fal. The gardens, which are open all year, were mainly the creation of Mr and Mrs Copeland (1937–55) but have been expanded since acquisition by the Trust. A profusion of rhododendrons, azaleas and hydrangeas and many fine trees – magnolias, cedars, beeches, oaks, maples – can be enjoyed by following the long Nature Trail or shorter walks along the river. A water tower of

c. 1860 looks like part of a Loire château. On the dunce's-cap roof the weathervane is surmounted by a squirrel, the crest of the Gilbert family (*see also* Compton Castle, Devon) who owned Trelissick from 1844 to 1913. The parkland slopes southward to the river and gives wonderful views over the great expanse of Carrick Roads.

Trerice (1/3B) A small Elizabethan manor house (National Trust) about 2 miles south of NEWQUAY, reached by turning off the A3058 at Kestle Mill. It was the home of a famous Cornish family, the Arundells, from the 14th century until devised to the Aclands of Broadclyst, Devon, in the 18th century. The National Trust acquired it in 1953 and carried out a scrupulous restoration. The house was built by the 4th Sir John Arundell in 1572–3 and is a typical E-shaped building of the period. The main (east) front has a three-storey, gabled porch, matching gables on the slightly projecting wings, two other gables of different design and an impressive array of mullioned windows. Most striking is the Great Hall window containing 576 panes of glass, many of them original. In the Hall are a fine plastered ceiling and a fireplace with the date 1572. The solar or drawing room on the south front has another original fireplace and even more elaborate plastering on the barrel-vault ceiling and frieze. The house is open to the public from April to October.

Tresco *see* Scilly, Isles of

Truro (1/3B) The cathedral town and administrative centre of the county at the head of the Truro river, 9 miles from both the north and south coasts, and also an important market town. It was a Stannary town and a busy port until FALMOUTH usurped most of its waterborne trade. It is a most pleasant place with gracious thoroughfares of late Georgian buildings, like Lemon Street and Boscawen Street, contrasting with the 'opes' or alleys (one named Squeezeguts) where tiny streams flow to join the Kenwyn and Allen rivers passing through the town. At one end of Lemon Street a statue of the Truro-born African explorer Richard Lander (1804–34) is by the Cornish sculptor Nevill Northey Burnard. Burnard's marble bust of the great Richard Trevithick is in the Royal Institution of Cornwall County Museum and Art Gallery in River Street, which has good collections of minerals and of relics from the county's prehistoric sites. In the Art Gallery are half a dozen paintings by John Opie, who was

The Great Hall, Trerice

born near ST AGNES in 1761. The Truro Pottery Museum is in Chapel Street.

The creation of the diocese of Truro in 1876 ended 800 years of reluctant submission to the Bishops of Exeter. The challenging task of building the first cathedral in England since Wren's St Paul's was given to John Loughborough Pearson (1817–97), an architect with experience of restoring other cathedrals, and its foundation stone was laid in 1880 by the future Edward VII. It was paid for by an unprecedented joint venture of all the religious denominations in the county and much local stone – granite, polyphant and serpentine – was used in the construction. The nave was finished and the 250 ft high central tower dedicated to Queen Victoria in 1903; the western towers with their fine spires named 'Alexandra' and 'Edward VII' were completed in 1910. Victorian architects can be castigated for their often ruthless restorations and opulent lack of taste but Truro Cathedral is a noble achievement in Early English style, of which Pearson was a master. Not all the building is modern. The old parish church of St Mary was pulled down to make room for the cathedral, but the early 16th-century south aisle

Zennor Quoit

was preserved to form an outer south choir aisle. It is a fine example of the decorative use of granite.

Veryan (1/3C) A pleasant village reached by lanes off the road to St Mawes (A3078). The name derives from Simphorian, an obscure saint to whom the beautifully sited but much-restored church is dedicated.

The Garden of Remembrance below the church takes the form of a delightful water garden. The village is widely known for its round, whitewashed, thatched cottages. Two stand at each end of the main street. They were erected early in the 19th century by a LOSTWITHIEL builder, Hugh Rowe, but look older. They quickly acquired a legend: having no north wall the Devil could not enter them nor the village. A cross at the apex of each roof warns him not to meddle. A mile south of the village a round barrow, one of the largest in southern England, occupies a prominent position on Carne Beacon. Still 15 ft high and with a diameter of 360 ft, it has not been excavated but is presumably an important Bronze Age burial.

Zennor (1/1B) A small village skirted by the coast road between ST IVES and ST JUST IN PENWITH (B3306). The exhibits in the little Wayside Museum reflect the village's history: agriculture since prehistoric times, early tin streaming all up the valley to Foage Farm, quarrying. The area is characterized by tiny, irregular fields marked out by stone hedges of surface granite, an Iron Age pattern with some larger fields created later with difficulty by removing dividing hedges. At the head of the valley near Foage excavation of a small settlement established earlier Bronze Age activity in the area. Zennor Quoit, a mile south-east of the village, is an even earlier relic, a Neolithic chamber tomb with an enormous capstone which covered five uprights and two other large stones marking the entrance to an antechamber.

The 12th-century church of St Senara, altered and enlarged in later medieval times, is famous for its two surviving bench ends which have been made into a seat. One of them depicts the beautiful mermaid of Zennor holding a looking glass in one hand and a comb in the other. She represents the best and most persistent of the mermaid legends, the story of a young man of the village lured from church to share the mermaid's home on the sea bed of nearby Pendour Cove.

Useful Information

Animal Sanctuaries, Aquaria and Zoos

Aqualand, Beacon Quay, Torquay, Devon

Brixham Aquarium, 12 The Quay, Brixham,
Devon (Easter–September)

Dartmoor Wild Life Park, Sparkwell, near
Plymouth, Devon

Donkey Sanctuary, Salcombe Regis,
Sidmouth, Devon

Exmoor Bird Garden, Blackmoor Gate, Devon

Gweek Seal Sanctuary, Cornwall

Ilfracombe Tropical Wild Life, Devon
(Easter–September)

Looe Aquarium, The Quay, East Looe,
Cornwall

Marine Biological Association Aquarium, The
Hoe, Plymouth, Devon

Newquay Zoo and Leisure Park, Trevemper
Road, Cornwall

Padstow Tropical Bird and Butterfly Gardens,
Fentonluna Road, Padstow, Cornwall

Paignton Seashore Aquarium, Devon (Easter,
May–September)

Paignton Zoological and Botanical Gardens,
Devon

Parke Rare Breeds Farm, Bovey Tracey,
Devon (April–October)

Teignmouth Aquarium, Devon (mid-May to
early October)

Woolly Monkey Sanctuary, Coombe Martin,
Devon (Easter–September)

Country Parks

Furway, near Honiton, Devon
(April–September)

Grand Western Canal, Tiverton, Devon

Mount Edgcumbe, Cremyll, near Millbrook,
Cornwall

Northam Burrows, Devon

River Dart, Ashburton, Devon (Easter–end of
September)

Stover, Newton Abbot, Devon

Factories and Craft Centres

Axminster Carpets, Devon

Bickleigh Mill Craft Centre and Farm, near
Tiverton, Devon

Coates & Co Ltd, Blackfriars Distillery,
Plymouth (May–September)

Colyton Tannery, Colyton, Devon

(Wednesday am May–September)

Cornish Ironcraft Co, Brentspool near
Kilkhampton, Cornwall

Dartington Glass, Great Torrington, Devon

Honiton Pottery, High Street, Honiton, Devon

Leach Pottery, Higher Stennock, St Ives,
Cornwall

Otterton Mill Centre and Gallery, Otterton,
Budleigh Salterton, Devon

Quince Honey Farm, North Road, South
Molton, Devon

Tremar Potteries, Penhale Grange, St Cleer,
Liskeard, Cornwall

Houses and Gardens *(not mentioned in the
Gazetteer)*

Bicton Park, East Budleigh, Devon
(April–October)

Chambercombe Manor, Ilfracombe, Devon
(Easter–September)

Glendurgan Garden (National Trust), Helford
river, Cornwall (Monday, Wednesday,
Friday March–October)

Godolphin House near Helston, Cornwall
(Thursday May–June, Tuesday, Thursday
July–September)

Pencarrow, near Croanford, Bodmin, Cornwall
(Easter–September)

Rosemoor Gardens, Torrington, Devon
(April–October)

Trelowarren, Mawgan-in-Meneage, Cornwall
(Wednesdays and Bank Holidays, Easter–
October; Sundays June–September)

Ugbrooke, Chudleigh, Devon (Sundays and
Bank Holidays in May, June–September)

Speciality Museums

CORNWALL

Automobilia, The Old Mill, St Stephen,
St Austell

Barbara Hepworth Museum, Barnoon Hill,
St Ives (Sculpture)

Barnes Cinematograph Museum, Fore Street,
St Ives

Bodmin Farm Park, Fletchers Bridge, Bodmin
(mid-May–September, not Saturdays)

Carnglaze Slate Caverns, near St Neot (guided
tours, summer)

Cornish Folk Museum, East Looe

The Blue Coaches timetable board, Ilfracombe

(May–September)
Dairyland, Tresilian Barton, Newquay
 (April–September)
Delabole Slate Quarry, Delabole

(April–September)
Duke of Cornwall's Light Infantry Regimental
 Museum, The Keep, Bodmin
Geevor Mine Museum, Pendeen, Penwith

(April–October)

Lanreath Mill and Farm, Churchtown,
Lanreath, south-west of Liskeard
(Easter–October)

Mr Thorburn's Edwardian Countryside,
Dobwalls Steam Park near Liskeard (wildlife
paintings, Easter–October)

Poldark Mine Museum, Wendron, near
Helston (April–October)

Shire Horse Farm and Carriage Museum,
Lower Grylls Farm, Treskillard, Redruth
(Easter–September)

Tolgus Tin, New Portreath Road, Redruth
(May–September)

Truro Pottery Museum, Chapel Street, Truro

Wheal Martyn China Clay Museum, Carthew,
St Austell (April–October)

DEVON

Alscott Farm Museum, Shebbear
(Easter–September)

Ashley Countryside Collection, Wembworthy
(Easter–September, Monday, Wednesday,
Saturday and Sunday)

Brixham Fisheries, Old Malthouse, The Quay,
Brixham (April–September)

Cobbaton Combat Vehicles (Second World
War), Chittlehampton (March–October)

Combe Martin Motorcycle Collection, Combe
Martin (Easter, mid-May–mid-September)

Cookworthy Museum, Kingsbridge (Easter–
mid-October)

Croyde Gem Rock and Shell Museum, Croyde
(March–October)

Devon Museum of Mechanical Music,
Thornbury, near Holsworthy
(Easter–September)

Devon Shire Horse Farm, Yealmpton near
Plymouth

Devonshire Regimental Museum, Wyvern
Barracks, Barrack Road, Exeter

Devonshire Collection of Period Costume,
Totnes (Spring Bank Holiday–September)

Exeter Maritime Museum, The Basin, Exeter

Finch Foundry of Rural Industry, Sticklepath,
Okehampton

Museum of Shellcraft, Buckfast
(Easter–mid-October)

Newcomen Engine House, Dartmouth
(Easter–October)

North Devon Maritime Museum, Appledore
(Easter–September)

Okehampton and District Museum of
Dartmoor Life, Okehampton
(April–December)

Old Quarries, Beer (guided tours, summer)

Torbay Aircraft Museum, Barton Pines,
Higher Blagdon, Paignton (Easter–October)

Totnes Motor Museum, The Quay, Totnes

Steam and Model Railways

Brixham Model Railway, 19 The Quay
(Easter–September)

Brunel Atmospheric Railway Exhibition, Old
Pumping House, Starcross, Devon
(Easter–October)

Dart Valley (Steam) Railway, Buckfastleigh to
Totnes. (Easter, June–mid-September)

Dawlish Warren Railway Museum and Model
Railway, Devon (Easter, May–
mid-September)

Dobwalls Steam Park near Liskeard, Cornwall
(Easter–October)

Gwinnear Outdoor Model Railway, Carnhell
Green, near Camborne, Cornwall
(Easter–September)

Kingsbridge Miniature Railway, Devon
(Easter, mid-May–mid-September)

Lappa Valley Railway and Leisure Park,
Newlyn East, near Newquay, Cornwall
(summer season)

Model Railway and Museum, Meadow Street,
Mevagissey, Cornwall (summer, and Sunday
pm winter)

Pecorama, Beer, Devon (all year; Pleasure
Garden May–September)

Seaton Electric Tramway, Devon

The Great Exmouth Model Railway, Devon
(Easter–October)

Torbay and Dartmouth Steam Railway,
Paignton to Kingswear, Devon (Easter,
June–September)

Miscellaneous

Canonteign Falls and Farm Park, Christow,
near Exeter, Devon (April–September;
Saturday, Sunday in winter)

Cornwall Leisure World, Carlyon Bay,
St Austell, Cornwall

Dartington Cider Press Centre, near Totnes,
Devon

Exmoor Brass Rubbing Centre, Lynton,
Devon (April–September)

Lelant Model Park, near St Ives, Cornwall

Model Village, Babbacombe, Torquay, Devon

Smeaton's Tower, The Hoe, Plymouth, Devon
(April–October)

St Agnes Leisure Park, St Agnes, Cornwall

The Gnome Reserve, Bradworthy, Devon
(Easter–October)

Wesley's Cottage, Trewint, Altarnun, Cornwall

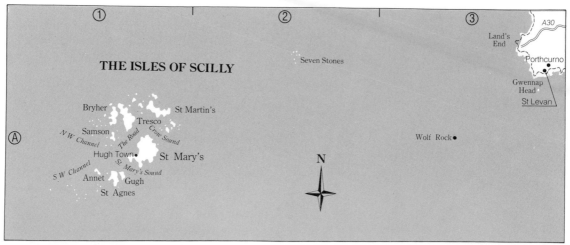

THE ISLES OF SCILLY

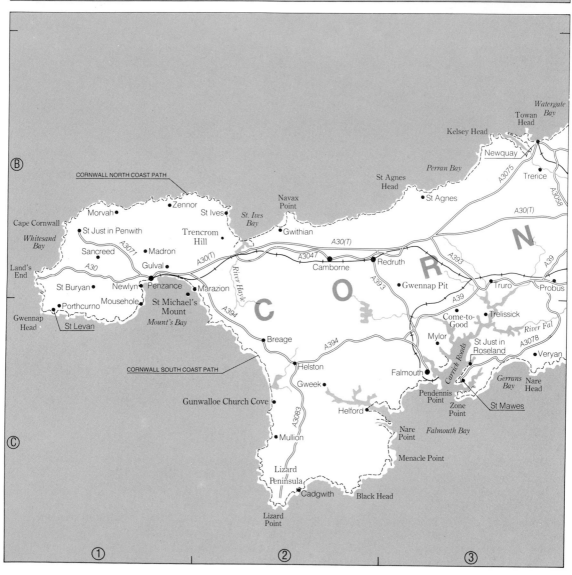

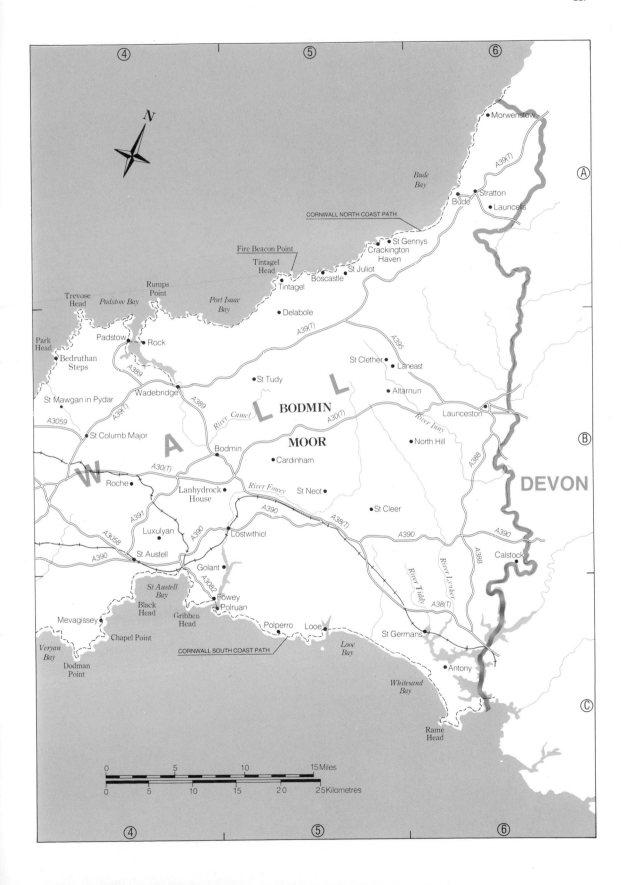

④ ⑤ ⑥

N

A

• Morwenstow

A39(T)

*Bude
Bay*

Stratton
Bude •
Launcells •

CORNWALL NORTH COAST PATH

• St Gennys

Crackington
Haven

Fire Beacon Point

Tintagel
Head

St Juliot •

Boscastle •

• Tintagel

Rumps
Point

Trevose
Head

Padstow Bay

*Port Isaac
Bay*

• Delabole

A39(T)

A395

St Clether •
Laneast •

Park
Head

Padstow •
• Rock

Bedruthan
Steps

A389

• Altarnun

Launceston •

St Mawgan in Pydar •

Wadebridge

A389

• St Tudy

L

BODMIN

River Camel

A30(T)

River Inny

B

A3059

A39(T)

L

MOOR

• North Hill

A388

St Columb Major •

A30(T)

Bodmin •

DEVON

• Roche

Lanhydrock
House •

River Fowey

• Cardinham

St Neot •

W A L L

A391

A3058

Luxulyan •

A390

Lostwithiel •

A390

A38(T)

• St Cleer

A390

A390

Calstock •

St Austell •

A390

Golant •

A3082

River Tiddy

River Lynher

A388

A38(T)

Mevagissey •

*St Austell
Bay*

Black
Head

Gribben
Head

Fowey
Polruan

Polperro •

Looe •

St Germans •

Chapel Point

CORNWALL SOUTH COAST PATH

*Looe
Bay*

*Veryan
Bay*

Dodman
Point

*Whitesand
Bay*

Antony •

C

Rame
Head

0   5   10   15 Miles

0   5   10   15   20   25 Kilometres

④ ⑤ ⑥

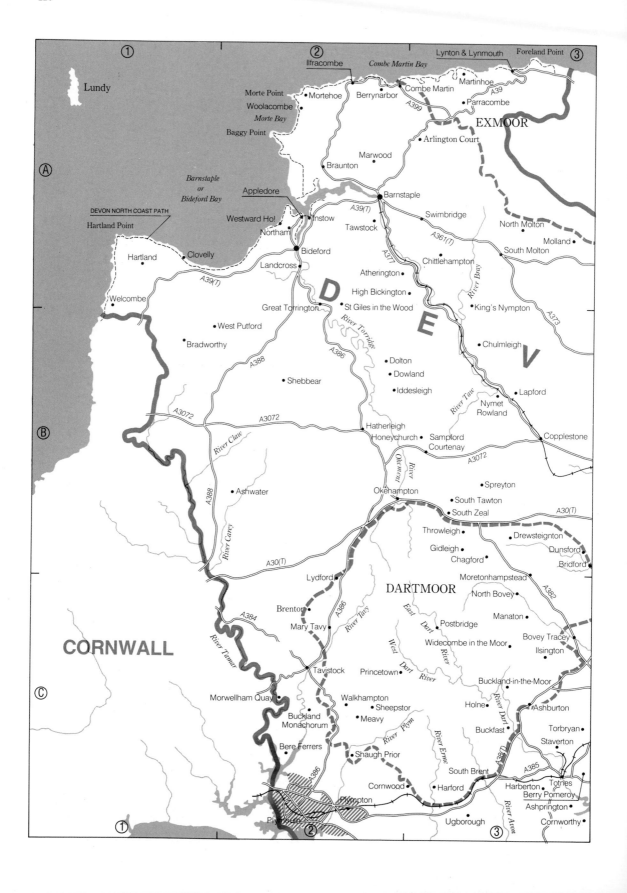

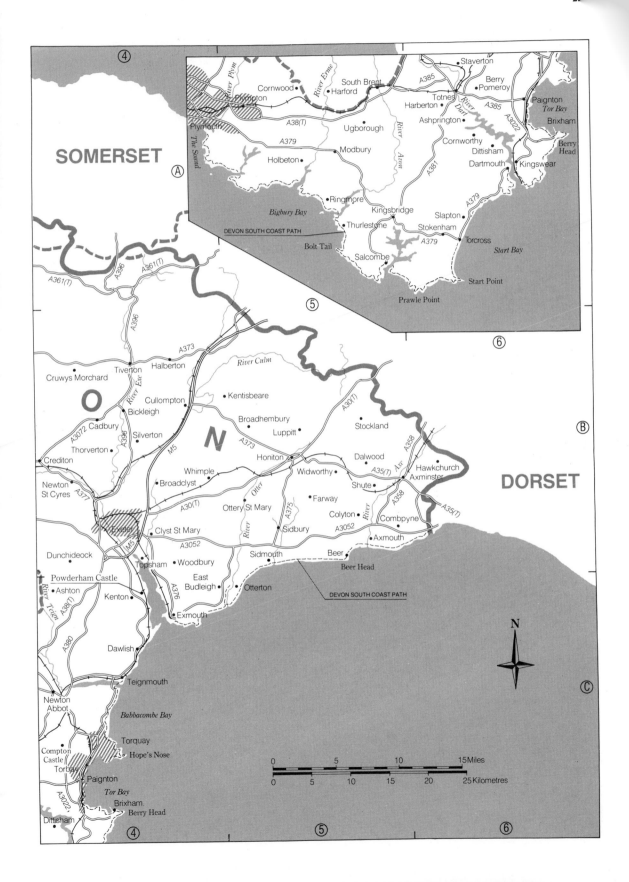

SOMERSET

DORSET

Inset map (top right):

Staverton
Cornwood
Harford
South Brent
A385
Berry Pomeroy
Totnes
Paignton
Tor Bay
Harberton
A385
Plympton
A38(T)
Ashprington
Brixham
A379
Ugborough
Cornworthy
Berry Head
Modbury
Dittisham
Holbeton
Dartmouth
Kingswear
The Sound
River Plym
River Erme
River Dart
River Avon
A381
A3022
Ringmore
Kingsbridge
Slapton
A379
Bigbury Bay
Thurlestone
Stokenham
Bolt Tail
Salcombe
A379
Torcross
Start Bay
DEVON SOUTH COAST PATH
Start Point
Prawle Point

Main map:

A396
A361(T)
A361(T)
A396
A373
Tiverton
Halberton
River Culm
River Exe
Cruwys Morchard
Cullompton
Kentisbeare
A30(T)
Bickleigh
Broadhembury
Stockland
A358
Cadbury
Silverton
Luppitt
Hawkchurch
A3072
M5
A373
Dalwood
Axminster
Thorverton
A35(T)
Honiton
A358
Crediton
Whimple
Widworthy
Shute
A35(T)
Newton St Cyres
Broadclyst
Farway
Colyton
Combpyne
A377
A30(T)
Ottery St Mary
River Otter
Sidbury
A3052
Exeter
Clyst St Mary
A375
Axmouth
M5
A3052
Sidmouth
Beer
Dunchideock
Topsham
Woodbury
Beer Head
Powderham Castle
East Budleigh
Otterton
DEVON SOUTH COAST PATH
River Teign
Ashton
Kenton
A38(T)
A376
Exmouth
A380
Dawlish
Teignmouth
N
Babbacombe Bay
Newton Abbot
Torquay
Compton Castle
Hope's Nose
Torbay
Paignton
A3022
Tor Bay
Brixham
Berry Head
Dittisham

O N

0   5   10   15 Miles
0 5 10 15 20 25 Kilometres

④   ⑤   ⑥
Ⓐ   Ⓑ   Ⓒ
④   ⑤   ⑥

Bibliography

Axford, E. C. *Bodmin Moor*. David and Charles 1975
Barnatt, J. *Prehistoric Cornwall*. Turnstone Press 1982
Barton, R. M. *A History of the Cornish Clay Industry*. Bradford Barton, Truro 1966
Berry, C. *Portrait of Cornwall*. Robert Hale 1974
Booker, F. *Industrial Archaeology of the Tamar Valley*. David and Charles 1971
Burrows, R. *The Naturalist in Devon & Cornwall*. David and Charles 1971
Burton, S. H. *The West Country*. Robert Hale 1972
Burton, S. H. *Devon Villages*. Robert Hale 1972
Crossing, W. *Guide to Dartmoor*. David and Charles. Reprint of 1912 edition
Doble, G. H. *The Saints of Cornwall*. Dean & Chapter of Truro – 5 parts 1960–70
Gill, C. *The Isles of Scilly*. David and Charles 1975
Gill, C. (ed) *Dartmoor. A New Study*. David and Charles 1984
Halliday, F. E. *A History of Cornwall*. Duckworth 1975

Harris, H. *Industrial Archaeology of Dartmoor*. David and Charles 1968
Hemery, E. *High Dartmoor*. Robert Hale 1983
Hoskins, W. G. *Devon*. David and Charles, new ed. 1972
Norman, D. and Tucker, V. *Where to Watch Birds in Devon and Cornwall*. Croom Helm 1984
Pearce, S. M. *The Archaeology of South West Britain*. William Collins 1981
Pettit, P. *Prehistoric Dartmoor*. David and Charles 1974
Pevsner, N. *The Buildings of England*. Penguin Books. *Cornwall*. 1970; *North Devon*, 1952; *South Devon* 1952
Rawe, D. R. *Cornish Villages*. Robert Hale 1978
South West Way Association *The South West Way* (A guide revised and updated annually)
Todd, A. C. and Laws, P. *Industrial Archaeology of Cornwall*. David and Charles 1972

Index

Numbers in *italics* refer to illustrations